THE
FAITHFUL
CHRISTIAN

THE
FAITHFUL
CHRISTIAN

An Anthology of Billy Graham

Compiled by
William Griffin
and
Ruth Graham Dienert

McCRACKEN PRESS
New York

McCracken Press™
An imprint of Multi Media Communicators, Inc.
575 Madison Avenue, Suite 1006
New York, NY 10022

Excerpts from *The Seven Deadly Sins* by Billy Graham © 1955 by Billy Graham Evangelistic Association. Permission granted.

Excerpts from *A Biblical Standard for Evangelists* © 1984 reprinted by permission of World Wide Publications.

Excerpts from *Calling Youth to Christ* © 1947, 1975 by Zondervan Publishing House and *the Chance of a Lifetime* © 1952 by Zondervan Publishing House reprinted by permission of Zondervan Publishing House.

Excerpts from *Peace with God* © 1953, 1984; *The Secret of Happiness: Jesus's Teaching on Happiness as Expressed in the Beatitudes,* © 1955, 1985; *Angels: God's Secret Agents,* © 1975, 1989; *The Holy Spirit: Activating God's Power in Your Life,* © 1978, 1988, 1989; *Till Armageddon: A Perspective on Suffering,* © 1981; *Approaching Hoofbeats: The Four Horsemen of the Apocalypse,* © 1983; *Facing Death—and the Life After,* © 1987; *Hope for the Troubled Heart,* © 1991; *Storm Warning,* © 1992: published by Word Publishing Inc., reprinted by permission.

For Bible copyrights see page 267.

Library of Congress Cataloging-in-Publication Data

Graham, Billy, 1918-
  The faithful Christian : 200 readings / Billy Graham.
      p .   cm.
  Includes bibliographical references.
  ISBN 1-56977-625-3: $16.95
    1. Theology, Doctrinal—Popular works. 2. Christian life—
Baptist authors. I. Title.
BT77.G77   1994   94-4840
239'.044—dc20   CIP

10 9 8 7 6 5 4 3 2 1

CONTENTS

FOREWORD

It is the best of times and the worst of times, writes the novelist who thinks that the world, this world, is a perfectible place.

But for the evangelist it is the other way around. It's the worst of times and the best of times. *Worst* in that this world is bubbling with imperfection—sin, war, rebellion, chaos, poverty, disease. *Best* in that there's a way out of sin and disease and the despair engendered by them, that the Bible describes the way, that Jesus Christ is the way as well as the truth and the life.

Such an evangelist is Billy Graham, who for almost half a century has preached from the Bible to audiences around the world. He's really an itinerant evangelist in the sense that he has sought souls all over the world. Traveling by plane, train, and ship, he has conducted crusades all over the United States and in most of the capitals of Europe, in South America and South Africa, as well as in the Far East. More than two million souls have accepted his invitation to publicly accept Jesus Christ as their Lord and Savior.

His shuttle evangelism is not unlike Saint Paul's. Traveling by horse, camel, and commercial grain ship, the Apostle of the Gentiles visited such international centers of the Roman empire as Jerusalem, Ephesus, Corinth, Caesarea, Galatia, Damascus, Antioch, Athens, and finally Rome, where he was eventually martyred. Everywhere he went he presented the hard and pure teaching of Jesus Christ.

At one point or another in their careers, theologians and preachers of all Christian denominations come to feel that

Christian doctrine has an inner clock, that its pendulum has been winding down, that its ticking has become less audible, less reliable, over the rough course of centuries and cultures.

There's a certain logic in this, but it's a logic not verified by fact. In the course of his own career, Graham has seen that the harder the doctrine, the more believable it is. And hence he has had no difficulty in presenting, much as Paul before him, the Gospel whole and entire—angels, miracles, virgin birth, atonement for sin, Heaven and Hell—to the people of the world in a literal, non-critical acceptance of the biblical narrative.

Graham's "one great failure" in life, according to an interview given to *Time* magazine on the occasion of his seventy-fifth birthday in 1993, was an intellectual one. He felt he hadn't devoted enough time and energy to the academic study of theology and Scripture, even when the opportunity presented itself. Instead, acknowledging his own lack of intellect, and indeed lack of appetite, for theologizing, he decided to make the Bible his text, and to stick to it.

And so he has. Billy Graham's preaching has presented the entire Bible, from the beginning to end, from Genesis to Revelation. He makes a variety of topical references along the way, dozens of them in any one sermon; if the great D. L. Moody could insert fourteen stories in one sermon, so Billy Graham could illustrate his own sermons with a swirl of stories, anecdotes, and headlines. But apart from each transitory reference, which was meant only to illustrate a point he was making, his preaching is still Jesus, the Word of God's word, the Bible.

Uncluttered, and indeed unfettered, by a social or theological agenda that might be fashionable one day but unfashionable the next, his preaching has had a certain purity of tone. It takes listeners back in time, to the apostolic time, where they have the distinct impression that they may be listening, not to a contemporary American evangelist with an urgent voice, but to Paul or Peter or Timothy talking with irresistible enthusiasm about this person named Jesus.

One gets the same impression reading Billy Graham's books. This is not to say that reading Graham is like reading the Gospel. But it is to say that this collection of excerpts from Graham's published works, *The Faithful Christian*, contains the evangelist's thoughts on the same topics chosen by the writers of the Gospels and Epistles in the New Testament.

Biographer William Martin, author of *A Prophet with Honor: The Billy Graham Story* calls Graham "an icon not just of American Christianity but of America itself." Perhaps that's because his influence has spread beyond his denomination. His form of Christianity, a centrist Christianity that can generally be believed by Bible churches as well as liturgical churches, has flowed through American Christianity like a mighty Mississippi, seeking whom it might nourish, whom it might serve, whom it might save.

William Franklin Graham, Jr., was reared on a North Carolina farm, where he learned piety from his parents. He didn't want to grow up to inherit the farm; he wanted to play baseball. But a conversion experience intervened. He wasn't knocked off his feet by a voice from a cloud, as Paul had been; rather it was like being picked off first base with too long a lead. "I didn't have any tears, I didn't have any emotion, I didn't hear any thunder, there was no lightning," he recalled for *Time* magazine. "But right there, I made my decision for Christ. It was as simple as that, and as conclusive."

He attended Bob Jones College, the Florida Bible Institute, and finally Wheaton College in Illinois. There he met Ruth Bell, the daughter of missionaries to China. She herself wanted to do big things for the Lord, like converting Tibet; instead, she accepted the proposal of the young man with high hopes and married him.

On his call to be an evangelist, he told *Time* magazine his wife was the greatest influence. "I thought *God* called you," interrupted his wife of fifty years. "Well, he told me through you too." And she has been an influence in his books. Countless are the references to her, to her experiences, to her wisdom; and many are the quotations from her poetry. The Grahams have six children and many grandchildren.

For many years the Grahams have lived in a comfortable log home in the mountains of North Carolina, 3,200 feet above sea level. "As much as my wife Ruth and I enjoy our home,. . . " Graham has written, "we spend very little time there because God has called us into the valley of life where the lost people are. If we spent all our time in the hills and on mountaintops, how would we effectively serve God?"

The excerpts in *The Faithful Christian* are drawn from articles and many of Billy Graham's published works from *Calling Youth to Christ* (1947) through *Storm Warning* (1993).

One virtually unknown title has proved to be invaluable when it comes to understanding Billy Graham the person as well as Billy Graham the evangelist. *A Biblical Understanding for Evangelists* (1984) is his commentary on the fifteen Affirmations made by four thousand participants at the International Conference for Itinerant Evangelists in Amsterdam, July 1983. The words of the Affirmations themselves form a sort of creed or code for the itinerant evangelists like Graham, and indeed through them, eventually, to their audiences. His commentary is not only on the wording of the Affirmations themselves but also the outline of his own teaching, ministerial life, and beliefs. "May we see a renewed dedication in this generation," he wrote in the Introduction, "to the priority of evangelism on the part of every child of God."

Near the end of every revival meeting, the evangelist invites members of the audience to come forward as a public sign of accepting Christ as his or her own Lord and

Savior. It's not a casual invitation; it's an crucial one. Graham always gives several, very excellent reasons for this. Jesus taught that there is an eternal destiny for each individual, either Heaven or Hell; they have no assurance of continued physical life tomorrow; and a delayed decision can result in a heart that's hardened to the call of God's Spirit.

In its way, this book, *The Faithful Christian*, is itself an invitation to meet, not only Billy Graham, for he has written all the words, but also Jesus Christ, Who is Himself the Word, Who spoke the Word of God Himself, and Who Himself promised eternal life.

—Bunny Graham Dienert

THE
FAITHFUL
CHRISTIAN

1

THE NATURE OF EVANGELISM

Challenge and Thrill

There are a lot of people who think that to be a preacher all you have to do is to preach twice a week and conduct prayer meetings—about an hour and a half's work per week. Many consider the ministry an easy and lazy profession and many have said, "If you cannot be anything else, be a preacher." But a preacher who is true to the Word of God must not only preach the Word (2 Timothy 4:2) but must expose false teaching (1 Timothy 1:3). A minister who is true to his calling must warn people against the danger of heresy and false doctrine. Many times he is tempted to soft-pedal because people may misunderstand and he may make enemies. That is why Paul said, "I am praying for you day and night, Timothy." Your pastor needs prayer that God will give him courage to stand true. Timothy was called upon to "reprove." That was a hard thing for a young man to do! Paul told him to "rebuke." That, too, is hard! First Timothy 5:19 tells us that Timothy was instructed to handle church discipline. All these problems are faced by a minister of the Gospel. Your pastor or evangelist carries a thousand and one problems and has hundreds of things to do that you never hear of. Yet Timothy was a young man, and Paul charged him with these great responsibilities. The greatest challenge and thrill in the world is to preach the Gospel—even though many times it costs!

Gift of the Evangelist

We must be clear about the nature and necessity for evangelism as it is presented to us in the Bible. We must be clear also on the legitimacy and importance of the call to be an evangelist.

How important is evangelism to the church? If a fire is raging in the world, how important is a fire truck? There would be no church without evangelism.

The gift of the evangelist is one of the major spiritual gifts God has given the church (Ephesians 4:11). The gift of the evangelist is just as valid and crucial for the church today as it was in New Testament times.

Paul in his last letter commanded the young pastor Timothy, "Preach the word; . . . do the work of an evangelist" (2 Timothy 4:2,5). Tragically, the church has often lost sight of the legitimacy and importance of the biblical evangelist. When it has, the church has grown stale and lifeless, shrinking in numbers and spiritual impact. But when it has rediscovered and encouraged the gift of the evangelist, God has blessed the church with spiritual harvests. May God grant that the gift of the evangelist will be seen once again as central in the world church, so that God's people may reach out more effectively to a world that, apart from God, is lost and dying.

God's call to the special ministry of evangelism is distinct from other callings in the ministry of the church. In Acts 21:8 we read that Philip is identified as "the evangelist." Now, this does not detract from the truth that all Christians are called to be witnesses to their Lord and Savior. And pastors, in addition to their shepherding, teaching, and administrative responsibilities, are to be involved in evangelism.

But he who is called to and set apart for the work of an evangelist is to devote his time and effort singlemindedly to this God-given task. He is not to be distracted by anything likely to deflect him from this. Persecution will not weaken his resolution. The persuasion of others will fall on deaf ears. Only the clear leading of God will cause him to change his ministry.

Invitation and Urgency

Every time I give an invitation I am in an attitude of prayer—because I know the situation is totally dependent on God. Incidentally, this is the moment in a meeting when I feel emotionally, physically, and spiritually drained. This is the part of the evangelistic service that often exhausts me in every way. I think one of the reasons may be the strong spiritual battle going on in the hearts of so many people. It becomes a spiritual battle of such proportions that sometimes I feel faint. There is an inward groaning and agonizing in prayer that I cannot possibly put into words. I am sure every true evangelist senses this.

Urgency is another ingredient of this aspect of the evangelist's ministry. Of course, whenever we preach, there is a sense of urgency in the message, but this comes to a climax at the moment of invitation. The urgency I feel at that time is compelling. I know there could be many who, if they leave without making their commitment to Christ, may never have another opportunity like this again. When the call for decision has been made and many are responding, I still feel a continuing sense of urgency for those who are holding back. I've felt the same urgency as I've shared Christ with an individual on a plane, or in an office. Urgency is an indispensable part of the work of an evangelist.

The urgency in calling people to a decision is based on three concerns.

First, Jesus taught that there is an eternal destiny for each individual—either Heaven or Hell (John 5:25–29). The eternal destiny of each individual depends on a decision made in this life (Luke 16:19–31)—to be followed by a life of obedience. No decision for Christ can be made after death. "It is appointed unto men once to die, but after this the judgment" (Hebrews 9:27).

Second, we have no assurance of continued physical life tomorrow (Proverbs 27:1). There is an urgency to the Gospel because life can end at any moment. Someone to whom we speak may never have another opportunity to hear the Gospel and accept Christ. "Behold, now is the accepted time; behold, now is the day of salvation" (2 Corinthians 6:2).

Third, a delayed decision can result in a heart that becomes hardened to the call of God's Spirit. The Bible warns us about being "hardened through the deceitfulness of sin" (Hebrews 3:13). The Bible also warns, "He, that being often reproved hardeneth his neck, shall suddenly be destroyed, and that without remedy" (Proverbs 29:1). So the evangelistic message always contains a note of urgency born out of the teaching of Scripture.

This urgency is expressed by the evangelistic call to all who hear the Gospel. This call is an integral part of the evangelist's responsibility; he does not merely preach truth but proclaims it with a view toward some of his hearers responding positively to the Gospel. Of course, the Gospel must be simply and understandably communicated, the issues made plain, the necessity of a response— positive or negative—clearly taught. At that point the evangelist is dependent on the power of the Scripture and the ministry of the Holy Spirit to work in and through the message in the hearts of all who hear.

While the evangelist is essentially a harvester, his message may be used by God in another way. It may be a preparation of some hearts for a subsequent positive response—a planting of the seed of the Gospel. For others, it may be a watering of that seed which leads to decision. God is sovereign and we cannot dictate to Him the stages through which He may choose to bring an individual to saving faith. Paul wrote, "I have planted, Apollos watered; but God gave the increase. So then neither is he that planteth anything, neither he that watereth; but God that giveth the increase" (1 Corinthians 3:6–7).

The call to decision is scriptural. It is found repeatedly throughout the Bible. It begins with God calling Adam and Eve (Genesis 3) when they hid from Him because of their sin. It ends with God's call by His Spirit through His witnesses and evangelists, "The Spirit and the bride say, 'Come.' And let him that heareth say, 'Come.' And let him that is athirst come. And whosoever will, let him take the water of life freely" (Revelation 22:17).

The Word of God is a re-echoing invitation to lost humanity to turn to Him.

Bible in Hand, Hill of Beans

I wish today that all the ministers in this country could stand behind the sacred desk and preach as having authority. I wish that every man who professes the name of Christ and holds this sacred Book in his hands could back up every word and say, "Thus saith the Lord." I believe it is the message of the hour, the message that needs to be proclaimed from the housetops, in the streets, down on the avenue, in the church, or wherever one might find professing Christians—"Thus saith the Lord." My illustrations don't amount to a hill of beans. What I think about them doesn't amount to a hill of beans. My ideas about philosophy, politics, or world events mean absolutely nothing. I believe that today men and women are hungry to hear "Thus saith the Lord." Today people want to hear what is on the pages of this Book. They want to know what God has to say. They want to know what the Bible says. Night after night in this campaign I have been trying, to the best of my ability, to tell you what God says instead of what man says. Instead of what philosophers or politicians say about world events, I have been trying to tell you what the Scriptures say.

Jesus spoke as a man having authority. Jesus stood up and spoke as the Son of God, and today we can follow Him and speak with authority concerning the Word of God. He was the greatest Teacher of all times.

2

THE GOOD BOOK

More Than Great Literature

There are those who regard the Bible principally as the history of Israel. Others admit that it sets forth the soundest ethics ever enunciated. But these things, important as they are, are only incidental to the real theme of the Bible, which is the story of God's redemption as it exists in Jesus Christ. In an editorial which appeared 30 June 1983, the *International Herald Tribune* recommended that the Bible should be read as literature because it is "The English language at its best." Those who read the Scriptures as magnificent literature, breathtaking poetry or history, and overlook the story of salvation miss the Bible's real meaning and message.

God caused the Bible to be written for the express purpose of revealing to man God's plan for his redemption. God caused this Book to be written that He might make His everlasting laws clear to His children, and that they might have His great wisdom to guide them and His great love to comfort them as they make their way through life. For without the Bible, this world would indeed be a dark and frightening place, without signpost or beacon.

The Bible easily qualifies as the only Book in which is

God's revelation. There are many bibles of different religions; there is the Muslim Koran, the Buddhist Canon of Sacred Scripture, the Zoroastrian Zend-Avesta, and the Brahman Vedas. All of these have been made accessible to us by reliable translations. Anyone can read them, comparing them with the Bible, and judge for themselves. It is soon discovered that all these non-Christian bibles have parts of truth in them, but they are all developments ultimately in the wrong direction. They all begin with some flashes of true light, and end in utter darkness. Even the most casual observer soon discovers that the Bible is radically different. It is the only Book that offers man a redemption and points the way out of his dilemmas. It is our one sure guide in an unsure world.

Sixteen hundred years were needed to complete the writing of the Bible. It is the work of more than thirty authors, each of whom acted as a scribe of God. Those men, many of whom lived generations apart, did not set down merely what they thought or hoped. They acted as channels for God's revelation; they wrote as He directed them; and under His divine inspiration they were able to see the great and enduring truths, and to record them that other men might see and know them too.

During these sixteen hundred years, the sixty-six books of the Bible were written by men of different languages, living in different times, and in different countries; but the message they wrote was one. God spoke to each man in his own language, in his own time, but His message basically in each case was the same. When the great scholars gathered together the many ancient manuscripts written in Hebrew, Aramaic, and Greek, and translated them into a single modern tongue, they found that God's promises remain unchanged, His great message to man had not varied.

Investing in a Bible

If you do not have a Bible in your home, go out and get one now—get the one that suits you best, get the size that is most comfortable for you to handle, get the type that is most pleasant for you to read, and then settle down and find out for yourself why this one Book has endured. Don't be afraid to invest in the best Bible you can afford—for that is what you are making: an investment. We spend our money for expensive clothing which perishes but hesitate to buy the best in Bibles which is an investment in eternity. Find out for yourself why it answers every human need, why it supplies the faith and strength that keeps humanity marching forward.

If you and the Bible have had a long absence from each other, it might be well for you to renew your acquaintance by reading again the Gospel of John. While this is considered one of the most profound books in the Bible, it is also the clearest and most readily understood. It was written for the very purpose of showing the how and the why of man's salvation, so that the questions of the mind as well as the gropings of the heart might be satisfied.

After reading the Book of John, you might acquaint yourself with the Gospel as taught by Mark, Luke, and Matthew, noting how these men of widely different personalities and writing styles set forth the eternal story of redemption through Jesus. You will become aware of the powerful, universal truth that underlies all Gospel teaching and be impressed anew with what the biblical writer meant when he said, "Jesus Christ the same yesterday, and today, and forever" (Hebrews 13:8).

When you have read each of the Gospels individually, start in at the beginning of the New Testament and read straight through all the books in order. When you have done that, you will have developed such a taste for Bible reading, you will have found it such a fountain of inspiration, such a practical counselor and guide, such a treasure chest of sound advice, that you will make Bible reading a part of your daily life.

A knowledge of the Bible is essential to a rich and meaningful life. For the words of this Book have a way of filling in the missing pieces, of bridging the gaps, of turning the tarnished colors of our life to jewel-like brilliance. Learn to take your every problem to the Bible. Within its pages you will find the correct answer.

But most of all, the Bible is a revelation of the nature of God. The philosophers of the centuries have struggled with the problem of a Supreme Being. Who is He? What is He? Where is He? If there is such a Person, is He interested in me? If so, how can I know Him? These and a thousand other questions about God are revealed in this Holy Book we call the Bible.

3

THE NATURE OF GOD

What is God Like?

A simple, straightforward answer to this very basic question is hard to find——unless we simply remind ourselves
that God is just like Jesus Christ! All the attributes of God
are seen in Jesus Christ: His love, mercy, compassion, purity, sovereignty, and might. This is why our faith in God
must always be Christ-centered. As Dr. Michael Ramsey,
the former Archbishop of Canterbury, wrote: "The heart of
Christian doctrine is not only that Jesus is divine, but that
God is Christlike and in him is no un-Christlikeness at all."

The greatness of God defies the limitations of language.

As I read the Bible, I seem to find holiness to be His
supreme attribute. However, love is also a prime quality.
The promises of God's love and forgiveness are as real, as
sure, as positive, as human words can describe. God is
holy love.

Behind the love of God lies His omniscience—His ability to "know and understand all." Omniscience is that
quality of God which is His alone. God possesses infinite
knowledge and an awareness which is uniquely His. At
all times, even in the midst of any type of suffering, I can
realize that He knows, loves, watches, understands, and,
more than that, He has a purpose.

As a boy I grew up in the South. My idea of the ocean was so small that the first time I saw the Atlantic I couldn't comprehend that any little lake could be so big! The vastness of the ocean cannot be understood until it is seen. This is the same with God's love. It passes knowledge. Until you actually experience it, no one can describe its wonders to you.

A good illustration of this is a story my wife told me about a man in China who was selling cherries. Along came a little boy who loved cherries; and when he saw the fruit, his eyes filled with longing. But he had no money with which to buy cherries.

The kindly seller asked the boy, "Do you want some cherries?" And the little boy said that he did.

The seller said, "Hold out your hands." But the little boy didn't hold out his hands. The seller said again, "Hold out your hands," but again the little boy would not. The kind seller reached down, took the child's hands, filled them with two handfuls of cherries.

Later, the boy's grandmother heard of the incident and asked, "Why didn't you hold out your hands when he asked you to?"

And the little boy answered, "His hands are bigger than mine!"

God's hands, also, are bigger than ours!

Some of our modern experts in theology have made attempts to rob God of His warmth, His deep love for mankind, and His sympathy for His creatures. But God's love is unchangeable. He loves us in spite of knowing us as we really are. In fact, He created us because He wanted other creatures in His image in the universe upon whom He could pour out His love, and who, in turn, would voluntarily love Him. He wanted people with the ability to say "yes" or "no" in their relationship to Him. Love is not satisfied with an automaton—one who has no choice but to love and obey. Not mechanized love, but voluntary love satisfies the heart of God.

Were it not for the love of God, none of us would ever have a chance in the future life!

Some years ago a friend of mine was standing on top of a mountain in North Carolina. The roads in those days were filled with curves, and it was difficult to see very far ahead. This man saw two cars heading toward each other. He realized that they couldn't see each other. A third car pulled up and began to pass one of the cars, although there wasn't enough space to see the other car approaching around the bend. My friend shouted a warning, but the drivers couldn't hear, and there was a fatal crash. The man on the mountain saw it all.

This is how God looks upon us in His omniscience. He sees what has happened, what is happening, and what will happen. In the Scriptures He warns us time after time about troubles, problems, sufferings, and judgments that lie ahead. Many times we ignore His warnings.

God sees all and knows all. But we are too limited by the finiteness of our minds and the short time we have on earth even to begin to understand the mighty God and the universe He has created.

The Trinity

When I first began to study the Bible years ago, the doctrine of the Trinity was one of the most complex problems I had to encounter. I have never fully resolved it, for it contains an aspect of mystery. Though I do not totally understand it to this day, I accept it as a revelation of God.

The Bible teaches us that the Holy Spirit is a living being. He is one of the three persons of the Holy Trinity. To explain and illustrate the Trinity is one of the most difficult assignments to a Christian. Dr. David McKenna once told me that he was asked by his small son, Doug, "Is God the Father God?"

He answered, "Yes."

"Is Jesus Christ God?"

"Yes."

"Is the Holy Spirit God?"

"Yes."

"Then how can Jesus be His own Father?"

David thought quickly. They were sitting in their old 1958 Chevrolet at the time. "Listen, son," he replied, "under the hood is one battery. Yet I can use it to turn on the lights, blow the horn, and start the car." He said, "How this happens is a mystery—but it happens!"

This is a terribly difficult subject—far beyond the ability of our limited minds to grasp fully. Nevertheless, it is extremely important to declare what the Bible holds, and be silent where the Bible is silent. God the Father is fully God. God the Son is fully God. God the Holy Spirit is fully God. The Bible presents this as fact. It does not explain it.

God the Father

Some see God as a harsh father, waiting to punish His children when they do something wrong. Others perceive God as unable to handle the evil on earth, or indifferent to the suffering caused by it.

God's love is unchangeable; He knows exactly what we are and loves us anyway. In fact, He created us because He wanted other creatures in His image upon whom He could pour out His love and who would love Him in return. He also wanted that love to be voluntary, not forced, so He gave us freedom of choice, the ability to say yes or no in our relationship to Him. God does not want mechanized love, the kind that says we must love God because it's what our parents demand or our church preaches. Only voluntary love satisfies the heart of God.

God is a God of love, and He is not blind to man's plight. He doesn't stand on a mountaintop, viewing the wrecks in our lives, without shouting a warning. Since man caused his own crash by his rebellion against the Creator, God could have allowed him to plunge into destruction.

From the very beginning of man's journey, God had a plan for man's deliverance. In fact, the plan is so fantastic that it ultimately lifts each man who will accept His plan far above even the angels. God's all-consuming love for mankind was decisively demonstrated at the cross, where His compassion was embodied in His Son, Jesus Christ. The word "compassion" comes from two Latin words meaning "to suffer with." God was willing to suffer with man.

In His thirty-three years on earth, Jesus suffered with man; on the cross He suffered for man. "God was reconciling the world to himself in Christ" (2 Corinthians 5:19). An important verse to memorize is: "God demonstrates His own love for us in this: While we were still sinners, Christ died for us" (Romans 5:8). God's love did not begin at the cross. It began in eternity before the world was established, before the time clock of civilization began to move. The concept stretches our minds to their utmost limits.

Can you imagine what God was planning when the earth was "without form and void"? There was only a deep, silent darkness of outer space that formed a vast gulf before the brilliance of God's throne. God was designing the mountains and the seas, the flowers and the animals. He was planning the bodies of His children and all their complex parts.

How could creation be by chance?

Even before the first dawn, He knew all that would happen. In His mysterious love He allowed it. The Bible tells us about the "Lamb that was slain from the creation of the world" (Revelation 13:8). God foresaw what His Son was to suffer. It has been said there was a cross in the heart of God long before the cross was erected at Calvary. As we think about it, we will be overwhelmed at the wonder and greatness of His love for us.

God's love liberated man from the beginning of time to

do his own thing, but whatever his choice, there were to be either benefits or consequences. Adam and Eve enjoyed the benefits for a while, but they forced every generation that would ever be born to face the consequences.

It was the love of God which put the Ten Commandments in the hands of His servant, Moses. It was His love which engraved those laws, not only in stone, but also upon the hearts of all people. Those commandments became the foundation of all civil, statutory, and moral law and the basis of conscience. It was God's love which knew that men were incapable of obeying His law, and it was His love which promised a Redeemer, a Savior, who would save His people from their sins.

It was the love of God which put words of promise into the mouths of His prophets, centuries before Christ came to this planet. It was God's love that planned the political conditions before the coming of Jesus Christ. Greece, as the great power during the four-hundred-year period before the birth of Christ, prepared the way for His message by spreading a common language throughout the world. Then the transportation problem had to be solved, and the great Roman Empire came into power and built a network of roads and developed a system of law and order. So by using the common language and the Roman roads and legal system, God spread His Word through the early Christians. The Scripture says that "when the time had fully come, God sent his Son" (Galatians 4:4).

God the Holy Spirit

THE HOLY SPIRIT, A PERSON

The Bible teaches that the Holy Spirit is a person. Jesus never referred to "it" when He was talking about the Holy Spirit. In John 14, 15 and 16, for example, He spoke of the Holy Spirit as "He" because He is not a force or thing but a person. Whoever speaks of the Holy Spirit as "it" is uninstructed, or perhaps even undiscerning. In Romans 8:16 the King James Version refers to the Holy Spirit as "itself." This is a mistranslation. Nearly all of the newer translations have changed "itself" to "himself."

We see from the Bible that the Holy Spirit has intellect, emotions, and will. In addition to this, the Bible also ascribes to Him the acts we would expect of someone who was not just a force, but a real person.

He speaks. "He who has an ear, let him hear what the Spirit says to the churches. To him who overcomes, I will grant to eat of the tree of life, which is in the Paradise of God" (Revelations 2:7). "And while they were ministering to the Lord and fasting, the Holy Spirit said, 'Set apart for Me Barnabas and Saul for the work to which I have called them'" (Acts 13:2).

He intercedes. "And in the same way the Spirit also helps our weakness; for we do not know how to pray as we should, but the Spirit Himself intercedes for us with groanings too deep for words" (Romans 8:26).

He testifies. "When the Helper comes, whom I will send to you from the Father, that is the Spirit of truth, who proceeds from the Father, He will bear witness of Me" (John 15:26).

He leads. "And the Spirit said to Philip, 'Go up and join this chariot'" (Acts 8:29). "For all who are being led by the Spirit of God, these are sons of God" (Romans 8:14).

He commands. "And they passed through the Phrygian and Galatian region, having been forbidden by the Holy Spirit to speak the word in Asia; and when they had come to Mysia, they were trying to go into Bithynia, and the Spirit of Jesus did not permit them" (Acts 16:6, 7).

He guides. "When the Spirit of truth comes, he will guide you into all the truth; for he will not speak on his own authority, but whatever he hears he will speak, and he will declare to you the things that are to come" (John 16: 13 RSV).

He appoints. "Be on guard for yourselves and for all the flock, among which the Holy Spirit has made you overseers, to shepherd the church of God which He purchased with His own blood" (Acts 20:28).

He can be lied to. "But Peter said, 'Ananias, why has Satan filled your heart to lie to the Holy Spirit, and to keep back some of the price of the land? While it remained unsold, did it not remain your own? And after it was sold, was it not under your control? Why is it that you have conceived this deed in your heart? You have not lied to men, but to God'" (Acts 5:3, 4).

He can be insulted. "How much severer punishment do you think he will deserve who has trampled under foot the Son of God, and has regarded as unclean the blood of the covenant by which he was sanctified, and has insulted the Spirit of grace?" (Hebrews 10:29).

He can be blasphemed. "Therefore I say to you, any sin and blasphemy shall be forgiven men, but blasphemy against the Spirit shall not be forgiven. And whoever shall speak a word against the Son of Man, it shall be forgiven him; but whoever shall speak against the Holy Spirit, it shall not be forgiven him, either in this age, or in the age to come" (Matthew 12:31, 32).

He can be grieved. "And do not grieve the Holy Spirit of God, by whom you were sealed for the day of redemption" (Ephesians 4:30).

Each of the emotions and acts we have listed are characteristics of a person. The Holy Spirit is not an impersonal force, like gravity or magnetism. He is a Person, with all the attributes of personality. But not only is He a Person: He is divine as well.

THE HOLY SPIRIT, GOD HIMSELF

Throughout the Bible it is clear that the Holy Spirit is God Himself. This is seen in the attributes which are given to the Holy Spirit in Scripture, for example. Without exception these attributes are those of God Himself.

He is eternal. This means that there never was a time when He was not. "How much more will the blood of Christ, who through the eternal Spirit offered Himself without blemish to God, cleanse your conscience from dead works to serve the living God?" (Hebrews 9:14).

He is all-powerful. "And the angel answered and said to her, 'The Holy Spirit will come upon you, and the power of the Most High will overshadow you; and for that reason the holy offspring shall be called the Son of God'" (Luke 1:35).

He is everywhere present (that is, omnipresent) at the same time. "Where can I go from Thy Spirit? Or where can I flee from Thy presence?" (Psalm 139:7).

He is all-knowing (that is, omniscient). "For to us God revealed them through the Spirit; for the Spirit searches all things, even the depths of God. For who among men knows the thoughts of a man except the spirit of the man, which is in him? Even so the thoughts of God no one knows except the Spirit of God" (1 Corinthians 2:10, 11).

The Holy Spirit is called God. "But Peter said, 'Ananias, why has Satan filled your heart to lie to the Holy Spirit, and to keep back some of the price of the land? While it remained unsold, did it not remain your own? And after it was sold, was it not under your control? Why is it that you have conceived this deed in your heart? You have not lied to men, but to God'" (Acts 5:3, 4). "And we all, with unveiled face, beholding the glory of the Lord, are being changed into his likeness from one degree of glory to another; for this comes from the Lord who is the Spirit" (2 Corinthians 3:18 RSV).

He is the Creator. The first biblical reference to the Holy Spirit is Genesis 1:2 (Moffatt) where we are told "the spirit of God was hovering over the waters." Yet Genesis 1:1 says, "In the beginning God created the heavens and the earth." And in Colossians 1 where Paul is writing to the Church at Colossae about the Lord Jesus Christ, among other tremendous truths he tells us, "For in Him all things were created, both in the heavens and on earth, visible and invisible, whether thrones or dominions or rulers or authorities—all things have been created through Him and for Him. And He is before all things, and in Him all things hold together" (Colossians 1:16, 17). Thus, God the Father, God the Son, and God the Holy Spirit were together creating the world. To understand and accept these facts is of the greatest importance to every Christian, both theologically and practically.

4

THE HOLY SPIRIT

Fruits of the Spirit

Of all the passages in the Bible which sketch the character of Christ and the fruit which the Spirit brings to our lives, none is more compact and challenging than Galatians 5:22, 23. "But the fruit of the Spirit is love, joy, peace, patience, kindness, goodness, faithfulness, gentleness, self-control."

LOVE

There should be no more distinctive mark of the Christian than love. "By this all men will know that you are My disciples, if you have love for one another" (John 13:35). "We know that we have passed out of death into life, because we love the brethren" (1 John 3:14). "Owe nothing to anyone except to love one another; for he who loves his neighbor has fulfilled the law" (Romans 13:8).

JOY

Returning from his young son's grave in China, my father-in law wrote to his mother in Virginia, "There are tears in our eyes, but joy in our hearts." The joy which the Spirit brings to our lives lifts us above circumstances. Joy can be ours, even in the midst of the most trying situations.

The Greek word for "joy" is used repeatedly in the New Testament to denote joy from a spiritual source such as "the joy of the Holy Spirit" (1 Thessalonians 1:6). The Old Testament likewise uses phrases like "the joy of the Lord" (Nehemiah 8:10) to point to God as the source.

PEACE

Peace carries with it the idea of unity, completeness, rest, ease, and security. In the Old Testament the word was shalom. Many times when I meet Jewish friends I greet them with "Shalom." And often, when I greet my Arab friends I use a similar term that they use for peace, *salam*.

Isaiah said, "Thou wilt keep him in perfect peace, whose mind is stayed on thee: because he trusteth in thee" (Isaiah 26:3 KJV).

PATIENCE

Patience is the transcendent radiance of a loving and tender heart which, in its dealings with those around it, looks kindly and graciously upon them. Patience graciously, compassionately, and with understanding judges the faults of others without unjust criticism. Patience also includes perseverance—the ability to bear up under weariness, strain, and persecution when doing the work of the Lord.

KINDNESS

Kindness, or gentleness is a term that comes from a Greek word referring to the kindness that pervades and penetrates the whole nature. Gentleness washes away all that is harsh and austere. Indeed, gentleness is love enduring. Jesus was a gentle person. When He came into the world, there were few institutions of mercy. There were few hospitals or mental institutions, few places of refuge for the poor, few homes for orphans, few havens for the forsaken. In comparison to today, it was a cruel world. Christ changed that. Wherever true Christianity has gone His followers have performed acts of gentleness and kindness.

GOODNESS

This is derived from a Greek word referring to that quality found in the person who is ruled by and aims at what is good, that which represents the highest moral and ethical values. Paul writes, "For the fruit of the light consists in all goodness and righteousness and truth" (Ephesians 5:9). He also says, "To this end also we pray for you always that our God may count you worthy of your calling, and fulfill every desire for goodness and the work of faith with power; in order that the name of our Lord Jesus may be glorified in you" (2 Thessalonians 1:11, 12). Again Paul says in commending the church in Rome, "And concerning you, my brethren, I myself also am convinced that you yourselves are full of goodness, filled with all knowledge, and able also to admonish one another" (Romans 15:14).

FAITHFULNESS

The reference to faithfulness (or "faith" in the KJV) is not to faith exercised by the Christian, but rather to faithfulness or fidelity, produced by the Holy Spirit in a yielded Christian life. The same word occurs in Titus 2:10 where it is translated "fidelity" in the King James Version. This trait of character is highly commended in Scripture. Fidelity in little things is one of the surest tests of character, as our Lord indicated in the parable of the talents: "You were faithful with a few things, I will put you in charge of many things" (Matthew 25:21). Morality is not so much a matter of magnitude, but of quality. Right is right, and wrong is wrong, in small things as well as in big things.

GENTLENESS

The word "gentleness" here (or in the KJV, meekness) comes from a Greek word meaning "mild; mildness in dealing with others." Jesus said, "Blessed are the gentle, for they shall inherit the earth" (Matthew 5:5). Nowhere in Scripture does this word carry with it the idea of being spiritless and timid. In biblical times gentleness or meekness meant far more than it does in modern day English. It carried the idea of being tamed, like a wild horse that has been brought under control. Until tamed by the Holy Spirit, Peter was a rough and ready character. Then all of his energy was used for the glory of God. Moses was called the meekest of men, but prior to God's special call to him he was an unbroken, high-spirited man who needed forty years in the desert before he was fully brought under God's control. A river under control can be used to generate power. A fire under control can heat a home. Meekness is power, strength, spirit, and wildness under control.

SELF-CONTROL

Self-control (temperance in the KJV) comes from a Greek word meaning strong, having mastery, able to control one's thoughts and actions. John Wesley's mother once wrote him while he was a student at Oxford that "anything which increases the authority of the body over the mind is an evil thing." This definition has helped me understand "self-control."

The Gift of Healing

The Holy Spirit gives the gift of healing (literally, the gift of cures). Many cases of healing appear in the Old Testament, and certainly the New Testament is full of instances when Jesus and His disciples healed the sick. Throughout the history of the Christian Church countless instances of physical healing have been recorded.

The ministry of physical healings through spiritual means is sometimes associated with faith healers. Many of these claim to have the gift of healing or at least some special power. Tens of thousands of people flock to these healers. And thousands more are urged to write certain radio and television preachers who claim to have this gift of healing. Indeed, mass attention has been focused in recent years on the Christian faith and physical healing.

However, we must distinguish the operation of what the Bible calls the gift of healing from a second method of healing. Some place their emphasis on the faith of the one who needs healing—telling him it will happen if only he believes. By this they mean more than those who believe that forgiveness, cleansing, and acceptance with God spring from the atoning work of Jesus on the cross. They think that any Christian who becomes ill can claim healing by faith. Note that this has nothing to do with the gift of healing as such. Such teachers may believe, for example, that physical healing for disease is in the atonement of Jesus Christ. To them the death of Christ on the cross not only results in the offer of forgiveness for our sins, but also physical healing for the body. Both, they believe, come to us by faith.

This kind of healing has to do with faith rather than just the gift of healing itself.

5

JESUS CONFRONTS

All of These Kids

Jesus' disciples were irritated. The Master was tired from teaching all day, and here were all of these little kids pushing Him around. Can't you imagine the scene? Their mothers wanted the boys and girls to touch Him, and the disciples sought to shoo the children away. But Jesus reached out and said, "Suffer little children, and forbid them not, to come unto me; for of such is the kingdom of Heaven" (Matthew 19:14 KJV).

Translated into modern vernacular, that meant, "Let the children alone, don't stop them from coming to Me. Don't you know that the kingdom of Heaven belongs to children?"

We must all enter the kingdom of Heaven with the simple faith and trust of a child, but a special place is reserved in the heart of the Lord for the young ones.

One mother of a child who died said, "I thank God for loaning us the little fellow for a few years, and for the knowledge that we will see him again when we are united with Christ after death. What a joyous reunion! What a wonderful Savior, to provide the gift of eternal life!"

How true it is that the Lord must love little children, because He calls so many of them home. Our hope that those who die as children are lovingly taken by God to heaven was expressed beautifully by King David when his infant son died: "I will go to him, but he will not return to me" (2 Samuel 12:23).

The Rich Young Man

Do you remember that moment in Jesus' life when a rich young man came up to Him and asked, "What must I do to inherit eternal life?" Jesus answered, "You know the commandments." The young man answered, "All these I have kept since I was a boy." It was quite a claim. Jesus must have looked carefully at the young man. He must have seen that this seeker was telling the truth. The rich man was sincere, a struggler, a lover of truth. So Jesus answered him, "Sell everything you have and give to the poor. . . . Then come, follow me." The young man couldn't do it. It would have cost him too much. So "he became very sad" (Luke 18:18–23) and turned away. He missed the chance of a lifetime. He asked for life and missed it. He clung to the standards of living to which he had become accustomed, to his security, and he lost everything. We must not let this happen to us.

This does not mean Jesus necessarily calls all of us to renounce all wealth. God may entrust wealth to some individuals who are to use it for His glory. But the rich young ruler's problem was not that he was wealthy, but that his wealth came before his commitment to Christ. Is there anything in your life that is keeping you from Him? If so, there is no shortcut. You must loosen your grip on it before you can reach out to Christ.

The Rich Man and Lazarus

Probably one of the most graphic descriptions of Hell in the Bible is given by Jesus in His parable of the rich man and Lazarus. During his life the rich man refused to help Lazarus, a poor beggar who yearned to eat the crumbs which fell from the rich man's table. When the beggar died, he was carried to Abraham's side, which was what we would describe as Heaven. The rich man was sent to Hell and was in torment. Jesus did not imply that having wealth means being doomed to Hell, nor did he say that being poor guarantees anyone the right to Heaven. However, it is a graphic description of the unbeliever's suffering apart from God.

According to the parable, the rich man looked up and saw Abraham, with the beggar by his side. He spoke through cracked, parched lips and pleaded for Abraham to ask Lazarus to dip his finger in some water and bring it to him to cool his tongue. "I am in agony in this fire," he cried.

But Abraham said there was a great chasm between the two worlds and it was "fixed," or permanent. No person on one side could cross over to the other. In other words, the one in Hell had been given a choice of direction during his life on earth, and now he had to suffer the consequences of his decision to live for himself instead of for God. There was no second chance.

The Good Shepherd

The wonderful picture of God as our Shepherd is found in many places in the Old Testament. One of the Psalms begins, "Hear us, O Shepherd of Israel, you who lead Joseph like a flock" (Psalm 80:1). It's great to think that the Everlasting God, the Almighty Creator, condescends to be the Shepherd of His people.

David makes the relationship a personal one in the best known of all Psalms. "The Lord is my shepherd," he cries exultantly, "I shall lack nothing" (Psalm 23:1). The rest of the Psalm tells us what we shall not lack. It speaks of the shepherd's provision as He leads us to the green pastures,

His guidance along the paths of righteousness (that means the right paths), His presence with us in the dark valley. No wonder David testifies, "My cup overflows" (verse 5)—such are God's boundless blessings.

Isaiah adds a further touch to the picture when he says, "He tends his flock like a shepherd: He gathers the lambs in his arms and carries them close to his heart" (Isaiah 40:11). The figure here indicates the tender care with which the Lord supports His people on their journey and the strong love with which He enfolds them.

In the New Testament, Jesus uses this same figure and applies it to Himself. He says, "I am the good shepherd. The good shepherd lays down his life for the sheep. The hired hand is not the shepherd who owns the sheep. So when he sees the wolf coming, he abandons the sheep and runs away. Then the wolf attacks the flock and scatters it. . . . I am the good shepherd; I know my sheep and my sheep know me" (John 10:11–14).

Note four things about Jesus the Good Shepherd.

He owns the sheep: they belong to Him.

He guards the sheep: He never abandons them when danger is near.

He knows the sheep, knows them each by name and leads them out (see verse 3).

And He lays down His life for the sheep, such is the measure of His love.

How thankful we should be, weak, wandering, and foolish as we are, that we have such a shepherd. Let's learn to keep close to Him, to listen to His voice, and follow Him. This is especially important in times of spiritual peril. Jesus tells us not to be misled by the voices of strangers (verse 5), and there are many strange voices being heard in the religious world of our day. Don't be deceived by false teachers. Jesus is the Good Shepherd: trust Him. And Jesus is the door of salvation: Enter by that door, and you will find the full and abundant life He came to bring (verses 7–10).

Miracles

The gift of performing miracles takes its key term, "miracles," from a Greek word meaning "powers" (2 Corinthians 12:12). A miracle is an event beyond the power of any known physical law to produce; it is a spiritual occurrence produced by the power of God, a marvel, a wonder. In most versions of the Old Testament the word "miracle" is usually translated "a wonder" or "a mighty work." Versions of the New Testament usually refer to miracles as "signs" (John 2:11) or "signs and wonders" (John 4:48; Acts 5:12; 15:12).

Clearly, the wonders performed by Jesus Christ and the apostles authenticated their claim of authority and gave certitude to their message. And we must remember that people did ask Jesus and the apostles this question, "How do we know that you are what you say you are, and that your words are true?" That was not an improper question. And at strategic moments God again and again manifested Himself to men by miracles so they had outward, confirming evidence that the words they heard from God's servants were true.

Jesus and the Intellectual

The intellectual. . . already has his mental outlook logically formed into a coherent system with all of the pieces fitting together in a neat mosaic, so that the removal of one piece destroys the pattern. The intellectual thinks he must be able to understand before he comes to Christ. The intellectual just cannot reach out and grasp a helping hand because he must have the situation explained in terms of his system of thought. He wants to know the source of that help, the manager of that help, because he has already committed himself to a set of assumptions that are rigid and all-inclusive. From his point of view, his system is complete.

Nicodemus was an intellectual. He, too, had a rigid philosophical and theological system worked out, and it was a good system. He had even included a belief in God. The intellectual structuring of his philosophical religious system excluded Jesus as the Son of God.

But what did Jesus tell this intellectual? He said something like this: "Nicodemus, I am sorry that I cannot explain it to you. You have seen something that troubles you. You have seen something that does not fit your system. You have seen me to be good, and you have heard me say that I am God, that I act with the power of God. This does not fit your system, but I cannot explain it to you because your assumptions do not allow for a starting point. Nicodemus, to you it is not logical. Nothing in your system permits it. I am sorry I cannot explain. You will just have to be born again" (John 3:1–5).

In other words, Nicodemus had to start without even being logical from his own point of view. He had to start without fitting what Jesus said into his system. He had to take a leap of faith into a new system.

If you are to find the answer to your search, you too may have to reject much of your old system and plunge into this new one. As Dr. [Kenneth L.] Pike says: "The intellectual needs to be told that his system as a whole must be replaced...that he must be born again. Christianity is not an accretion, it is not something added. It is a new total outlook which is satisfied with nothing less than penetration to the furthest corners of the mind and the understanding."

Conflict, Not Coziness

Jesus Christ spoke frankly to His disciples about the future. He hid nothing from them. No one could ever accuse Him of deception or making false promises.

In unmistakable language, He told them that discipleship meant a life of self-denial and the bearing of a cross. He asked them to count the cost carefully, lest they should turn back when they met with suffering and privation.

Jesus told His followers that the world would hate them. They would be arrested, scourged, and brought before governors and kings. Even their loved ones would persecute them. As the world hated Him, so it would treat His servants. He also warned, "a time is coming when anyone who kills you will think he is offering a service to God" (John 16:2).

The Christian therefore must expect conflict, not an easy, cozy life. He is a soldier, and as it has been said, his captain never promised him immunity from the hazards of battle.

Many of Christ's early followers were disappointed in Him, for, in spite of His warnings, they expected Him to subdue their enemies and set up a world political kingdom. When they came face to face with reality, they "turned back and no longer followed him" (John 6:66). But the true disciples of Jesus all suffered for their faith.

We are told that the early Christians went rejoicing to their deaths, as if they were going to a marriage feast. They bathed their hands in the blaze kindled for them and shouted with gladness. One early historian, witnessing their heroism, wrote, "When the day of victory dawned, the Christians marched in procession from the prison to the arena as if they were marching to Heaven, with joyous countenances agitated by gladness rather than fear."

How true were the words of Paul to the early Christians: "We must go through many hardships to enter the kingdom of God" (Acts 14:22).

Someone has said that these are God's "permitted contradictions" in our lives. However, there is a drastic difference between God's permissive will and His perfect will for our lives. We strayed from that perfect will when Adam chose to disobey God in the Garden.

As life hits us head-on, we can respond with resentment,

resignation, acceptance, or welcome. We are the living examples of our responses.

The Great Commission

It is hard to imagine what must have been passing through the minds of that little band of eleven disciples as they clustered around the risen Lord Jesus Christ on a mountain somewhere in Galilee. They recently had gone through the misery of apparent defeat, watching helplessly as Jesus was nailed to a cross. Their dreams of a world kingdom under Christ's rule were shattered. Then came the reports from the women who had visited the tomb early on that first Easter morning—reports that He was alive! At first they doubted; but as time went on, they knew the reports to be true, for Jesus Himself appeared to them many times. Finally, He comes to them and issues the greatest challenge they—or we—could ever hear: "All power is given unto me in heaven and in earth. Go ye therefore, and teach all nations, baptizing them in the name of the Father, and of the Son, and of the Holy Ghost: Teaching them to observe all things whatsoever I have commanded you: and, lo, I am with you always, even unto the end of the world" (Matthew 28:18–20).

These words of commission need to be restudied and obeyed by the whole church, and especially by those of us who are evangelists. In that one statement the Master summarized all that we require for our task.

Jesus commanded—Go with My power. "All power [authority] is given unto me in Heaven and in earth. Go . . . !" (Matthew 28:18–19). Without that announcement of His authority, the Great Commission would have lacked justification and motivation. But under that authority, we can direct divine power from Heaven and destroy demonic power on earth. Jesus has all power in Heaven and on earth! As John Stott put it (at the World Congress on

Evangelism in Berlin in 1966), "The authority of Jesus Christ extends over all creatures, whether human or superhuman, over the church, over nations, over the devil and his works."

Jesus commanded—Go with My program. "Go . . . make disciples of all the nations, baptizing them in the name of the Father, and of the Son, and of the Holy Spirit: Teaching them to observe all things whatsoever I have commanded you" (Matthew 28: 19–20, NKJV). We are to evangelize men and women. The New English Bible renders this, "Make all nations my disciples" (Matthew 28:19, NEB). That personal pronoun makes it clear that our task is not only to call for decisions for Christ, but to make disciples for Christ. Also, we are to baptize men and women. We are to bring converts into the fellowship of the church. This is the significance of the One name of the Father, Son, and Holy Spirit. We are to catechize men and women. We are to "[warn] every man, and [teach] every man in all wisdom; that we may present every man perfect in Christ Jesus" (Colossians 1:28).

Jesus commanded—Go with My presence. "Lo, I am with you always, even unto the end of the world" (Matthew 28:20). In the person of the Holy Spirit, Jesus has promised to be with us every day, and come what may—until the task is finished—and to the end of time. What a promise, what a comfort!

6

THE NATURE OF MAN

The Great Quest

You started on the Great Quest the moment you were born. It was many years perhaps before you realized it, before it became apparent that you were constantly searching—searching for something you never had—searching for something that was more important than anything in life. Sometimes you have tried to forget about it. Sometimes you have attempted to lose yourself in other things so there could be time and thought for nothing but the business at hand. Sometimes you may even have felt that you were freed from the need to go on seeking this nameless thing. At moments you have almost been able to dismiss the quest completely. But always you have been caught up in it again—always you have had to come back to your search.

At the loneliest moments in your life you have looked at other men and women and wondered if they too were seeking—something they couldn't describe but knew they wanted and needed. Some of them seemed to have found fulfillment in marriage and family living. Others went off to achieve fame and fortune in other parts of the world. Still others stayed at home and prospered, and looking at them you may have thought: "These people are not on the

Great Quest. These people have found their way. They knew what they wanted and have been able to grasp it. It is only I who travel this path that leads to nowhere. It is only I who goes asking, seeking, stumbling along this dark and despairing road that has no guideposts."

But you are not alone. All mankind is traveling with you, for all mankind is on this same quest. All humanity is seeking the answer to the confusion, the moral sickness, the spiritual emptiness that oppresses the world. All mankind is crying out for guidance, for comfort, for peace.

Man the Searcher

The Bible tells us that man began in the image of God and lost his way. A good indication of the human predicament today is a sign on the rear window of an automobile: "Don't follow me. I'm lost." Carl Jung, the eminent psychologist, once said: "Man is an enigma to himself."

There is within every man a certain sense of frustration. Voices echo from within the inner chambers of his soul: "I ought not to be the way I am. I was made for something higher. There must be a supreme being. Life was not meant to be this empty." These voices, often unconscious and unarticulated, cause man to struggle onward toward some unknown, unnamed goal. We may try to evade this quest; we may detour into fantasy; we may revert to the lower levels of life and seek escape from this laborious truth. Indeed, we may even give up temporarily, throw up our hands, and say: "What's the use?" But always some inner compulsion drives us back, and invariably we take up the quest again.

Men in every culture are engaged in this eternal search. I took some of my college work in anthropology, where we studied primitive societies. We never found a tribe anywhere in the world, no matter how primitive, that was not engaged in this search. It is a search to find purpose and meaning in life. It is a search to find truth and reality. It may be crude, primitive, or even vulgar; but it is still part of the search!

Walking and Talking with God

In the beginning, God and man were friends. They walked together and talked together. They made great plans as to how this planet was to be populated and developed. The planet earth was to show God's glory to the entire universe. It was to be the center of God's activities in His partnership with man.

It is quite evident that God desired the fellowship of a creature like man. Thus man was created with a high and exalted purpose, a high and exalted destiny. Man was to be God's closest friend, His partner in cultivation and development of the earth.

God did not create man a piece of machinery so that He could push a button and man would obey Him. Man was no robot. Man was a "self." He had dignity and he had ego. He could choose whether he wanted God's friendship and fellowship or not. God did not want His creature to love Him because he was forced to do so. This would not be true love. He wanted man's love and fellowship because man chose to love God.

Thus from the very beginning God proceeded to test man's love and friendship. This is why He put the tree in the garden. He said: "Of every tree of the garden thou mayest freely eat: but of the tree of the knowledge of good and evil, thou shall not eat of it: for in the day that thou eatest thereof thou shalt surely die" (Genesis 2:16,17).

God promised to reward man with "the tree of life" if he obeyed, but God invoked the penalty of death for disobedience. We do not know all that "the tree of life" implies, but the reward must have been something far beyond our comprehension. If we accept the Genesis account, which Christ certainly accepted, then all of life has meaning.

True and False Religions

The two altar fires outside Eden illustrate the difference between true religion and false religion. One belonged to Abel who brought of the firstling of his flock as the offering to the Lord God. He offered it in love, in adoration, in humility, and in reverence. And the Bible says that the Lord had respect unto Abel and his offering. The other belonged to his older brother Cain, who had brought a bloodless, cheap offering to the altar, and the Bible says that "unto Cain and his offering God had not respect." How could the Lord God be so capricious? After all, did not Cain attempt to please God, and was he not perfectly sincere?

This story was put in the Bible to teach that there is a right way and a wrong way to make contact with God. Abel made his sacrifice humbly, reverently, and sacrificially, bringing his very best to God—and he came in God's way. Cain made his sacrifice grudgingly, selfishly, and superficially—but he also disobeyed God in the way he came for he came without faith. When God did not sanction and bless his sacrifice, Cain became angry and killed his brother. Abel truly loved God and worshiped Him. Cain's worship was a meaningless religiosity, as empty and hollow as his whole life became. Leaving his family, he walked the earth embittered, crying unto the Lord: "My punishment is greater than I can bear" (Genesis 4:13).

Here we see the emergence of a stream of religiosity, branching off from the mainstream of true worship of the Lord God. Throughout history this stream is destined to become an ever-widening river. Man is eternally torn between the true and the false, the worship of idols and the worship of the Lord God, the lure of religiosity or the recognition of the plain biblical teaching of the way of salvation.

Even while Moses was on Mount Sinai receiving the tablets of stone "written with the finger of God," humanistic religion was breaking out in the camp of Israel. The people said to Aaron: "Up, make us gods which shall go before us." Aaron submitted to their demands and said: "Break off the golden earrings, which are in the ears of your wives, of your sons, and your daughters, and bring them unto me. . . . And he received them at their hand, and fashioned it with a graving tool, after he had made it a molten calf: and they said, 'These be thy gods, O Israel, which brought thee up out of the land of Egypt'" (Exodus 32:1–4).

As time moved forward, other idolatrous tributaries flowed into the mainstream of religion—Baal, the god of tribes of Canaan; Chemosh, the god of Moabites; Dagon, the god of Philistines; and Molech, the god of the Amorites. If all the gods of history were listed by name, a good-sized volume would be needed to hold them all.

The inescapable implication of a counterfeit is that the real thing exists. No one ever counterfeited a seventy-five-dollar bill. Every counterfeit bears witness to the reality of the currency it copies. So in the midst of all the plan and programs men have devised to satisfy their religious urge, true religion does exist and is available for all who will come to God on His terms.

Babylon

I want to take you in your imagination back twenty-five hundred years. Babylon rules the world. Situated at the top of the Fertile Crescent, enclosed within walls so thick that four chariots could ride abreast, pierced by a hundred bronze gates where sentinels stand watch day and night.

Babylon, mighty Babylon, on the left bank of the Euphrates River, the mightiest city in the world, at the crossroads of antiquity; the center of world commerce; the richest city on earth. Out on the far-flung battlefields of the world her armies were gaining victory after victory under the leadership of the victorious general Nabonidus.

The hanging gardens of Babylon were one of the seven wonders of the world and were built by Nebuchadnezzar for his Median queen the beautiful daughter of Xerxes, who had helped his father conquer Nineveh. These gardens were constructed on several tiers of arches, one over another, each bearing a solid platform four hundred feet square. The terraces were covered with flowers, shrubs, trees and gardens. Underneath, in the arches, were luxurious apartments.

As one looks at the ruins today, he finds it hard to realize that there once stood the great Babylon, a city of extravagance and luxury beyond imagination, unsurpassed in the history of the world, but now a scene of utter desolation and ruin.

The king of Babylon at this particular time was Belshazzar (Daniel 5). He was young and handsome, a haughty, proud and high-spirited young man, puffed up with false glory that he had never earned. He was the kind of young fellow who never gave the serious things of life a second thought. His motto was: "Eat, drink and be merry, and have a good time." God was far from his thinking. He was determined to sow his wild oats and to have his fling. Although God had said, "The wages of sin is death" and, "Whatsoever a man soweth, that shall he also reap," Belshazzar thought he could beat the game of sin. He thought he could get away with it.

Thus, in spite of the warning of God's servants, he determined to have a banquet, a party that would be second to none that the world had ever seen.

The luxury, the splendor, and the brilliance of his extravagance would be the talk of the empire. One day he called his chief servant and said, "I am going to put on a party that will be the biggest that this old world has ever seen. I want you to get the finest foods, the rarest wines, the best orchestra, the hottest dancers, and send invitations to a thousand of my lords and noblemen. I will show them." Thus the preparations got under way.

Could he get away with it? Could he disregard God in his life? Could he flout sin in God's face? Only a few years ago God had thrown his grandfather, Nebuchadnezzar, from the throne because of sin. Could any man beat the game of sin? Could any young man go on, have his fling, sow his wild oats and never have to pay for it? Let's see!

The day dawns. The sky is an oriental blue. This day has been declared a holiday throughout all Babylon. The king is throwing a party for a thousand of his lords and noblemen. It will be the most extravagant banquet the world has seen. Everyone is excited. Bands are playing the national airs. Flags are unfurled. There is dancing in the streets. Gaily colored costumes are evident everywhere. Jeweled chariots are coming in from every part of the empire bringing ambassadors, army officers, nobles, lords and men of high distinction to Belshazzar's banquet.

The evening shadows gathered, and hundreds of people line the walks and streets to see the notables enter the great banquet hall. Belshazzar is the host. The soft oriental music excites the mind and flesh. Dancers dance; wine flows freely. The party continues into the night. The orchestra plays wilder tunes. The dancing gets faster and faster. Immorality and disgusting sin are evident everywhere.

A cloud comes over the moon that has been riding high in the sky as if to hide its face from the wicked scene below. A soft breeze sweeps over Babylon as if the elements are trying to blow away the shameful stench of sin.

It is almost midnight. Suddenly the intoxicated mind of the young king seems to have gone wild. He calls a servant to him, whispers in his ear, and the servant leaves the hall. In a few moments the servant comes back bearing in his arms the gold and silver vessels of God. What is the young king about to do? Does he dare to shake his fist in God's face? Are not these the vessels that had been dedicated to the use of God in the Temple at Jerusalem? Are they not sacred? Does he dare to desecrate them?

He stands and orders the servants to pass the vessels. Then he proposes a toast to the gods of silver and gold, of brass, iron, wood and stone. The guests are breathless. They did not think that the young king would dare to go this far but in their wild, intoxicated, carefree spirit they assent with ungodly laughter. The party grows wilder and wilder.

Again Belshazzar stands to propose a toast and holds in his hand one of the ornate golden vessels of God. Suddenly the vessel crashes to the table. Belshazzar's face turns white. The joints of his loins are loosed, and his knees smite one against the other. A deathlike silence grips the banquet hall. Women scream and faint. Every person's eye is riveted to one spot on the wall. An armless hand is writing over against the candlestick upon the plaster of the wall. The young king has come face to face with the supernatural for the first time in his life, and he is afraid.

He has an army, but he is afraid. His coffers are filled with silver, gold, and precious jewels, but he is afraid. He is surrounded by his best friends, but he is afraid.

Belshazzar was frightened. He tried to interpret the writing on the wall, but he could not. He called in the astrologers, the Chaldeans, and the soothsayers and said to them, "Whosoever shall read this writing, and shew me the interpretation thereof, shall be clothed with scarlet, and have a chain of gold about his neck, and shall be the third ruler in the kingdom" (Daniel 5:7). They were an overconfident lot. They were the scientists, the philosophers, and the psychologists of the day. Certainly they could read and interpret anything. Confidently, they set about their work. Soon their faces turned white, and trembling they left the banquet hall one by one. They could not read the writing. Why? I will tell you. It is impossible for a man outside of God to read God's handwriting (1 Corinthians 2:14): "But the natural man receiveth not the things of the Spirit of God: for they are foolishness unto him: neither can he know them, because they are spiritually discerned."

By this time Belshazzar's mother came. . . . [she] realized the predicament of her young son and said, "O king, live forever: let not thy thoughts trouble thee, nor let thy countenance be changed: there is a man in thy kingdom, in whom is the spirit of the holy gods; and in the days of thy father light and understanding and wisdom, like the wisdom of the gods, was found in him; whom the king Nebuchadnezzar thy father, the king, I say, thy father, made master of the magicians, astrologers, Chaldeans, and soothsayers; forasmuch as an excellent spirit, and knowledge, and understanding, interpreting of dreams, and shewing of hard sentences, and dissolving of doubts, were found in the same Daniel, whom the king named Belshazzar: now let Daniel be called, and he will shew the interpretation."

Immediately Belshazzar took his mother's advice and sent for Daniel. Daniel was brought in. Though they put him in a lions' den, he would stand true to God. He was strong, magnificent, of sterling character. His righteous, piercing eye convicted Belshazzar before either had spoken.

"Daniel! Do you see that writing on the wall? If you can read that writing I will put a gold chain around your neck. I will make you the third ruler in the empire, and I will put royal robes on you." Notice Daniel's answer. There was no weakness here!

Then Daniel answered and said before the king, Let thy gifts be to thyself, and give thy rewards to another; yet I will read the writing unto the king, and make known to him the interpretation. O thou king, the most high God gave Nebuchadnezzar thy father a kingdom, and majesty, and glory, and honor: and for the majesty that he gave him, all people, nations, and languages, trembled and feared before him: whom he would he slew; and whom he would he kept alive; and whom he would he set up; and whom he would he put down. But when his heart was lifted up, and his mind hardened in pride, he was deposed from his kingly throne, and they took his glory from him: and he was driven from the sons of men; and his heart was made like the beasts, and his dwelling was with the wild asses: they fed him with grass like oxen, and his body was wet with the dew of heaven; till he knew that the most high God ruled in the kingdom of men, and that he appointeth over it whomsoever he will. And thou his son, O Belshazzar, hast not humbled thine heart, though thou knewest all this; but hast lifted up thyself against the Lord of Heaven; and they have brought the vessels of his house before thee and thou, and thy lords, the wives, and thy concubines, have drunk wine in them; and thou hast praised the gods of silver, and gold, of brass, iron, wood, and stone, which see not, nor hear, nor know: and the God in whose hand thy breath is and whose are all thy ways, hast thou not glorified: then was the part of the hand sent from him; and this writing was written. And this is the writing that was written, MENE, TEKEL, UPHARSIN. This is the interpretation of the thing. MENE: God hath numbered thy kingdom, and finished it. TEKEL: Thou art weighed in the balances, and art found wanting. PERES: Thy kingdom is divided, and given to the Medes and Persians.

Belshazzar quaked and cringed. He was afraid. His heart was pierced with conviction at his own folly. God's words came back to him: "Whatsoever a man soweth, that shall he also reap"; "The wages of sin is death"; "The soul that sinneth, it shall die."

The piercing scream of a sentry could be heard at the gate. While the party had been at a high pitch the great Medo-Persian army had changed the course of the great Euphrates River and had marched under the walls of Babylon. That night Belshazzar the king was slain. His soul went out into eternity without God and without hope to a place of everlasting punishment! God had said, "Thou art weighed in the balances, and art found wanting."

Notice, he wasn't weighed in the balance of what other people thought of him or even in the balance of his own thinking. He was weighed in God's balance. He didn't weigh enough. He didn't measure up. He didn't stack up. He was like the man of whom Jesus tells who looked from one moonlit field to the other and said, "Soul, thou hast much goods laid up for many years; take thine ease, eat, drink, and be merry."

The king retired to bed. An agonizing scream pierced the midnight air. The servants rushed here and there. Finally one of them said, "It is the master's room." Breaking down the door, they found the master writhing and dying. His hands were folded in a strange manner as though he had been holding on to something and suddenly it had slipped away. Then a voice from Heaven was heard which said, "Thou fool, this night thy soul shall be required of thee." The king had been weighed in the balance of God and found wanting.

Tonight God is weighing you! How much do you weigh?

Man vs. God

Modern man is in conflict with the truth of God at this point. Cod speaks of a fall and a condemnation, and His key word is "grace." Modern man speaks of the soul's native goodness, its aspirations and natural good will. Man's key word is "works."

God speaks of the depths into which men have fallen and the depravity of the natural man. Man boasts of his nobility, his ideals, and his progress.

God calls men to believe in Christ or be lost. Man says that it is enough to try to be like Christ. Man's goal is imitation, not redemption.

God says that Christ is the Savior of the world. Man says that Christ is just a great example.

Slowly we have drifted away from the biblical truth: "Without the shedding of blood there is no forgiveness" (Hebrews 9:22). Modern man would like to make of the cross a thing of sentiment—a trinket to be worn around the neck—an ornament on a church steeple or an emblem stamped in gold on our Bibles. A certain romantic interest has gathered around the story of the cross. But it is the suffering and sacrifice of Christ on Calvary that symbolize man's utter helplessness to save himself. The cross as the supreme symbol of suffering reveals two basic facts that cannot be denied: the depth of man's depravity and the immensity of God's love.

Loneliness

First, there is the loneliness of solitude. I have felt the loneliness of the ocean where there is never a sound except the booming of the surf along rock-strewn shores. I have felt the loneliness of the prairie with only the occasional mournful howl of the coyote. I have felt the loneliness of the mountains broken only by the sighing of the wind.

[Second, there is] the loneliness of society. . . . That poor creature living in the dingy tenement who never receives a letter, who never hears one word of encouragement, who never experiences the handclasp of a friend—that wealthy society leader whose money has bought everything but love and happines— each knows a loneliness few can understand.

Third, there is the loneliness of suffering. Some years ago we received a letter from a radio listener who for five years had been crippled into a sitting position by arthritis. For five long, weary, painful years she was unable to stretch out or to lie down, yet she wrote, "I have spent many a day alone, but never a lonely day." Why? It was Christ who made the difference. With Christ as your

Savior and constant companion, you too, although alone, need never be lonely.

Fourth, there is the loneliness of sorrow. In the eleventh chapter of John, we read of Mary and Martha. Their brother Lazarus was dead. Jesus had not yet come. They stood beside the body of their brother and wept. For you, too, perhaps the world has become a vast cemetery containing but one grave. You have stood in the sick room and watched the one dearer than all the world to you slip beyond your reach. You crave fellowship. You want someone to come along with a strong hand to help wipe the tears away and put the smile back on your face, and give you joy through the sorrow. Jesus can do just that. The Bible says, "Casting all your care upon him, for he careth for you" (1 Peter 5:7). God loves His children. If you are willing to trust Him and give yourself to Him, He can carry your sorrow.

Fifth, there is the loneliness of sin. . . . Perhaps you at one time thought you knew the joy and peace of being born into God's family. You experienced the sweet fellowship of God's people. You tasted the complete happiness and satisfaction of Christ's presence with you, but you sinned. You went out from the presence of Christ, and you have found that it is night. You have neither the fellowship of Christians nor the fellowship of sinners, and certainly you no longer have the fellowship of Christ. Perhaps there is no loneliness quite so bitter as the loneliness of a backslidden Christian. Yet there is forgiveness for you. As you confess and forsake your sins, your fellowship with Christ will be restored. "If we confess our sins, he is faithful and just to forgive us our sins, and to cleanse us from all unrighteousness" (1 John 1:9).

Last, there is the loneliness of the savior. Thousands of human beings were swarming around Him. There was great joy at the Passover season everywhere, but Jesus was "despised and rejected of men; a man of sorrows and acquainted with grief: and we hid as it were our faces from him; he was despised, and we esteemed him not. Surely he hath borne our griefs, and carried our sorrows: yet we did esteem him stricken, smitten of God, and afflicted. But he was wounded for our transgressions, he was bruised for our iniquities: the chastisement of our peace was upon him; and with his stripes we are healed. All we like sheep have gone astray; we have turned every one to his own way; and the Lord hath laid on him the iniquity of us all" (Isaiah 53: 3–6).

Jesus was alone. He had come to His own, and His own received Him not. "But all this was done, that the Scriptures of the prophets might be fulfilled. Then all the disciples forsook him, and fled" (Matthew 26:56). The crowds who had so recently shouted, "Hosanna," had that very day shouted, "Crucify him. Crucify him." Now even His loyal twelve had left.

And at last we hear Him cry out, "My God, my God, why hast thou forsaken me?" (Mark 15:34). Not only had He been forsaken by His human companions, but now in that desperate and lonely hour, He—because He was bearing our sins in His own body on the cross—had been forsaken by God as well. Jesus was enduring the suffering and judgment of Hell for you and me.

Searching in the Wrong Places

Over 2500 years ago the prophet Isaiah looked out on a people who longed for happiness and security but were looking for it in the wrong places. They were running to the marketplace and to places of amusement, spending their money madly for things which brought them no permanent satisfaction.

He stood before them one day and gave them the Word of God. "Ho, every one that thirsteth, come ye to the waters, and he that hath no money; come ye, buy, and eat; yea, come, buy wine and milk without money and without price. Wherefore do ye spend money for that which is not bread? And your labor for that which satisfieth not? Hearken diligently unto me, and eat ye that which is good, and let your soul delight itself in fatness" (Isaiah 55:1, 2).

Isaiah didn't speak negatively and berate them for their sins in this particular sermon. He didn't grab the bottle from the drunkard's hand, he didn't lecture them about the evils of gluttony, he didn't shame them for their immoral practices. He overlooked that for the moment. He simply asked them: "Are you getting what you want out of life? Why do you spend your money for that which is not bread and your labor for that which does not satisfy?"

If Isaiah were living today he would probably stand at Forty-second and Broadway in New York, in the Loop in Chicago, or on Market Street in San Francisco, and simply ask the milling, restless throngs: "Are you getting what you want? Are you finding satisfaction?"

He would ask the actress, surfeited with fame and fortune, but peering out on life hungrily: "Are you getting what you want?" He would say to the eminently successful financier who commands his fleets and controls his industries: "Are you getting what you want?"

He would say to the laborers and workmen of America who are enjoying the highest standard of living in history: "Are you getting what you want?" He would ask the youth of America: "Are you getting what you want?"

He would say to the consumers of America who have the best homes, the most comfortable furniture, the finest food, the cleverest gadgets, and the smoothest, most powerful automobiles: "Are you getting what you want?"

Isaiah did not leave them with an unanswered question. He went on to tell them that there is a satisfying way of life, if they would seek it. He exhorted them to abandon their vain searching for pots of gold at the end of mythical rainbows, and to start searching for happiness where it is really found, in a right relationship with God.

Two Sets of Eyes

The Bible teaches that you and I have two sets of eyes. Your physical eyes may have 20/20 vision, but your spiritual eyes may be blinded. In fact, the Bible teaches that we have been blinded by a supernatural power. The Scripture says in 1 Corinthians 2:14, "But the natural man (that's the ordinary man) receiveth not the things of the Spirit of God for they are foolishness unto him; neither can he know them, because they are spiritually discerned."

The Bible says in 2 Corinthians 4:4, "In whom the god of this world hath blinded the minds of them which believe not, lest the light of the glorious gospel of Christ, who is the image of God, should shine unto them."

In other words there's a supernatural veil over our minds and over our spiritual eyes, and that's why a person can never come to Christ or to God by intellect alone. The Gospel just doesn't make sense. You'll never be able to figure it out logically step by step because sin has affected your thinking processes. Your normal intellectual life is conformed to this materialistic, secular world. And that's why the Gospel is "foolishness," the Bible says. The Bible says the preaching of the Cross is "foolishness" to them that perish.

Rationalizing God

If you try to rationalize God exhaustively, you will fail. There are mysteries about God that we will never understand in this life. How can the small and finite, limited to time and space, understand an infinite God! We should not think it strange that it is impossible to comprehend God intellectually, when it is equally impossible to explain many mysteries in the realm of matter. Who can explain why objects are always attracted to the center of the earth?

Who can fathom the law of gravity? Newton discovered it, but he could not explain it.

There are many arguments we could marshal to give evidence of the existence of God. There is scientific evidence pointing to God's existence. For example, whatever is in motion must be moved by another, for motion is the response of matter to power. In the world of matter there can be no power without life, and life presupposes a being from which emanates the power to move things such as the tides and the planets.

Or there is the argument that says nothing can be the cause of itself. It would be prior to itself if it caused itself to be, and that is an absurdity.

Then there is the law of life. We see objects that have no intellect, such as stars and planets, moving in a consistent pattern, cooperating ingeniously with one another. Hence it is evident that they achieve their movements not by accident but by design. Whatever lacks intelligence cannot move intelligently. An arrow would be useless without a bow and an archer. What gives direction and purpose and design to inanimate objects? It is God. He is the underlying, motivating force of life.

Thus many evidences and many arguments could be advanced to indicate that there is a God. Yet the plain truth is this: God cannot be proved by mere rationalization. He cannot be contained in a tiny man-made test tube or confined to an algebraic formula. If God can be fully proved by the human mind, then He is no greater than the mind that proves Him.

Just Enough Natural Religion

There, back in the very beginning, was the introduction of natural religion upon the human scene as an effort to circumvent God's plan. Natural religion, however, is not always a crude invention of early man. Today it is the full-time effort of many intellectuals to circumvent God's plan. Some of them are professors of religion in our universities; others are even leaders in the church.

The Apostle Paul said of man's corruption of God's general revelation into a naturalistic religion: "For the invisible things of him from the creation of the world are clearly seen, being understood by the things that are made, even his eternal power and Godhead; so that they are without excuse: because that, when they knew God, they glorified him not as God, neither were thankful; but became vain in their imaginations, and their foolish heart was darkened. Professing themselves to be wise, they became fools...who changed the truth of God into a lie, and worshipped and served the creature more than the Creator, who is blessed for ever" (Romans 1:20–25). This is a biblical picture of man's perversion of God's revelation, with all its primitive crudity, sensuality, fetishism, superstition, and magic. It has passed through many refinements and much refurbishing. Today it presents itself in the forms of intellectual respectability, but in primitive cultures it still exists in the same forms of debasing sensuality and deceit.

Natural religion is opposed to divine revelation, which accepts the Bible as the authoritative source of the ideas of sin and justification by faith in the atoning death of Christ. Natural religion rejects almost everything in the Apostles' Creed.

This is not to say that natural religion does not contain elements of truth, or embody some high ethical standards and moral values. Some of its followers at times employ terms that recall the language of the Bible. While the morality encouraged by natural religion may win the approval of men, it neither secures acceptability with God nor reflects His full moral demands. In fact, some of the crudest immorality in human history has had the sanction of natural religion, as the Apostle Paul reminds us in the Epistle to the Romans.

The Bible teaches that Satan can transform himself into an "angel of light," adapting himself to every culture and every situation, even at times deceiving true believers. Counterfeiters always try to make their counterfeit money look exactly like the real thing. This is how Satan operates today. Thousands of people have been herded even into the church without a vital experience with Jesus Christ. They have substituted good works, community effort, social reform or a religious rite for personal salvation. Many people have just enough natural religion to make them immune to the real thing. Every time I go to the Far East I take cholera shots, and usually I get sick from the shots. Actually I get a small case of cholera, which makes me immune to the dreaded disease should I come in contact with it in my travels. This is true of most vaccinations. And it is also true in the realm of religion. There are many people who have just enough religion to be immune from a genuine personal experience with Jesus Christ. Therein lies the grave danger for thousands of professing Christians.

7

SIN AND TEMPTATION

Seven Deadly Sins

Pope Gregory the Great, at the end of the sixth century, divided all the sins under seven heads. He said that every sin that a man commits can be classified by seven words. He named the sins: pride, anger, envy, impurity, gluttony, slothfulness, and avarice. They have been called down through the centuries "the seven deadly sins." These sins are nowhere collectively mentioned in a single passage in the Bible, and yet they are all condemned separately in many places. Thomas Aquinas and most of the great theologians have agreed with Pope Gregory, and these seven deadly sins have become a recognized part of moral theology.

These sins also became the subjects of poets. The scheme of Dante's *Purgatory* follows the order of the seven deadly sins. They are also discussed fully in Chaucer's "Parson's Tale" and in Marlowe's *Doctor Faustus.* Even a recent Italian movie was entitled *The Seven Deadly Sins.*

PRIDE

The first of the seven deadly sins is pride. It naturally comes first—for as we read in Proverbs 16:18, "Pride goeth...before a fall." Pride is thus the mental and moral condition that precedes almost all other sins. All sin is selfishness in some form or other, and pride consists essentially in undue self-esteem, delighting in the thought of one's own superiority over his fellows. The Scripture says in Proverbs 16:5, "Everyone that is proud in heart is an abomination to the Lord: though hand join in hand, he shall not be unpunished." Again in Proverbs 29:23 we read, "A man's pride shall bring him low: but honor shall uphold the humble in spirit."

The pride that God loathes is not self-respect or a legitimate sense of personal dignity. It is a haughty, undue self-esteem out of all proportion to our actual worth. It is that repugnant egotism which is repulsive to both man and God. It is that revolting conceit which swaggers before men and struts in the presence of the Almighty. God hates it. It is an abomination unto Him, which means that it makes Him shudder. God has said in Psalm 101:5, "Him that hath a high look and a proud heart will not I suffer." God cannot stand or endure pride. He hates it.

Pride may take various forms, but it all emanates from the haughty human heart. Some take pride in their looks, others in their race, others in their business, others in their social life. In other words, pride may be spiritual, intellectual, material, or social. The most repugnant of these four is spiritual pride. This pride of the spirit was the sin that caused Lucifer, the Devil, to fall. This is where sin actually began.

We read in Isaiah 14:12–15, "How art thou fallen from heaven, O Lucifer, son of the morning! How art thou cut down to the ground, which didst weaken the nations!

"For thou hast said in thine heart, I will ascend into Heaven, I will exalt my throne above the stars of God: I will sit also upon the mount of the congregation, in the sides of the north:

"I will ascend above the heights of the clouds; I will be like the most High. Yet thou shalt be brought down to

Hell, to the sides of the pit."

Here we find Lucifer saying, "I will," five times. "I will be above God." It was the pride of his heart that was the first sin ever committed in the universe. When we, like Lucifer, begin to feel that we are self-contained and self-sufficient, we are on dangerous ground.

ANGER

Anger is one of man's most devastating sins. This is one sin which everyone is capable of committing. The tiny baby has a fit of temper and loses its dinner. The little boy has a tantrum and upsets the family decorum. The wife loses her temper and develops a sick headache. The husband gets angry and loses his appetite. Every member of the family is subject to its blight. No one is by nature immune to this dispositional disease of human nature.

Anger breeds remorse in the heart, discord in the home, bitterness in the community and confusion in the state. Homes are often destroyed by the swirling tornadoes of heated domestic anger. Business relations are often shattered by fits of violent temper when reason gives way to venomous wrath. Friendships are often broken by the keen knife of indignation, which is sharpened by the whetstone of anger.

Anger is denounced by the church and condemned by the sacred Scriptures. It murders, assaults, and attacks—causing physical and mental harm to its victims. Its recoil, like a high-powered rifle, often hits back at the one who wields it, doing equal damage to the offender and the offended.

Because anger has brought so much unhappiness and confusion to the world, God loathes it. In Psalm 37:8 we read, "Cease from anger, and forsake wrath; fret not thyself in any wise to do evil." Jesus condemned it in no uncertain terms and classed it with the heinous sin of murder. He said in Matthew 5:22, "I say unto you, That whosoever is angry with his brother without a cause shall be in danger of the judgment: and whosoever shall say. . . Thou fool, shall be in danger of Hell fire." The wise Solomon said in Proverbs 16:32, "He that is slow to anger is better than the mighty; and he that ruleth his spirit [is better] than he that taketh a city." The Bible again says in James 1:19, "Wherefore, my beloved brethren, let every man be swift to hear, slow to speak, slow to anger."

ENVY

Envy and jealousy can ruin reputations, split churches, and cause murders. Envy can shrink our circle of friends, ruin our business and dwarf our souls. Procrastination may be the thief of time, but envy is the murderer of souls. We read in Job 5:2 that it can kill a person (modern psychiatry bears this out), "For wrath killeth the foolish man, and envy slayeth the silly one."

There is a Greek story about a man who killed himself through envy. His fellow citizens had erected a statue to one of their number who was a celebrated champion in the public games. But this man, a rival of the honored athlete, was so envious that he vowed that he would destroy that statue. Every night he went out into the darkness and chiseled at its base in an effort to undermine its foundation and make it fall. At last he succeeded. It did fall—but it fell on him. He fell, a victim of his own envy.

The Bible, whose counsel is wiser than top psychiatrists, tells us not to be envious of the rich. In Psalm 49:16 we read, "Be not thou afraid when one is made rich, when the glory of his house is increased." Envying those who are more prosperous than we are does not add one dollar to our assets, but it bankrupts the soul. The envious man somehow feels that other people's fortune is his misfortune, that their success is his failure and that their blessing is his curse. The irony of it all is that if he builds up such a case in his mind and soul, his failure is inevitable. I have never seen a man who profited in any way by being envious of others, but I have seen hundreds cursed by it. You cannot have a full orbed personality and harbor envy in your heart. We are told in Proverbs 14:30, "A sound heart is the life of the flesh, but envy the rottenness of the bones." Envy is not a defensive weapon—it is an offensive instrument used in spiritual ambush. It wounds for the sake of wounding and hurts for the sake of hurting.

IMPURITY

There are three facts about the sin of impurity which I would like for you to notice. *First,* the sin of impurity marks. In the days of slavery a slave could be identified by the marks of his master. When men become mastered by sin, it is inescapable that the marks of sin are upon them. The reddened eyes and bloated cheeks of the alcoholic, the nervous twitch of the dope fiend, the lewd stare of the impure, and the haughty look of the proud are all imprints of inner wickedness. Immorality, which is the sin of perversion and unnaturalness, has a way of making those who harbor it unnatural appearing. The shifty eye, the embarrassed blush, the suggestive glance—these are all marks of the impure. They are the outward signs of inward impurity.

But the outward marks are slight compared to the blemishes which impurity etches on the personality and upon the soul. Guilt complexes and bad consciences are fashioned in the fires of lustful passion. Out of unbalanced practices of impurity grow phobias which alarm even our most skilled psychiatrists. But worse than all, impurity mars the souls. The Bible says in Galatians 5:19, "The works of the flesh are these; adultery, fornication, uncleanness, and lasciviousness." The Bible says that the sin of impurity is the result of the deceitfulness of sin. The Bible teaches that "There is none that doeth good, no not one" (Psalm 14:3), and that the entire human race has been tainted by the disease of sin. The Bible also teaches that those who are guilty of this sin of impurity shall not inherit the kingdom of God. Jesus interpreted the Seventh Commandment which says, "Thou shalt not commit adultery," when He said, "Whosoever looketh upon a woman to lust after her hath committed adultery with her already. . ." (Matthew 5:28). Jesus said that a person can be guilty of this sin by thought and word, as well as deed. There are thousands today who are guilty, whose souls have been marred by the sin of impurity, and who have become separated from God because of this besetting sin.

Next, impurity mocks or deceives. Paul, writing to Titus, indicates that even he knew the deceitfulness of immorality before he came to know Jesus Christ. He said in Titus 3:3, "For we ourselves also were sometimes foolish, disobedient, deceived, serving divers lusts and pleasures. . ." It has deceived kings, prophets, sages, and saints. Do not think for one moment that you are immune to its blight! Even the wise Solomon, who through experience had every reason to know, said, "Fools make a mock of sin" (Proverbs 14:9).

Too many people underestimate the power of impurity. Samson toyed with it, made sport of it and thought he had it under control, but in the end it controlled him and ruined his life. David, chosen of God, came under its subtle spell and in a moment of weakness was deceived by the overcoming powers of impurity—and he was years climbing back to God up the steep stairway of repentance. Homes have been lost in a fleeting moment of weakness, kingdoms have been bartered for a transient pleasure, and an eternal heritage has been squandered for an hour of Hell's diversion.

Impurity mocks those who harbor it in their hearts. Impurity mocks when its harvest is gathered. In Galatians 6:7-8 we read, "Be not deceived, God is not mocked; for whatsoever a man soweth, that shall he also reap. For he that soweth to his flesh shall of the flesh reap corruption. . . ."

Impurity, when it is finished brings forth remorse. Some of the most miserable men I know are those who are haunted by the memory of the wasted, wanton years of impurity. God is willing to forgive them, but they are not willing and able to forgive themselves. The magnitude of their sin has grown through the years, and it has born its fruit of regret and remorse. They have sown to the flesh, and of the flesh have reaped corruption. Their impurity mocks them, haunts them and derides them. Like every other device of the Devil, it has taken away from them all that is good and has given them nothing in return. Satan drives a hard bargain!

Then, impurity masters. The Bible says in Romans 6:16, "Know ye not that to whom ye yield yourselves servants to obey, his servants ye are to whom ye obey?" Many people are mastered by impurity because they have given themselves to impurity.

GLUTTONY

Gluttony is a sin, first, because it is a physical expression of the philosophy of materialism. It laughs at righteous restraint and scorns temperance and decency. It cries, "Eat, drink and be merry, for tomorrow we die." It makes no room for God and has no consideration for eternity. It lives for the present, and its philosophy is, "You live only once, so live it up."

Jesus gave us a classic example of a man who lived for this life only. In his prosperity he said, "I will pull down my barns and build greater; and there will I bestow all my fruits and my goods. And I will say to my soul, Soul, thou hast much goods laid up for many years; take thine ease, eat, drink, and be merry" (Luke 12:18,19). His philosophy was little different from our materialistic philosophy of today. Build bigger...take it easier...drink more...eat more...enjoy life more.

We hear this philosophy blaring out of our radio and

television sets from morning till night. The accent is on comfort, ease and the satisfying of our appetites. We see it pictured in our magazines. Everywhere we are encouraged to easier living and more and better food—with the accent on the things of this world. Temperance, restraint, and self-discipline are being forgotten in the rush toward ease and plenty. This generation, shot through with the materialistic philosophy, is trying in vain to drink its way to happiness, fight its way to peace, spend its way to prosperity and enjoy its way to Heaven. How easy it is in this day to fill our minds with rubbish, our stomachs with trash—and starve our souls. God has said in Deuteronomy 8:3, "Man shall not live by bread alone, but by every word that proceedeth out of the mouth of God."

Gluttony is a perversion of a natural, God-given appetite. We must fix in our minds the fact that sin is not always flagrant and open transgression. It is often the perversion and distortion of natural, normal desires and appetites. Love is often distorted into lust. Self respect too often is perverted into godless ambition. When a God-given, normal hunger is extended greedily into abnormality so that it harms the body, dulls the mind, and stultifies the soul, it becomes sin. In Proverbs 23:21 we read, "For the drunkard and the glutton shall come to poverty; and drowsiness shall clothe a man with rags."

The gratification of our fleshly appetites is not to receive first importance in our lives. Jesus said, "Take no thought saying, What shall we eat? or, What shall we drink? . . . But seek ye first the kingdom of God, and His righteousness; and all these things shall be added unto you" (Matthew 6:31, 33).

Most of us have disregarded Jesus' warning about putting our fleshly appetites first. Too many of us spend our lives in the pursuit of the material, crowding Christ out altogether; and then in the last frenzied, hurried moment of life we cry, "God have mercy on my soul!" I ask you: is it fair, is it intelligent, to wait until the last second of life upon this earth to transact life's most urgent business—settling your account with God? Of course it is not fair, and I seriously doubt the genuineness of such a deathbed repentance. God may give a man a chance on his deathbed to repent of sin if the man has never been warned and has never heard the plan of salvation clearly explained. But to a man who has deliberately rejected Christ and continued in his sins, there is little hope that he can find peace with God in his last hours. The Bible warns that a day will come when a person will seek Him but will not find Him, and call on Him but He will not hear.

SLOTHFULNESS

The Bible indicates that the sin of slothfulness engenders a negative kind of life which is stagnant and ineffective and which renders a person unworthy of being a follower of Jesus Christ. Spiritual laziness is not only a sin against God—it is a sin against yourself. It measures the distance between what you ought to be and what you actually are. It shows the difference between the person you are and the person you could be.

Slothfulness is the destroyer of opportunity and the murderer of souls. It kills stealthily and silently, but it kills just the same.

The slothful man is like driftwood floating downward with the current—effortlessly and heedlessly. The easy way is the popular way, the broad way, the way of the crowd. It takes no effort, no strength, no manhood to be lost.

A drifting boat always goes downstream—never up. A drifting, slothful soul inevitably is drifting toward an eternity of destruction.

Many a man has lost his life in an automobile accident, not because he was a bad driver, but because he was a good driver—asleep. Many persons are fighting losing battles spiritually, not because they are really bad, but because they are spiritually slothful, sleepy, and drowsy.

Ephesians 5:14 declares, "Awake, thou that sleepest, and arise from the dead, and Christ shall give thee light."

Many persons have lost their health and their life, not because they have abused their bodies by sin, but because they have neglected their bodies. They were just too lazy to take care of themselves.

Slothfulness reaps its annual harvest of thousands of deaths on the highways, thousands of physical breakdowns, and a staggering amount of suffering and misery across the world.

The sin of doing nothing has been called in the Scriptures the sin of omission—which is just as dangerous as the sin of commission.

You do not have to do anything to be lost—just be slothful about your soul—just do nothing. Jesus said that it is easy to be lost. He said, "Wide is the gate, and broad is the way that leadeth to destruction, and many there be which go in thereat" (Matthew 7:14).

In the parable of the talents given by Jesus, we read not only of the reward of the faithful servant, but of the judgment of the slothful servant. His judgment for doing nothing was as great as the judgment of those that had committed adultery and murder. Matthew 25:26–30 records His sentence: "Thou wicked and slothful servant...take therefore the talent from him...and cast ye the unprofitable servant into outer darkness: there shall be weeping and gnashing of teeth." The unprofitable servant had done no outward wrong—he simply was too slothful to carry out the responsibility which had been assigned to him. His sin was the sin of slothfulness, the sin of doing nothing.

The chief sin of the ten virgins was not immorality, lying, or cheating—it was slothfulness. They simply neglected to provide themselves with oil. They were judged, not for flagrant sin, but for laziness and unfaithfulness. When the bridegroom came, the door of opportunity slammed shut, and the voice of God echoed in judgment, "I know ye not" (Matthew 25:12).

In every area of life the slothful person is the loser. The slothful, lazy student who spends his time loafing in the campus store can never hope to be on the honor roll. Diplomas are usually awarded for faithful work and diligent study—not for native talent or ability. It is usually the person who is willing to work who wins the applause of his professors. On the farm, in business, in the school, in the shop, and in every area of our lives, slothfulness is judged and faithfulness is rewarded.

Slothfulness is a destroyer in everyday life. On its account, lives have been lost, cities have been ravaged by fire, and homes have been broken. It has kept the hobo from a life of respectability, the prostitute from living a life of purity, and the thief from being honest.

Someone has aptly said, "It isn't the thing you do, friend; but the thing you leave undone, that gives you a bit of a heartache at the setting of the sun."

The encouraging word we might have spoken to a discouraged friend, the helpful deed that would have made someone's burden a little lighter, the bit of money pressed lovingly into the hand of the needy—these are the neglected things that bring remorse and rob others of the help they need. When through slothfulness we fail to do that loving deed, Jesus' words of judgment ring in our ears, "Inasmuch as ye did it not unto one of the least of these, ye did it not unto me" (Matthew 25:45).

AVARICE

Avarice, the close relative of covetousness, is probably the parent of more evil than all the other sins. In fact, 1 Timothy 6:10 says that the "love of money is the root of all evil." Men driven by avarice have robbed, assaulted, attacked, embezzled, slandered and murdered. Covetousness was one of the first sins to raise its venomous head in the Garden of Eden. In Genesis 3:6 we read that "when the woman saw that the tree was good for food, and pleasant to the eyes, and a tree to be desired, she took of the fruit thereof, and did eat." This sin of avarice is as much a part of the natural man as breathing. From babyhood to old age it motivates our actions and shapes our behavior patterns.

It has also forced its way into our ethical ideology. Such catch phrases as "self preservation is man's first instinct," "self protection is the first law of life," "look out for number one" are all adages of avarice.

The Garden of Eden was a place of indescribable beauty until the sin of avarice crept in. After that it was an eerie swamp with a flaming sword of judgment which turned every way. Life can never be hallowed with the bliss of Eden, and man can never know the fellowship of God until he finds victory over the blighting sin of greed and selfishness. No sin can rob life of its beauty and radiance as thoroughly as the sin of avarice.

Scan through the pages of the Bible and note the trail of abject misery which this deadly sin has made through human history. It was an unholy, unnatural lust for selfish gain that caused King Ahab to covet Naboth's vineyard and eventually to murder to achieve his avaricious end. But the voice of God came to Ahab, saying, "In the place where dogs licked the blood of Naboth shall dogs lick thy blood" (1 Kings 21:19).

Avarice first claims our souls, then seals our destiny. Ahab little dreamed that the innocent seed of greed in his heart would in the end bring forth a harvest of death and judgment. Joseph's brothers sowed the tiny seed of avarice and greed when they sold their godly brother into slavery, but little did they foresee the harvest of famine and misery which they were to reap when avarice came into full bloom.

The rich man of whom Jesus spoke sowed a crop of selfishness and greed, and Jesus said that it brought forth plentifully. This rich man soon came to know the futility which comes from full barns, full pockets, but an empty heart. He was soon to drop dead with a voice from heaven saying, "Thou fool, this night thy soul is required of thee" (Luke 12:20).

Judas, driven by avarice, sold his Lord for thirty pieces of silver but found out that life was not worth living without Him. Throwing the tarnished silver at the feet of the greedy with whom he had made a poor bargain, he went out and hanged himself; but long before the life was choked out of the body, his soul was dead—it had been strangled by greed and avarice. To all the Ahabs, the Judases, the foolish men of every age who live selfishly and greedily, Christ says in Luke 12:21, "So is he that layeth up treasures for himself and is not rich toward God."

Sinners By Choice

While the tendency to sin has been passed on to us from our first parents, we are also sinners by choice. When we reach the age of accountability and are faced by the choice between good and evil, we all at some time or other choose to get angry, to tell a lie, to act selfishly. As David said: "Behold I was shapen in iniquity, and in sin did my mother conceive me" (Psalm 51:5). This does not mean that he was born out of wedlock, but rather that he inherited the tendency to sin from his parents. Thus Jeremiah said: "The heart is deceitful above all things, and desperately wicked: who can know it?" (Jeremiah 17:9).

A seventeen-year-old boy stabbed an old man to death in Brooklyn. Later at the police station he said: "I don't know why I did it." "There is," said a great lion tamer, "no such thing in the world as a tamed lion. A lion may be on good behavior today and a whirlwind of ferocity tomorrow." None of us can really trust our hearts. The Bible vividly puts it like this: "Sin croucheth at the door" (Genesis 4:7 RV). Given the right circumstances, most of us are capable of almost any transgression.

This does not mean that every person is devoid of all qualities pleasing to men. Man may have certain moral qualities. He may be a gentleman in every sense of the word. However, the Scriptures teach that every person is destitute of that love for God that is the fundamental requirement of the law. It means that the average man is given to prefer "self" to God.

Because man fails to meet God's requirements, he is guilty and under condemnation. Being guilty means that he deserves punishment. God's holiness reacts against sin, because He is a holy God. Thus there is "the wrath of God" (Romans 1:18).

Evil Imaginations

You can commit immorality by evil imaginations. In Genesis 6:5 we read: "And God saw that the wickedness of man was great in the earth, and that every imagination of the thoughts of his heart was only evil continually." God is concerned with our imaginations, for they in a large measure determine what kind of a persons we are to be.

Solomon said: "As [a man] thinketh in his heart, so is he" (Proverbs 23:7). If our thoughts are evil, then our acts will be evil. If our thoughts are godly, then our lives will be godly. Robert Browning said: "Thought is the soul of the act." Ralph Waldo Emerson said: "Thought is the seat of action, the ancestor of every action is thought."

If God destroyed the world during Noah's time for its continual evil imaginations, is it not reasonable to believe that all of the sin, lust, and licentiousness rampant today grieves His heart just as it did in that day?

Many people dream of sin, imagine sin, and if granted the opportunity would indulge in sin. All they lack is the occasion to sin. So in the sight of God they are sinners as great as though they had actually committed immorality.

Spiritual Pride

Spiritual pride, because it trusts in one's own virtue rather than the grace of God, is earmarked for God's judgment. It induces in us a contempt for others, and makes us contemptible to those about us. It says with the repulsive Pharisee of old, "God, I thank Thee that I am not as other men are." It is smug, self-satisfied and full of conceit. God loathes spiritual pride because it presumes to be good in its own right. It is the strutting of a tramp clad in filthy rags who imagines that he is the best dressed of all men. Spiritual pride would be humorous if it wasn't so tragic. God has sounded a stern warning for these descendants of the Pharisees. He has said in James 4:6, "God resisteth the proud, but giveth grace unto the humble."

There are some people who think they have a corner on the Gospel. They have become conceited, smug, proud and pharisaical. There are others that glory in their self-righteousness, and think that they are better than other people. They don't do this, and they don't do that. They keep the letter of the law, but have long since forgotten the spirit of the law. They are guilty of spiritual pride. There are also others who think themselves to be pure and all others impure. They have forgotten that there is no such thing as a completely pure church. Jesus taught that the chaff and the wheat would grow together and that we would not be able to distinguish them until the end of time. Yet we have many Pharisees today going about trying to throw the chaff out of the wheat, doing that which God said could never be done until Christ comes again. We have many going about pulling specks out of other people's eyes when they have beams in their own eyes. They have a haughty, superior, "chip on the shoulder" attitude. They spend their time criticizing and gossiping about others. This is the worst pride of all.

Intellectual Pride

Another form of pride is intellectual pride. The Bible says to those who suffer from this kind of spiritual delusion in 1 Corinthians 8:1–2, "...Knowledge puffeth up, but love edifieth. And if any man think that he knoweth anything, he knoweth nothing yet as he ought to know." This kind of pride manifests itself in arrogance toward the unlearned, the illiterate and the oppressed. It forgets that our mental capacities were given by God, and that the knowledge we attain is largely the labor of others. Is this reason for intellectual arrogance? Paul says in Romans, "...Mind not high things, but condescended to men of low estate..."

Intellectual pride is too often the enemy of the Gospel of Christ because it gives its possessor self-confidence rather than God-confidence. We read in Proverbs 3:5, "Trust in the Lord with all thine heart; and lean not unto thine own understanding." But the intellectually proud are not like that. They like to put God in a test tube; and if He cannot be put in a test tube, then they cannot accept Him. They do not like to lean on Him and trust Him. They cannot understand that faith goes beyond learning, knowledge, and even reason, and accepts that which may not even appear logical to the mind. To have knowledge without faith is to use only half of your mind. The Psalmist says in Psalm 111:10, "The fear of the Lord is the beginning of wisdom..."

True religion, contrary to the conception of some, increases your intellect rather than distracts from it. Paul, himself an intellectual, said in Romans 12:2, "...be ye transformed by the renewing of your mind..." The kind of intellectual pride that is given to intolerance, bigotry, and smugness, God hates. God abhors intellectual pride. He says in Proverbs 26:12, "Seest thou a man wise in his own conceit? There is more hope of a fool than of him."

False Religions

Suppose a neighbor of yours or a member of your family has become involved in a religious group and is urging you to look at it seriously and become a member. Or suppose someone knocks on your door and with a warm smile asks to share a few ideas about their religious group with you or give you some religious literature. What should you do to avoid being deceived and led astray from the truth of Christ? Let me suggest three questions you should ask.

First, is Christ worshiped as Lord and Savior? The central question today is still the same as that Jesus asked almost two thousand years ago: "What do you think about the Christ? Whose son is he?" (Matthew 22:42). Some cults dismiss Christ completely or suggest He was only a great teacher. Some claim salvation is not to be found in Christ, but only in their leader or founder, or in their teachings. Many cults claim to have a high view of Christ, but deny that He rose again from the dead, or that He was the unique and divine Son of God, or that we are saved only through His atoning death on the cross.

But Jesus declared, "I am the way and the truth and the life. No one comes to the Father except through me" (John 14:6). The apostle Peter summarized the consistent message of the New Testament from beginning to end: "Salvation is found in no one else, for there is no other name under heaven given to men by which we must be saved" (Acts 4:12). Don't be deceived! No human leader, no group, no set of religious teachings or philosophical ideas can save you from your sins and reconcile you to God. Only Christ can do that—and He will, for all who turn in simple faith and trust to Him as Lord and Savior.

Second, is the Bible central as the one true guide to faith and practice? Cults and false religions often ignore or even deny the full inspiration and authority of the Bible as the Word of God. They often substitute instead another book or a set of teachings that are not based on the Bible. Some cults pay lip service to the Bible as the Word of God, but then add a second book to "interpret" the Bible "correctly" according to their own man-made teachings. One prominent cult in America claims it bases its teachings on the Word of God—but has made its own "translation" of the Bible which twists the meaning of the Bible's clear teaching.

The Bible is God's Word, and as such it is our authoritative source of truth about God. It is not the product of men's imaginations—although God used men to write it—but comes from the Spirit of God Himself. "Above all, you must understand that no prophecy of Scripture came about by the prophet's own interpretation. For prophecy never had its origin in the will of man, but men spoke from God as they were carried along by the Holy Spirit" (2 Peter 1:20, 21).

Third, is participation in a local Christian fellowship encouraged and practiced. One common characteristic of many cults is that they claim that they, and they alone, have the whole truth. They therefore strongly discourage their members from participating in the worship and instruction of a Christian church—and may even take violent measures to prevent it.

Science Doesn't Satisfy

Out of the new age of science and technology there has been emerging a new faith of scientism that displaces biblical faith. This nuclear age has greatly reduced the faith that was woven deeply into the culture of the past. One scientist said: "The world picture of the nuclear age does not include God. The cultivated man today finds no God in his reactor, and he finds none through his telescope. God is not among the rushing electrons, and He is not visible in outer space." There is no doubt that there are new powers of science that respond to the touch of a button at the shrine of computers, rather than at the word of our prayers or at the altars of our churches. In our hands is a power that seems to our finite minds as great as that we once attributed to God. To many this is the power of a god, and in a new way we hear again the words of the serpent to our first parents: "Ye shall be as gods" (Genesis 3:5). Yet like the other gods of our generation, science does not satisfy the deep longings of the human soul. The more man learns, the less he knows. Thus many of our leading scientists have come to express their faith in God.

To Adapt or Not to Adapt

In all my evangelistic ministry I have never felt a need to "adapt" Jesus to the many and varied nationalities, cultures, tribes, or ethnic groups to whom I have preached. I believe in contextualization. That is that we adapt our methods and terminology to the people to whom we are ministering. I try to adapt illustrations or emphasize certain truths that will help a particular audience understand the Gospel more clearly in light of their cultural background. But the essential truths of the Gospel do not change. All things were created by Him, and He sustains all creation, so the message of His saving grace is applicable to all. The facts concerning His virgin birth, His sinless life, His sacrificial and substitutionary death, His resurrection and ascension to the right hand of the Father, and the glorious hope of His return must not be diluted or distorted in any way.

Jesus is not only the Christ, He is also "God, our Lord and Savior." This is a staggering, almost incomprehensible truth: God Himself has come down on this planet in the person of His only Son. The incarnation and the full deity of Jesus are the cornerstones of the Christian faith. Jesus Christ was not just a great teacher or a holy religious leader. He was God Himself in human flesh—fully God and fully man.

Christianity for Skeptics

There is no doubt that naturalistic religion has invaded the church today. Many of our concepts of the church are secular. Even the mission of the church is often changed from a biblical basis to a secularized one.

There is a strong movement, especially in Protestantism, to recast the Christian message in order to make it acceptable to modern man. These people contend that the intellectuals reject Christianity today because "they cannot accept certain traditional beliefs which were really the envelope in which the message was sent, rather than the message itself." Yet these modern theologians fail to agree among themselves as to which part of the New Testament is to be retained and which part is to be thrown out. Many of them seem to agree that the miracles were myths. They regard the resurrection as a subjective experience of the disciples rather than as an objective historical event. These theologians call God "the ground of being." They deny absolutely that Jesus Christ was supernatural. They say that He was a man who was so good and unselfish that God's love shone through His humanity rather than in the biblical terms of the Incarnation. . . . In trying to make Christianity plausible for skeptics, they have succeeded only in making it meaningless.

All the way through the Bible we are warned against false prophets and false teachers. In the Sermon on the Mount, Jesus said: "Beware of false prophets, which come to you in sheep's clothing, but inwardly they are ravening wolves. . . wherefore by their fruits ye shall know them" (Matthew 7:15, 20). Sometimes it is very difficult even for a Christian to discern a false prophet. There is a close resemblance between the true and the false prophet. Jesus spoke of false prophets who "shew great signs and wonders; insomuch that, if it were possible, they shall deceive the very elect" (Matthew 24:24). Paul tells of the coming Anti-Christ, whose activity in the last days will be marked by "signs and lying wonders" (2 Thessalonians 2:9). Satan's greatest disguise has always been to appear before men as "an angel of light" (2 Corinthians 11:14).

Who Said Life Was Fair?

Have you ever heard a child wail, "It's not fair!" There are those who have made their fortunes on other people's misfortune. The Bible never promised that life would be fair. Christian living that sounds like an article on the lifestyle page of the newspaper may leave us unprepared for a world where Hell does break loose. We are in a battle on this earth, and there is no one who is excused from service. As we pray and give thanks for the end of the Berlin Wall and the opening of Eastern Europe to democracy and religious freedom, we also realize that new tyrannies challenge the Christian faith. We must not become complacent in our sanctuaries.

In some churches and religious television programs, we see an effort to make Christianity popular and always positive. This may be a comfortable cushion for those who find the hard facts too difficult. Within the New Testament, there is no indication that Christians should expect to be healthy, wealthy, and successful in this present age. Jesus said, "If the world hates you, keep in mind that it hated me first" (John 15:18). Christ never told his disciples that they would get an Academy Award for their performances, but He did tell them to expect to have troubles.

This age is interested in success, not suffering. We can identify with James and John who wanted choice seats in the kingdom. We might even ask for reclining chairs and soft music.

Our Lord was ridiculed, insulted, persecuted, and eventually killed. In the face of opposition, He went about "doing good." Even His enemies could find no fault in Him. He became the greatest teacher of moral values the world has ever known, but after only three years of public ministry He was executed as a criminal.

"Good" people do not escape suffering in this life. The Bible lists in Hebrews 11 the heroes of the faith, both Jew and Gentile, who were tortured, imprisoned, stoned, torn apart, and killed by the sword. They didn't wear designer jeans but went about in animal skins, destitute and tormented. Those early believers wandered in deserts, crossed mountains, and hid in caves. They were the homeless of that time, without even a cardboard shelter.

In America today, being a Christian is sometimes equated with having good health. Some popular nutrition and psychology publications recommend that a sound body may require a strong spiritual life. Many of these writers lean toward a hybrid of Eastern religious thought and humanistic psychology, but others have been biblically sound. I believe that exercise and proper eating habits are very important, since the Bible says that the body is God's holy temple, but I don't think that superbodies equate with committed Christian discipleship. Some of the greatest saints I've known have been those with physical infirmities.

The Wreckage of Sin

The Bible teaches that sin affects the mind. "The natural man receiveth not the things of the Spirit of God . . . neither can he know them, because they are spiritually discerned" (1 Corinthians 2:14). While a man may be brilliant in some things, he may be grossly confused about spiritual realities. The Bible teaches that there is a veil over his mind. Before a person can be converted to Christ, this veil must be lifted. This is done by the supernatural power of the Holy Spirit. Without this "veil-lifting" there is no possibility of a man's coming to God. The Gospel of Jesus Christ is not anti-intellectual. It demands the use of the mind, but the mind is affected by sin. It is in the service of a rebellious will. In the final analysis a man must submit his mind to the Lordship of Christ.

The Bible teaches that sin affects the will. Jesus said: "Whosoever committeth sin is the servant of sin" (John 8:34). There are vast numbers of persons living under the tyranny of pride, jealousy, prejudice, or perhaps they are living under the bondage of alcohol, barbiturates, or narcotics. Even some who do not want to do the things they are doing are powerless to quit. They have become slaves. They cry for freedom, but there seems to be no escape. But Christ said: "Ye shall know the truth, and the truth shall make you free" (John 8:32). He is the truth. He can set you free.

Sin also affects the conscience, until one becomes slow to detect the approach of sin. The Bible talks about the deceitfulness of sin. Psychologists have learned that they can put a frog in hot water and he will jump out. However, if they put a frog in lukewarm water and gradually heat it they can boil him without his jumping. So it is with sin. There was a time when you were disturbed and conscience-smitten about a certain sin. It may have been immorality. It may have been a lie. It may have been the first time you cheated in school. But now your conscience bothers you hardly at all. Your heart has become hardened. You no longer have a sensitivity to things you know to be wrong. You have built up a rationalistic system to keep your conscience quiet. In the first chapter of Romans the Apostle Paul said that because men were so given over to their sins, "God gave them up." God once said concerning Ephraim: "Ephraim is joined to idols; let him alone" (Hosea 4:17).

A Form of Insanity

You know the Bible teaches that sin is a form of insanity? The Bible says if our Gospel is hid or veiled, the veil must be in the minds of those who have spiritually died. The spirit of this world has blinded the minds of those who do not believe and who prevent the light of the glorious Gospel of Christ, the image of God, from shining in there. Notice, "The spirit of this world." There is an evil spirit in our world that blinds us to the reality of what God can do. It blinds us to our own condition. Then the Holy Spirit comes along and convinces us of our sins, and we sit and think about it, and we are disturbed and unhappy about our condition. We don't know where to escape. We don't know which way to go. But [the prodigal son] decided to do the right thing. He decided to get up and go back. He said, "I have sinned against Heaven." He didn't just say, "I have sinned against my father." He said, "I have sinned against God." That's your problem. Your problem is not a family relationship. Your problem is not really a race problem. Your problem is a problem with God. You get the problem with God straightened out, and you will have a new perspective on how to straighten out some of the other problems. That's the real problem. The real hangup in your life is what to do about God, what to do about Christ. Let Him come and change and transform your life and see the fulfillment and the power and the strength you will have.

Invitation to Do Wrong

Nowhere in the Bible will you find immunity from temptation promised. It is common to all and will be with us to the end. Every Christian can and should expect temptation.

Being tempted is not sin. Yielding to temptation is sin. Temptation comes from without the mind; sin comes by cooperation from within the mind. Realize that temptation is not synonymous with guilt. Our Lord was tempted of the devil, but certainly He knew nothing of guilt. Because He was seeking to do His Father's will at all times, Jesus was able to defeat the devil when He was tempted in the wilderness. All who seek to have the mind of Christ are armed to meet temptation.

Temptation in the sense of an invitation to do wrong never comes from God. "Let no man say when he is tempted, I am tempted of God: for God cannot be tempted with evil, neither tempteth He any man" (James 1:13). God allows us to be tempted, however, so that we may be victorious and gain strength for future conflicts, and so that our characters may be developed and our usefulness increased. In the same chapter we read, "Blessed is the man that endureth temptation: for when he is tried, he shall receive the crown of life which the Lord hath promised to them that love him" (James 1:12).

Dr. F. B. Meyer once said, "Don't fear temptation. Don't fear that you will fail. Don't dread defeat. Instead, know that the moment a poor trembling heart lays itself at the feet of Christ, and one thin languid hand touches the hem of His garment, that moment virtue streams in to be the complement of even twelve years of weakness."

"The Lord is faithful, Who shall establish you, and keep you from evil" (2 Thessalonians 3:3).

Sexual Sin

Some say that the sexual revolution is slowing down. People are seeing the ravages of AIDS and adjusting their life-styles. Charles Colson said, "There is painful irony in the fact that it took AIDS to accomplish what no amount of pulpit pounding could do. People have a greater fear of disease than of God's judgment!"

A loving God ordained monogamous marriage and the sanctity of what we call the traditional family. Within the bounds of marriage, sex is a gift of God, but when it is misused the possibilities are frightening. This is nothing new in our generation. Sexual immorality has always been a cause of death, judgment, and Hell. AIDS has clearly reminded our society of that, but the reality is not limited to AIDS.

Fatal Attraction, a popular movie of recent years, told the story of a supposedly respectable man who decided one short affair outside his marriage wouldn't hurt. The beautiful woman with whom he slept turned out to be a borderline psychotic who then crosses the border. In the film's terrifying climax, she nearly kills his wife. The story reflects what deep within our hearts we already know; if we want our lives to be good, indulging in what is unholy is risky business, to put it mildly. The gift of sex is misused with reckless disregard for the consequences. Tragically, within the Christian ministry we see occasional examples of that abuse. What was meant by God to be beautiful within the bounds of marriage is degraded in everything from advertisements for perfume to comic strips. How much further, oh God, can it go?

The Bible shows Jesus dealing with sexual sin in several stories. The woman described in John 8 is one. Jesus had been praying all night before this event took place. He was teaching on the porch of the Temple, and a crowd had gathered. Suddenly there was a rude interruption as the Pharisees dragged before Him a poor woman who had been taken in immorality. She was crying. She expected to be stoned. It was a setup to trap Jesus by asking Him what should be done with the woman.

Jesus' dilemma was this. If He said yes to stone her, He would be in trouble with the Roman authorities, because they alone held the power of capital punishment. If He said not to stone her, He would break the law of Moses. He would be caught either way. So Jesus stooped down and wrote something on the ground. We can only guess what He wrote in the sand that day. Could it have been that He wrote the Ten Commandments?

He said, "If any one of you is without sin, let him be the first to throw a stone at her" (John 8:7). Imagine those religious leaders shifting from one foot to another, their eyes on the ground, not daring to look at one another. None of them could cast the first stone, because they were all guilty. They had dragged themselves to judgment, just as they had dragged the woman. Unfortunately, some Christians have treated those with AIDS in the same way, trying to make a point in an argument, instead of seeing the victim as one more of us sinners needing to be forgiven and cared for.

We understand this story, because we know we are, in our own way, standing in the crowd needing forgiveness, too. We may not be guilty of adultery, but we may be guilty of idolatry, lust, greed, or whatever our private or personal sin is. We may not carry the AIDS virus ourselves, but God forbid as modern-day Pharisees we should condemn others while carrying the virus of our own unconfessed and unrepented sins.

When Sigmund Freud began writing in the early part of this century, he complained of the narrowness of the Victorian era and attributed many neuroses to the sexual repression of his society. But if Freud were to come back today, he might reverse his stand and attribute our modern mania to the license and lack of sexual boundaries.

Historically the church, for the most part, has tried to teach that guilt and suffering are a result of sexual immorality. That is why there is no such thing as "safe sex." It may be sterile and clinically free of disease, but it is not safe from the pain of heartbreak it may cause. However, what right does any church have even attempting to approve of life-styles or certain acts for which God prescribed the death penalty in the Old Testament?

Why did God make us sexual beings?

I was speaking to the cadets at West Point, and as we were driving away, the chaplain said to me, "You know, God gave us one of the most difficult things ever to handle...sex." He asked me if I knew why. I said I thought I did.

In the first place, God has given us sex to attract us to

the opposite sex. That is natural and normal. In the very beginning, He looked at all He had made and called it good.

Second, sex was given for the propagation of the race. None of us would be here if it weren't for sex. That is the way God intended it, and it is the way He meant, within the bonds of matrimony, to produce children.

God has given us our sexuality as a means of expressing our love. This is why sex is not just for playboys to amuse themselves; it is the deepest way we can say to our spouse, "I love you and only you. I give myself completely to you alone."

Human sexuality was given as a glorious contribution to married love. It was given so that a man and a woman could express the unity that binds them together. We find ourselves in emotional quicksand if we go outside those rules of marriage, frequently resulting in depression, despair, or possibly disease.

Sin has a great impact on sex. It follows that if sin affects your sex life, it will also affect the rest of your life. Often it drives people to seek refuge in further sexual activities and other diversions, instead of turning to God.

Rebels against God who have misused the gift of their human sexuality are a growing army during our day. What God has given us as a gift of joy has often been turned into an instrument for our own destruction. But there is the wonderful good news of God's compassion, like that of Jesus speaking to the woman who was dragged before Him for her adulterous acts. Jesus told her to leave her life of sin and that she would not be condemned.

Rebels against God come in many forms. Some believe every disease, every accident, is caused by sin. Their judgmental attitude causes heartache in many lives. Other rebels defy God's laws and cause pain for themselves that may multiply in the lives of others.

Pious and judgmental attitudes will not soothe troubled hearts. The hope is in Jesus Christ, the light sent into this hopeless world.

Works of the Flesh

In Galatians 5 there is a catalog of fifteen works of the flesh which range from sexual sins to drunkenness and include idolatry and sorcery. What strikes terror in every Christian heart is the knowledge that these sins can easily creep into our lives unless we are spiritually vigilant and strong. "Therefore let him who thinks he stands take heed lest he fall" (1 Corinthians 10:12). With this in mind, let us look at the list of sins Paul lists in Galatians 5, so we will be better prepared to fight against the flesh.

Some have suggested that these can be divided into three categories, or sets. The first set are sexual immorality, impurity, and sensuality (Galatians 5:19).

1. Immorality. The Greek word here is broad enough to cover all kinds of sexual wickedness and is, incidentally, the word (*porneia*) from which the word "pornography" comes. Premarital sex, extramarital sex, abnormal sex, incest, prostitution, and surely sex sins in the heart are part of what the apostle has in mind here.

2. Impurity. Here the Greek word suggests any kind of impurity, whether in thought or deed. It might even include unnatural lust as described by Paul in Romans 1:24. It surely would cover some of the modern films, pornographic literature, and "evil imaginations." William Barclay describes it as the pus of an unclean wound; a tree that has never been pruned; material that has never been sifted.

3. Sensuality. This Greek word can be thought of as wantonness or debauchery. But there may be more to it than that. It has in it the notion of reckless shamelessness, or even an open indulgence in impurity. The same word is used in 2 Peter 2:7 when the apostle speaks of the licentiousness of Sodom and Gomorrah. It can be no less than lewdness and sensuality of any kind.

The second set of the works of the flesh enumerated by Paul are these:

1. Idolatry. The Greek word for idolatry is the worship of false gods of which there are many today. By implication we think of it as including anything that comes between us and God. Money can become an idol if we worship it above our worship of God. Pleasure can become an idol, even a relationship to another person can become an idol if it takes the place of God.

2. Sorcery. The Greek word here can be translated "witchcraft"; the idea especially is the administering of magical potions and drugs. Thus it is related also to the use of drugs; we get our word *pharmacy* from this Greek word, *pharmakia*. Throughout Scripture, witchcraft and sorcery are condemned. This evil is spreading rapidly in Western societies at an alarming rate.

3. Enmities. The Greek word for enmities has to do with hatred. Hatred contains within it the idea of something latent, like an animal ready to spring on its prey. Hostility, antipathy, antagonism, animosity, rancor, and intense dislike are all comparable terms for what is translated here as hatred.

4. Strife. The Greek word refers to variance, contentions, strife, fighting, discord, wrangling, and quarreling. Many churches are hard hit by internal discord that divides laymen from pastors, and laymen from laymen. When members of a congregation do not speak to each other and when they fight with one another, this sin is at work and the Spirit of God is quenched. Numerous families are infected by this spirit. Many marriages, even Christian ones, are being destroyed by this sin.

5. Jealousy—a very common sin. It involves envy when someone gets an honor we wanted, or it can mar a marriage relationship when a husband or a wife is jealous of his or her partner. We read of murders being committed because of jealousy, of friends who have not spoken for years. On the other hand, there is the beautiful example of

Jonathan who was not jealous of David (1 Samuel 20).

6. Outbursts of anger. The Greek word for "wrath" means unrighteous fits of rage, passionate outbursts of anger and hostile feelings. John uses the same root word in the Apocalypse about the righteous wrath of God. Man's wrath can be righteous or unrighteous, but God's wrath is always righteous for He cannot sin. There is a righteous wrath, but it is not a fit of anger. Here anger or wrath is a sin we must cast out of our lives. Someone has well said, "Righteous indignation is usually one part righteous and nine parts indignation."

7. Disputes. This Greek word for "disputes" or "strife" means selfish ambition, self-seeking, and selfishness. This violates both parts of the Ten Commandments (Exodus 20). First, it is a sin against God when selfish ambition replaces the will of God for our lives. Then it violates the command to love our neighbors, for acts of self-seeking are always committed at someone else's expense.

8. Dissensions. The Greek word means seditions, dissensions, or divisions. Believers are to be of one mind. "He is the God that maketh men to be of one mind in an house" is the Prayer Book version of Psalm 68:6. Unless principles are at stake or the Word of God is threatened, then discord can become sinful. We are to contend for the faith, but even when doing so we are not to be contentious. Truth often divides, but when truth is not at stake, God's people should be able to live together in love by the grace of the Holy Spirit.

9. Factions. The Greek word for "factions," or "heresies," has to do with sects and sectarianism. It means to choose that which is bad, or to form an opinion contrary to the revelation of God in Scripture. This is the same word found in 2 Peter 2:1 (NIV): "But there were also false prophets among the people, just as there will be false teachers among you. They will secretly introduce destructive heresies, even denying the sovereign Lord who bought them—bringing swift destruction on themselves."

Thus this is a serious sin. As Alexander said, "Error is often plausibly dressed in the outer garb of truth."

10. Envyings. This Greek word means resentment at the excellence or good fortune of another, a jealous spirit. We may envy someone his beautiful voice, his great wealth, his superior position, or his athletic attainments. Or we may begrudge a girl her beauty, a person his position in public office. Envy has been the downfall of many a Christian. Normally, there can be no envy that does not involve covetousness.

11. Drunkenness. This Greek word means overindulgence in alcohol. Alcohol may be used for medicine, but it can also become a terrible drug. The way it is used in our world is probably one of the great evils of our day. It is a self-inflicted impediment that springs from "a man taking a drink, a drink taking a drink, and drink taking the man." Distilled liquors as we have them today were unknown in Bible times. This modern use of alcohol is far more dangerous than the use of wine, which was also condemned when taken to excess. Teetotalism or nonteetotalism cannot be proven from Scriptures. Whatever we do, we should do it to the glory of God (1 Corinthians 10:31).

12. Carousings. In the Greek this means "orgies." In Romans 13:13 and 1 Peter 4:3 it is associated with illicit sex, drunkenness, and other evils in which no Christian should indulge.

There may be someone reading this who has been guilty of one, or even all of the sins listed here. Does this mean you can never enter the kingdom of Heaven; that the door is forever closed to you? Certainly not. The Bible says that by repentance and faith anyone can be forgiven (1 John 1:9).

However, Galatians 5:21 constitutes the most serious warning to those who may think they can sin that grace may abound. The apostle sternly says, "Those who practice such things [i.e. those things just enumerated] shall not inherit the kingdom of God."

Where Did Pain Begin?

Could God have created a world without suffering? Yes, He could, and He did.

In millenniums past there was a time when the universe and its undiscovered galaxies were in a state of complete harmony with their Maker. It was an existence beyond the comprehension of our finite minds; we cannot imagine a world that is older than we can even think and which existed without a hint of the suffering to come. However, into this Paradise came Satan, probably the most misunderstood person in the universe. Before Satan there was no sin, and before sin there was no pain.

Who is Satan? He is underestimated and frequently caricatured. Some think he is only a spiritual force, others have imagined him as a goblin or dismissed him as a myth. Today, however, when Satan worship is increasing at an alarming rate, we had better be aware of him, his origin, his aims, his abilities, and his limitations.

Satan was once a dazzling creature. The prophet Ezekiel called him "the model of perfection, full of wisdom and perfect in beauty" (28:12). This incredible person was once one of the "sons of God" (Job 38:7 NASB).

Lucifer (meaning "morning star" in Hebrew) was an angel created to glorify God, but this was not the role he wanted. His heart's desire was to be the chief authority; he wanted to sit on God's throne and rule the universe. Isaiah 14:12–14 tells us: "How you have fallen from heaven, O morning star, son of the dawn! You have been cast down to the earth, you who once laid low the nations! You said in your heart, I will ascend to heaven; I will raise my throne above the stars of God; I will sit enthroned on the mount of assembly, on the utmost heights of the sacred mountain. I will ascend above the tops of the clouds; I will make myself like the Most High."

When Lucifer asserted his desire to be more than God, a great revolution took place in the universe. Many angels joined with Lucifer and became his rebel army. Evidently when God judged Lucifer's crimes, God changed his name to Satan, the Evil One, and sentenced him to eternal exile.

Satan didn't lose any of his beguiling ways when he became the fallen prince. He took his charm, his subtleties, and his clever plots to use on us. When he made his decision to battle God to the death, he took his band of rebel angels with him as his combat soldier. The battlefield is known as earth.

Before the great polluter spread his poison throughout this new territory, God chose to beautify this planet with light and darkness, seas and skies, land and vegetation, sun, moon and stars, air, and land animals.

In a time when we are concerned about our polluted earth, can you imagine what Paradise was like? Every flower that grew was perfect; no blight was on them. The fertilizers and bug sprays we keep in our garden shed were not needed. Visualize a fruit tree laden with juicy apples or pears, without a bug in any piece. Imagine the sky so clear you could see every galaxy and constellation. No trash, no unpleasant odors, no litter. The lakes would have waters so clear you could see the color of every fish. God designed this glorious earth garden for His perfect children. When Adam and Eve were created they brought human beauty into this world of perfection.

God wanted someone with whom He could have fellowship. So He created Adam and Eve. No couple since then has had the ideal union that those two lovers had.

In the middle of the garden were two special trees, the Tree of Life and the Tree of the Knowledge of Good and Evil. The Lord God told the man, "You are free to eat from any tree in the garden; but you must not eat from the tree of the knowledge of good and evil, for when you eat of it you will surely die" (Genesis 2:16–17). Monsignor Knox translates it even more emphatically: "Thy doom is death!"

A river flowed out of Eden, dividing into four rivers, two of which were the Tigris and the Euphrates. So the

Garden of Eden was somewhere in present-day Iraq. . . . It became God's daily practice to walk with man in the garden in the cool of the day (Genesis 3:8). What an idyllic existence! How could anyone want more? And yet the first couple did.

God gave Adam and Eve more than beauty and a perfect environment. He gave them one of the most precious things man can have. Freedom. John Milton said, "When God gave Adam reason, He gave him freedom to choose . . . otherwise, he would have been a mere artificial Adam, such as an Adam in the puppet shows." Adam and Eve could have been created to walk where God directed them, speak the words God gave them—just mere puppets. However, God gave them, just as He has given us, freedom to choose.

Satan entered the garden in the form of a serpent. We can only speculate how this happened, but we do know that he had been on the prowl, searching for ways to destroy God ever since the time of his banishment from Heaven. And here was his opportunity to hurt two who were dear to the heart of God. He started in the same subtle way he uses today.

He cast doubt on what God had said. He worked on Eve first when he said, "Did God really say. . .?" (Genesis 3:1). The next strategy Satan used was an appeal to the ego. He told Eve she wouldn't die when she ate of that certain tree, she would simply be like God. So Eve took the fatal bite and passed some over to Adam, and he ate. This is called the Fall of man, and it has been a long way down ever since. God said to Adam, "Have you eaten from the tree that I commanded you not to eat from?" (Genesis 3:11). Adam answered by saying, "The woman you put here with me—she gave me some fruit from the tree, and I ate it" (Genesis 3:12).

Ever since, man has been passing the blame. A boy sins, his parents are blamed. A person is murdered, his environment is blamed. Someone cheats, the system is blamed. Passing the blame is as old as the Garden of Eden.

Even worse, man keeps asking, How can a just and loving God allow so much suffering in the world—natural disasters—man's inhumanity to man? Somehow, like Adam, man tries to blame God.

Who's On Trial?

In past generations it was thought that mankind was on trial before a holy God. Now it seems that the reverse is true; people imagine God on trial for all the terrible things that happen....It is human to question, "Where is God when...?" and you can finish the sentence with your own cry.

When Jesus Christ was on the cross, His blood draining the life from His body, He knew what it was like to be alone, questioning God when He was wracked with pain. But His pain was the suffering of the sins of the ages, the greatest darkness of the soul ever known to man.

Why did Jesus suffer? For you. For me. That we might have life eternal and His peace in the midst of storms. "Peace I leave with you; my peace I give you. I do not give to you as the world gives. Do not let your hearts be troubled and do not be afraid" (John 14:27).

Suffering has no meaning unless we can believe that God understands our pain and can heal it. In the suffering of Jesus we have that assurance!

Sin in Every Sickness

Some people see sin in every sickness. They make their friends miserable by probing for hidden sins whenever suffering enters their lives. Although there may be some truth in their questioning, it also could be a cruel response to another's time of pain. They are like Job's so-called friends who pointed out all of his wrongs. Job called them "miserable comforters."

A child was dying of leukemia, and all hope had been abandoned. Her parents received a call from a woman who said she was a "healer." Grasping for any way to help their daughter or prolong her life, they asked the woman to come to their home. When she arrived, she asked a few questions, looked briefly at the weak, bedridden child, and then pronounced, "There's something wrong here. I detect sin in this house." The little girl heard these words and began to cry, "Make her leave, make her leave."

It is unkind to attribute every accident, every illness and sorrow to God's punishment for wrong behavior. It is appalling how many Christians approach suffering friends with that principle. They visit first with words of comfort, and then leave a load of guilt behind ("What could you have done to deserve this?") or pious advice ("Perhaps you need to pray harder").

Suffering people can be tormented with questions of guilt; however, if all suffering is punishment for sin, then God's signals must be mixed, for accidents occur at random and disease strikes without any relationship to a person's moral or immoral life-style.

God's teaching doesn't attribute all suffering to sin or punishment for human mistakes. I have no right to tell a suffering person that it is because he sinned that his child died, or that he has cancer, or that his house burned.

In John 9, the followers of Jesus pointed to a man born blind and asked, "Who sinned, this man or his parents?" Jesus told them that neither the man nor his parents sinned, "But this happened so that the work of God might be displayed in his life." The disciples wanted to look back, to probe into the behavior of the blind man or his parents, but Jesus pointed them to the future and the hope that even suffering can be used to glorify God.

Avoiding Temptation

There are some temptations from which we should flee and others which we must endure and conquer. However, good advice is to avoid temptation whenever possible. Our rule of life should be not to see how near we can live to the world and still keep the name of Christian, but on the contrary, to keep just as far away as possible. . . . We are not to see how much we can tamper and meddle with the things of the world, but to see how far away we can keep from those things which would be displeasing to God. If the will is kept firm, God comes to the rescue. He grants grace to do His bidding and to overcome temptation. We fail to overcome temptation when we forget to trust the Lord or when we are too lazy or too proud to call on His strength. Oscar Wilde was right when he said that the easiest way to get rid of a temptation is to yield to it. The natural, easy, pleasing way is self-indulgence and moral softness. The hard way is self-denial and self-discipline, which, incidentally, is commanded in the Word of God. We have too many soft Christians today!

One of the best ways to overcome temptation is to keep busy for the Lord. Find something to do for Him. Seek to serve Him. Once you are willing, He will open innumerable doors of service for you.

One good rule to follow is: Any pleasure which tends to make us more companionable with unbelievers and less sociable with believers is to be avoided.

In fact, avoidance of danger when it comes to temptation is a principle in itself.

8

THE ANSWER

Revelation

When a spacecraft returns from its orbital flight, there is a blackout period of about four minutes when all communications are broken. This is due to the intense heat generated by the spacecraft's reentry into the earth's atmosphere.

The Bible teaches that man is in a period of spiritual blackout.

Spiritually, he is blind. "We grope for the wall like the blind, and we grope as if we had no eyes: we stumble at noonday as in the night; we are in desolate places as dead men" (Isaiah 59:10). "The God of this world hath blinded the minds of them which believe not" (2 Corinthians 4:4).

Spiritually, man is also deaf. "They have ears to hear, and hear not" (Ezekiel 12:2). Jesus went so far as to say: "If they hear not Moses and the prophets, neither will they be persuaded, though one rose from the dead" (Luke 16:31).

Spiritually, man is even dead. "Who were dead in trespasses and sins" (Ephesians 2:1).

All of this means that the communication between God and man is broken. There is a wonderful world of joy, light, harmony, peace, and satisfaction to which millions of persons are blind and deaf, and even dead. They long for serenity, they search for happiness, but they seem never to find it.

Many give up the search and surrender to pessimism. Often their despondency leads to a frantic round of cocktail parties where vast amounts of alcohol are imbibed. Sometimes it leads them to narcotics. It is all part of man's desperate search to find an escape from the cold realities of a sin-blighted existence. All the while God is there speaking and beckoning. The television set may be sitting in your room cold, dark, and lifeless, but this is not the fault of the television industry. They are sending forth programs from many transmitters, and their sending stations are in perfect order. But you must turn the dials of your set; you must tune in on the right channel. God is sending forth His message of love, but you must tune in. You must be willing to listen and to receive His message and then to obey it.

Many persons want to hear what God says just out of curiosity. They want to analyze and dissect it in their own test tubes. To these persons God may remain the great cosmic silence "out there somewhere." He communicates to those who are willing to hear and receive Him and willing to obey Him. Jesus said that we must become humble as little children, and God has most often revealed Himself to the meek and humble—to a shepherd boy like David, to a rough desert man like John the Baptist, to shepherds watching their flocks, to a girl named Mary.

How does God speak? How can a blind man see? How can a deaf man hear?

From the beginning God spoke to man. Adam heard the voice of the Lord in the Garden of Eden. Adam had two sons, Cain and Abel, and God spoke to them. Cain spurned that which was revealed to him, but Abel was obedient to the word of God. Abel's response showed that a man tainted and handicapped by sin could respond to God's overtures. Thus in the very beginning God began by revelation to build a bridge between Himself and man.

REVELATION IN NATURE

God reveals Himself in nature. "The heavens declare the glory of God; and the firmament sheweth his handiwork. Day unto day uttereth speech, and night unto night sheweth knowledge. There is no speech nor language, where their voice is not heard" (Psalm 19:1–3). There is a language in nature that speaks of the existence of God. It is the language of order, beauty, perfection, and intelligence. Some time ago a scientist told me that when he gave serious thought to the majestic order of the universe and its obedience to unchanging law, he could not help but believe in God. He had become aware that God was speaking through nature.

God speaks in the certainty and regularity of the seasons; in the precision of the movements of the sun, the moon, and the stars; in the regular coming of night and day; in the balance between man's consumption of life-giving oxygen and its production by the plant life of the earth; and even in the cry of a newborn child with its ever new demonstration of the miracle of life.

REVELATION IN CONSCIENCE

God has revealed Himself also in the conscience. Conscience has been described as the light of the soul. What causes this warning light to go on inside me when I do wrong?

Conscience is our gentlest counselor and teacher, our most faithful friend, and sometimes our worst enemy. There are no punishments or rewards comparable to those of the conscience. The Scripture says: "Man's conscience is the lamp of the eternal" (Proverbs 20:27 Moffatt). In other words, conscience is God's lamp within man's breast. In his *Critique of Pure Reason*, Immanuel Kant said there were just two things that filled him with awe—the starry heavens and conscience in the breast of man. The conscience in its varying degrees of sensitivity bears a witness to God. Its very existence within us is a reflection of God in the soul of man. Without conscience we would be like rudderless ships at sea and like guided missiles without a guidance system.

REVELATION IN SCRIPTURE

God has revealed Himself also through the Scriptures. God has two textbooks, one the textbook of nature and the other the textbook of revelation. The laws of God revealed in the textbook of nature have never changed; they are what they were since the beginning. They tell us of God's mighty power and majesty.

In the textbook of revelation, the Bible, God has spoken verbally; and this spoken word has survived every scratch of human pen. It has withstood the assaults of skeptics, agnostics, and atheists. It has never bowed its head before its discoveries of science. It remains supreme in its revelation of redemption. The more the archaeologist digs and the more the scientist discovers, the greater the confirmation of the truth of the Bible.

The writers of the Bible claim repeatedly that God gave them their material. Two thousand times in the Old Testament they said that God spoke. In the first five books we find such expressions as these:

> "The Lord God called unto Adam and said"
> "The Lord said unto Noah"
> "God spake unto Israel"
> "These are the words which the Lord hath commanded"
> "God said"
> "The Lord spake saying"
> "The Lord commanded"
> "The word of the Lord"

Over and over the Old Testament prophets used such expressions as these:

"Hear the word of the Lord"
"Saith the Lord"
"I heard the voice of the Lord saying"
"The word of the Lord came unto me"
"Whatsoever I command thee thou shalt speak"
"I have put my words into thy mouth"
"The Word of the Lord came unto me saying"

Either God did speak to these men as they wrote by inspiration, or they were the most consistent liars the earth ever saw. To tell more than two thousand lies on one subject seems incredible, and more than two thousand times the writers of the Bible said that God spoke these words! Either He did just that, or they lied. If they were mistaken in this emphasis, why should we honor their witness at any point?

Jesus quoted frequently from the Old Testament. He never once indicated that He doubted the Scriptures. The Apostles quoted the Scriptures often. The Apostle Paul said: "All Scripture is given by inspiration of God" (2 Timothy 3:16). The Apostle Peter said: "For the prophecy came not in old time by the will of man: but holy men of God spake as they were moved by the Holy Ghost" (2 Peter 1:21).

Thus God speaks to man through the Scriptures. This is why it is so important to read the Bible for yourself. So many take the Bible secondhand, and they have only a caricature of what the Bible says, only vague ideas about its teachings.

REVELATION IN JESUS CHRIST

Finally, God speaks in the person of His Son Jesus Christ. "God . . . hath in these last days spoken unto us by his Son" (Hebrews 1:1, 2). The idea that God would some-day visit this planet is an ancient truth that is no doubt an oral remnant of the original revelation God gave to Adam of a promised salvation (Genesis 3:15). We find crude references to it in most other religions of the world, indicating that man at some time had heard or sensed that God would visit the earth. However, it was not until the "fullness of the time" when all the conditions were right, when all the prophetic considerations were fulfilled, that God "sent forth his Son, made of a woman" (Galatians 4:4).

Every hope we have of God, every prospect we have of eternal life, every anticipation we have of Heaven, every possibility we have of a new social order—all must be linked to Jesus Christ. It is as we come to Jesus Christ that the unknown becomes known; and not only that, but as we come to Jesus Christ, we experience God Himself. Our limited darkened lives receive the light of the eternal presence of God, and we see that there is another world beyond the confusion, limitation, and frustration of this world.

A Scarlet Thread

"Without shedding of blood is no remission," declares the Word of God. There is a scarlet thread of blood from Genesis to Revelation, for God taught man from the very beginning that the only approach to God was by the blood.

Any man who accepts the Bible as the Word of God must come to the conclusion that Christianity is a religion of atonement. Its redemption feature distinguishes Christianity from any and all other religions. If you separate this distinctive religious doctrine from its creed, this supreme religion is brought down to the level of many other prevailing religious systems. Christianity is not merely a system of ethics. It is the story of redemption through Jesus Christ.

Let us make a hasty sketch of this doctrine of blood

which is taught in the Word of God. Even in the Garden
of Eden we see it. Adam and Eve had sinned. God had
said, "In the day that thou eatest thereof thou shalt surely
die." They believed Satan's lie rather than God's truth.
They ate. Thus they died. Immediately they saw themselves naked. They were afraid. Instead of becoming gods,
as Satan had told them, they found that in actuality they had
broken God's law and were now naked, alone and fearful.
They ran into the bushes to hide, but they were still afraid.
They gathered huge fig leaves, sewed them together, and
made themselves aprons to cover their nakedness.

Often in the cool of the day God would come to walk
with Adam and Eve. This time they hid from His presence. God called to Adam and said to him, "Where art
thou?" and Adam said, "I heard thy voice in the garden,
and I was afraid, because I was naked; and I hid myself."
Immediately the earth, the serpent, the man and the
woman were cursed.

God is a holy God! He is purer than to behold evil and
cannot behold iniquity (Habakkuk 1:13). He went into the
forest and the Scripture says in Genesis 3:21, "Unto Adam
also and to his wife did the Lord God make coats of skins,
and clothed them." Thus blood was shed for the first time.
God was teaching man in the very beginning that the only
way he could possibly approach a holy God was through
shed blood.

Adam and Eve were sinners; thus they begat sinners:
Cain and Abel. "Wherefore, as by one man sin entered into
the world, and death by sin; and so death passed upon all
men, for that all have sinned" (Romans 5:12).

Cain and Abel were reared together; they lived together; they had the same advantage, the same environment,
the same heredity. Cain decided to be a farmer. Abel
became a rancher. The time of the year came when they
were to bring their first fruits to God. Cain had worked
hard to make the first fruits of his crop as attractive as possible. Abel went out into the herd, slew a lamb, and

brought it to God as a sacrifice. God had already taught them that the only way they could approach Him was by blood. Cain had ignored it. He came in his own way. He brought the fruit of the ground. Though he had labored long and hard, yet his righteousness was counted as filthy rags. It must be God's way or not at all. God rejected it! Abel's sacrifice was accepted. He probably did not work as hard as Cain, but his sacrifice was blood. He had come in obedience and God accepted his sacrifice.

There are thousands of people today that are coming to God on the merits of their own works. Either they are sewing on fig leaves or bringing the fruits of their own labors. But God sees through the fig leaves and denounces their works. Salvation is by blood, and by blood alone! Man has no merit or work that God can accept.

The first thing Noah did after leaving the ark was to offer a sacrifice: "Noah builded an altar unto the Lord; and took of every clean beast, and of every clean fowl, and offered burnt offerings on the altar" (Genesis 8:20). Noah, too, walked the highway of blood.

In every house of Egypt the firstborn would be smitten by the destroying angel who, at midnight, would pass through the land. God said, "The blood shall be to you for a token upon the houses where ye are: and when I see the blood, I will pass over you, and the plague shall not be upon you to destroy you, when I smite the land of Egypt." This story of the Passover is well known to us all. The Egyptians and the Israelites in many cases dwelt near each other, and so a sign must be set on the door of every Israelitish house that the destroying angel might not enter there to slay.

The sign was the blood of a lamb slain by the father of the family. It was to be sprinkled on the doorpost. It was to be an assurance by which the Israelite might have entire confidence concerning the safety of his family. The blood was to be a token of redemption. The death of the lamb was to be considered as taking the place of the death which each man had deserved by sin. That night in Egypt they were busy buying and selling, eating and drinking, living delicately and boasting about their power and wisdom. The devil had lulled thousands to sleep by the business and enjoyment of the day. Hundreds had not believed the Word of God. They were not prepared. The blood was not sprinkled! God had said, "When I see the blood, I will pass over you," not "when I see your good works," not "when I see your good intentions or motives." The only thing that counted that night was whether the blood was sprinkled on the doorpost or not!

It is recorded that on the Passover night there was an old gray-haired man who lived in the house of his firstborn son, and he himself was the firstborn son of his father. His son also had a firstborn son. Thus there were three firstborn sons in the house, all of whom must die if the destroying angel entered the house. The old man lying on his bed, sick, but he heard with interest everything his son told him about God's command to Moses. Toward evening he was often restless as he thought of their danger, and he said, "My son, are you sure that you have done everything that has been prescribed?" His answer was: "Yes, Father, everything." For a moment he was satisfied. Then he asked again, "Are you sure? Has the blood been sprinkled on the door?" Again the answer was, "Yes, Father, everything has been done according to the command." The nearer it came to midnight, the more restless he became. Finally, he cried, "My son, carry me out if you please, that I may myself see it, and then I can rest." The son carried his father to a place where he could see the blood on the sideposts and the lintel. "Now I am satisfied," he cried. "Thank God! Now I know that I am safe!"

In the awful day of judgment when you stand alone before God, the only thing that will count is the blood of the Crucified One. Has it been sprinkled by faith on your heart's door? Soon the death angel will be passing by. Be sure the blood is there.

Results of the Atonement

First: It redeems—1 Peter 1:18–19: "Forasmuch as ye know that ye were not redeemed with corruptible things, as silver and gold, from your vain conversation received by tradition from your fathers; but with the precious blood of Christ, as of a lamb without blemish and without spot."

Second: It brings us nigh—Ephesians 2:13: "But now in Christ Jesus ye who sometimes were far off are made nigh by the blood of Christ."

Third: It makes peace—Colossians 1:20: "And having made peace through the blood of his cross, by him to reconcile all things unto himself; by him, I say, whether they be things in earth, or things in Heaven."

Fourth: It justifies—Romans 5:9: "Much more then, being now justified by his blood, we shall be saved from wrath through him."

Fifth: It cleanses—1 John 1:7: "But if we walk in the light, as he is in the light, we have fellowship one with another, and the blood of Jesus Christ his Son cleanseth us from all sin."

The Beginning of Sorrows

So Jesus sat down with them and began to teach these things. His answer, recorded in Matthew 24:3–37, offers a dramatic portrait of the last days of planet Earth. Here Jesus revealed the fate of Jerusalem, which was carried out to the letter when it was sacked and burned by the legions of Emperor Titus in A.D. 70. Jesus spoke of the coming of a godless, secular society, and He spoke of the dangers of the heresies conceived by false teachers who would try to pervert the simple message of truth Christ came to deliver. He said to them: "Take heed that no one deceives you. For many will come in My name, saying, 'I am the Christ,' and will deceive many" (Matthew 24:4–5 NKJV).

The rest of the passage, which speaks to the troubles of our own times, reads as follows: "And you will hear of wars and rumors of wars. See that you are not troubled; for all these things must come to pass, but the end is not yet. For nation will rise against nation, and kingdom against kingdom. And there will be famines, pestilences, and earthquakes in various places. All these are the beginning of sorrows."

Gethsemane

Gethsemane means "oil press." Most of us are familiar with olive oil as an ingredient in salads or cooking. In Palestine it was, and is, a valued staple. The Mount of Olives is frequently mentioned in the New Testament and is intimately connected with the devotional life of Jesus. It was on the Mount of Olives that He often sat with His disciples, telling them of events yet to come. And it was to the Mount of Olives that He retired each evening for prayer and rest, after the weary work of the day.

The oldest olive trees in Palestine today are those which are enclosed in the Garden of Gethsemane. Visitors to Jerusalem today can look at them, but they can't get close enough to touch them. Too many curious people have tried to deface those ancient, gnarled trees as they sought a special souvenir from the Holy Land.

When olives are harvested, they are squeezed, pressed, and pulverized under an enormous revolving stone which mashes the fruit to pulp and recovers the valuable oil. It was in the Garden of Gethsemane that the wheel of humiliation, defeat, and eventually death would grind Jesus to the point of His greatest personal agony. Emotional torment is many times more difficult to bear than physical torment. At Gethsemane, the place of the press, the mental anguish was so intense that Jesus pleaded with His Holy Father for release. But only if it was the Father's will.

How we need friends in time of testing! Jesus demonstrated His humanity when He asked His disciples to stay with Him. He wanted and needed them in His time of greatest trial. "My soul is overwhelmed with sorrow, to the point of death; stay here and keep watch with me" (Matthew 26:38). Jesus moved a short distance from His friends, the ones who confidently said they would follow Him, the ones who said they would never deny Him, and He fell on the ground to pray. It couldn't have been too long before His heavy-lidded friends dozed off. The sleepy disciples who had said they would do anything for Him couldn't even sit up and console Him.

As Jesus prayed, His agony was great, "and being in anguish, he prayed more earnestly, and his sweat was like drops of blood falling to the ground" (Luke 22:44). Does that seem impossible? Medical dictionaries describe this condition as "chromidrosis," a state in which intense emotional stress may actually cause the blood vessels to expand so much that they break where they come in contact with the sweat glands. Personally, I cannot begin to comprehend such overpowering emotion.

Jesus prayed three times, "My Father, if it is possible, may this cup be taken from me. Yet not as I will, but as you will" (Matthew 26:39).

Was there a way out? Could Jesus be delivered from the horrors of such a death—at least for a time?

Jesus did not take delight in His approaching crucifixion; He loved life on this earth. He enjoyed the pleasures of walking with His disciples, holding children on His knees, attending a wedding, eating with friends, riding in a boat, or working in the temple at Passover time. To Jesus, death was the enemy. When He prayed, "If it is possible," He wanted to confirm once again if His imminent death were truly the Father's will. Was there some other way?

But what did He mean by His plea to "let this cup pass from me"?

In the Scriptures, "cup" is used figuratively to describe either God's blessing (Psalm 23:5) or God's wrath (Psalm 75:8). Since Jesus would not have prayed for God's blessing to be taken from Him, it is obvious that His use of "cup" here speaks of the divine wrath that Christ would suffer at the Cross as He bore the sins of mankind upon Himself.

How unthinkable it seems to us for Jesus, who knew no sin, to have to bear the sin and guilt of all men. "God made him who had no sin to be sin for us" (2 Corinthians 5:21). Was there no other way of accomplishing the will of the Father without drinking that cup of wrath?

This was the question Jesus was asking—and in complete obedience to the Father's sovereign will Jesus voluntarily accepted the answer. No, there was no other way for a just and loving God to deal with our sins.

Sin must be punished; if God were simply to forgive our sins without judging them, then there would be no justice, no accountability for wrongdoing, and God is not truly holy and just. And if God were simply to judge us for our sins as we deserve to be judged, then there would be no hope of eternal life and salvation for any of us—for "all have sinned and fall short of the glory of God" (Romans 3:23). His love would have failed to provide a way for our salvation.

The cross was the only way to resolve this awesome dilemma. The conflict of the ages was about to reach its climax. On one hand, our sins were about to be placed on Christ, the sinless One. He would be "clothed" in our sins like a filthy, tattered old garment, and on the cross those sins would be judged—your sins, my sins. He would be the final atoning sacrifice for sin. On the other hand, however, Christ's perfect righteousness would be given to us, like a spotless, gleaming set of new clothes. Sin was therefore judged, and God's justice was satisfied. The door of forgiveness and salvation was opened, and God's love was satisfied. "God made him who had no sin to be sin for us, so that in him we might become the righteousness of God" (2 Corinthians 5:21).

Even as Jesus, in His humanity, struggled within Himself over this awesome predicament, He finally prayed, "Thy will be done." This was not a prayer spoken with a sigh of resignation, but with a strong voice of complete trust. Jesus knew this meant total and absolute surrender to the will of the Father and to the needs of others. Yet, there is a mystery here that we cannot fully understand. Jesus surely experienced the overwhelming awareness of His inevitable sacrifice for the sins of the world. He knew this was His primary mission on earth, for He had said, "For even the Son of Man did not come to be served, but to serve, and to give his life as a ransom for many" (Mark 10:45).

The Garden of Gethsemane is the place where Jesus was revealed to be a true man. He was face-to-face with the choice between obedience or disobedience. He was not a robot programmed to obey God automatically. He can sympathize with our weaknesses, "For we do not have a high priest who is unable to sympathize with our weaknesses, but we have one who has been tempted in every way, just as we are—yet was without sin" (Hebrews 4:15). Satan tempted Jesus all through His ministry, but the temptations in the wilderness at the beginning of His ministry can scarcely compare to those in the garden. After three years of selfless giving and the stress of that final week, Jesus was never more vulnerable than at this moment of time.

Some skeptics have said that Jesus' suffering in Gethsemane was a sign of weakness. They point out that many martyrs, for instance, died without the intense emotional wrestling of Jesus.

But it is one thing to die for a cause, or to die for country or for another person. It is quite another to die for an entire world, all the accumulated sins of generations past and generations to come. Jesus was to become guilty of murder, adultery, cheating, lying, and all other evil human behavior. It's more than our finite minds can ever comprehend.

The Full Armor

Paul, referring to the conflict with "the spiritual forces of evil," wrote, "Therefore put on the full armor of God, so that when the day of evil comes, you may be able to stand your ground, and after you have done everything, to stand" (Ephesians 6:13).

Here are five points to use as a checklist in determining the strength of your "full armor." Write them down, refer to them daily, and act upon them.

LOOK GODWARD

First, we must make sure of our relationship to God. As Amos the prophet saw the day of judgment fast approaching for Israel, he warned the people to prepare to meet God (Amos 4:12). The word "preparedness" should be a key word for everyone.

WALK WITH GOD

Second, we should learn how to walk with God in our daily life. Abraham walked with God and was called a friend of God (Isaiah 41:8; James 2:23). Walk with God as Noah did; when the flood came, Noah was saved. Walk with God as Moses did in the solitude of the desert; when the hour of judgment fell upon Egypt, Moses was prepared to lead his people to victory. Walk with God as David did as a shepherd boy; when he was called to rule his people he was prepared for the task of kingship. Daniel and his three young friends walked with God in Babylon, and when trouble came, God was beside them— whether it was in the lions' den or in the fiery furnace.

WORK WITH THE WORD

Third, we need to fortify ourselves with the Word of God. Begin reading, studying, and memorizing Scripture as never before. Paul says, "Stand firm then, with the belt of truth buckled around your waist" (Ephesians 6:14). The truth is the Word of God. He also says, "Take the...sword of the Spirit, which is the word of God" (verse 17). We are to be girded and undergirded with the Word. To achieve this, we must read it, assimilate it, feed on it. We must let it be our staff and strength. It is quick and powerful—the bulwark of the soul.

PRACTICE WITH PRAYER

Fourth, we need to fortify ourselves with prayer. The Bible, referring to "the evil day," says, "Pray in the Spirit on all occasions with all kinds of prayers and requests" (Ephesians 6:18). If we are to stand uncompromisingly for Christ when a national crisis comes, we must rediscover the power of prayer. Jesus taught us that we should "always pray and not give up" (Luke 18:1). The early church knew the value and necessity of prayer. Earnest, fervent prayer preceded every major triumph. Prayer preceded Pentecost.

PRACTICE THE PRESENCE OF CHRIST

Fifth, we must fortify ourselves by realizing the nearness of the Lord at all times. Spurgeon once said, "There have never been fifteen minutes in my life when I did not sense the presence of Christ." I regret I cannot say that. We must learn again to practice the presence of Christ, not only in days of testing and suffering, but always.

9

THE JOURNEY TO CHRIST

The Inward Journey

The inward journey is that lifelong pilgrimage of spiritual growth and maturity. Too often we see conversion as the end rather than the beginning of life's struggle to know God and to do His will. For example, going forward in a crusade or church to receive Jesus Christ as Lord and Savior is the first step of the long inward journey. The study of God's Word, the practice of prayer, wide reading of Christian books and articles, memorization of Scripture, poetry, and hymns, gathering together in Christian community, participation in small nurture groups, building intimate and honest Christian friendships—all of these activities are necessary to grow in Christian faith. Yet too often we just assume that people understand and practice these disciplines on their own.

The Outward Journey

The outward journey is an expression that I think originated with Elizabeth O'Connor, the historian of the Church of the Savior in Washington. To grow on an inward journey, the journey to know God, is not enough.

We are also called to follow Christ onto our streets and into our neighborhoods. We are called to serve Christ in bringing His message of redemption to the world. The outward journey, that journey which takes us beyond our own small world to the world in need, is the inevitable outworking of a genuine inward journey. The cross points in two directions—toward God and toward my neighbors.

The Church of the Savior requires that each member be actively working in an outreach project—whether evangelism through a coffee house, a retreat ministry, rebuilding houses or feeding the poor, caring for orphans, widows, and transients, being involved in the primary concerns of education, public housing or environment. Sometimes we act as though attending church on Sunday morning and putting an offering in the basket are all that God requires of us. We make the faith seem undemanding. And we forget Jesus standing before the rich young man saying, "sell everything you have and give to the poor.... Then come, follow me" (Mark 10:21).

Vulnerability

Perhaps you have read the words I have written...about Satan's way of deceiving, such as through false teachings or through his appeal to our lusts and our pride. Possibly, however, you have said to yourself, "This is all very interesting, but Satan could never deceive me. I'm not a member of some false religion. I'm not involved in any sinful lifestyle." The Bible warns us, however, "So, if you think you are standing firm, be careful that you don't fall!" (1 Corinthians 10:12). Satan never gives up in his efforts to deceive.

First, we must admit to ourselves that Christians, too, are vulnerable to deception.

The Scriptures are filled with wonderful promises: "Do not be afraid, little flock.... My grace is sufficient.... You have overcome the evil one" (Luke 12:32; 2 Corinthians

12:9; 1 John 2:13). We must remember these promises and believe them. But we must also remember God's warnings. Jesus Himself said that in the last days "false Christs and false prophets will appear and perform signs and miracles to deceive the elect—if that were possible" (Mark 13:22). Paul wrote, "See to it that no one takes you captive through hollow and deceptive philosophy" (Colossians 2:8). Jesus warned us, "Watch out that you are not deceived" (Luke 21:8). God will complete in us what He has begun, and yet we must be on our guard against deception.

Second, we are vulnerable at the point of authority figures.

We Christians sit in pews facing the front of the church. We listen—and then we get up and leave. How often do we pause to think about what was said? Do we ask questions of those who address us? Most of the authority figures in our lives can be trusted. And that means that there is all the more reason for us to ask questions. A trustworthy authority figure welcomes our honest questions and will answer them frankly. A cult figure is not interested in questions; he wants loyalty. A cult figure doesn't want to give us options; he wants power over our lives.

Of course, the basic test of the Spirit in an authority figure is clearly stated in the Scriptures: "This is how you can recognize the Spirit of God: Every spirit that acknowledges that Jesus Christ has come in the flesh is from God, but every spirit that does not acknowledge Jesus is not from God" (1 John 4:2–3). Unfortunately, however, this test alone may not prove adequate, for many—in fact most—cult leaders would acknowledge Jesus in just such a way before going on to replace His authority over us with their own authority.

Victims are often from religious homes and churches in which people are not instructed to question authority figures nor taught to make decisions on their own. When the rider who deceives rides into town, we need to ask him who he really is and what he really wants from us. In all likelihood we will quickly detect why he must not be trusted—why he is a false messiah who would lead us to our deaths.

Third, we are vulnerable at the point of money.

It is common for false religious leaders to be very secretive about the finances of their organization. Unfortunately, when legitimate Christian organizations and churches refuse to be completely open about finances they are conditioning people to accept unquestioningly the contention of the cult leader that he is not accountable to anyone for his financial dealings. What is the least attended meeting of the church year? The annual business meeting, of course. Too often even those who attend rush superficially through the budget with little understanding of what it says or means. Yet the annual budget is one document that enumerates our priorities. Without understanding the budget, we don't understand who we are or what we are doing. Worse, by not understanding or questioning the budget, we are setting each other up for a leader who doesn't want us to know where the dollars are going. If you give to any Christian charity (including the Billy Graham Evangelistic Association) and you don't insist on an understandable financial accounting of your gift, you are in danger of falling prey to the horseman who deceives.

Fourth, we are vulnerable at the point of time.

Too many of us are so busy that we stumble about in a daze, exhausted, too tired to think, let alone to question. False religious leaders keep their members busy. Exhaustion sets in. Deception follows. At the heart of the Christian calendar is a day of rest. And at the heart of that Sabbath day is God's understanding of His creation. Unless we maintain our physical strength, we will lose our spiritual and psychological stamina as well. At the heart of brainwashing is exhaustion. The rider on the white horse loves to see us too tired to resist. That makes his deception all the easier.

Fifth, we are vulnerable at the point of human relationships.

False religious leaders separate family from family and friends from friends. They know that when we are lonely and cut off from each other, we cannot share our questions or raise the issues that would set us free. Modern culture, with its sound and fury (even sometimes within the church), doesn't really honor friendship or the time and energy it takes to maintain those intimate ties with a husband or a wife, a friend or a colleague. So, become active. Commit yourself to a small circle of friends. Honor and build friendship whatever the cost.

Wet Blanket vs. Dry Christian

By retreating and avoiding sin, you will in reality be advancing in your Christian experience. To yield to temptation is to ensure its recurrence. When we presumptuously put ourselves in the way of temptation, we deserve to fall. If we parlay with sin, we will surrender. Remember, "God is faithful, who will not suffer you to be tempted above that ye are able" (1 Corinthians 10:13).

Never act upon a wrong desire. It will always lead to sin. To maintain the right, however, strengthens you for the future. "The righteous also shall hold on his way, and he that hath clean hands shall be stronger and stronger" (Job 17:19).

Never feel ill at ease or embarrassed when you have to refuse to do certain things or to go into certain places when the crowd does so. Don't be afraid to say "no." One of the most important lessons we can learn is how to say "no." Doing so will intensify our determination to witness for Christ. Close your mind to temptation. Ask for God's grace to turn from it. Remember, it is better to be a so called "wet blanket" than a "dry Christian"—one who is not separated from the ungodly to the Lord and whose life is therefore "like the heath in the desert" and like "the parched places in the wilderness, in a salt land and not inhabited" (Jeremiah 17:5–6).

We must "endure hardness as a good soldier of Jesus Christ" (2 Timothy 2:3–4). If hard experiences come and indications of the enemy at work are seen, do not give up the fight, but by His grace endure hardness and "strength with His strength oppose." Prepare for the stumbling blocks which may appear in your path. Your ability to resist temptation will depend to a great extent upon your spiritual attitude when sin presents its ugly head. The problems you face will test your faith and will make you stronger. "My brethren, count it all joy when ye fall into divers temptations; knowing this, that the trying of your faith worketh patience. But let patience have her perfect work, that ye may be perfect and entire, wanting nothing" (James 1:2–4).

Tiny Blades of Opportunity

The Bible reminds us further that our days are as grass (Psalm 103:15). They are filled with tiny golden minutes with eternity in them. We are exhorted to redeem the time because the days are evil (Ephesians 5:16). As C. T. Studd, the famous Cambridge cricketer and missionary pioneer, wrote while still a student at Cambridge,

> Only one life, 'twill soon be past;
> Only what's done for Christ will last.

Life is a glorious opportunity if it is used to condition us for eternity. If we fail in this, though we succeed in everything else, our life will have been a failure. There is no escape for the man who squanders his opportunity to prepare to meet God.

Our lives are also immortal. God made man different from the other creatures. He made him in His own image, a living soul. When this body dies and our earthly existence is terminated, the soul or spirit lives on forever. One hundred years from this day you will be more alive than you are at this moment. The Bible teaches that life does not end at the cemetery. There is a future life with God for those who put their trust in His Son, Jesus Christ. There is also a future Hell of separation from God toward which all are going who have refused, rejected, or neglected to receive His Son, Jesus Christ.

Victor Hugo once said, "I feel in myself the future life." Cyrus the Great is reported to have declared, "I cannot imagine that the soul lives only while it remains in this mortal body." Nothing but our hope in Christ will take the sting out of death and throw a rainbow of hope around the clouds of the future life. Our anchor is in Jesus Christ, who abolished death and brought life and immortality to light through the Gospel.

Lips vs. Lives

Preaching is not the only way we declare the Gospel of Christ. Our lives also should be witnesses to others of the reality of Christ. Those who have affected me most profoundly in my life have not necessarily been great or eloquent preachers, but men and women of God whose lives were marked by holiness and Christ-likeness. The Gospel must be communicated not only by our lips but by our lives. This is a visual proof that the message we preach actually can change lives.

Our world today is looking for men and women with integrity, for communicators who back up their ministry with their lives. Our preaching emerges out of what we are. We are called to be a holy people—separated from the moral evils of the world. The Bible commands, "As he which hath called you is holy, so be ye holy in all manner of conversation" (1 Peter 1:15). The apostle John wrote, "Love not the world neither the things that are in the world. If any man love the world, the love of the Father is not in him. For all that is in the world, the lust of the flesh, and the lust of the eyes, and the pride of life, is not of the Father, but is of the world. And the world passeth away, and the lust thereof: but he that doeth the will of God abideth for ever" (1 John 2:15–17).

10

HOW TO BE BORN AGAIN

How to Become Born Again

First, realize that you are a sinner in God's eyes. You may not consider yourself a bad person, because you know you have lived a fairly decent life. On the other hand, you may be carrying a burden of guilt over some sins committed in the past. Whatever your background, the Bible tells us "there is none righteous, no, not one" (Romans 3:10 KJV). We have all broken the Law of God, and we all deserve nothing but God's judgment and wrath.

Second, realize that God loves you and sent His Son to die for you. You deserve to die for your sins, but Christ died in your place. "For Christ also died for sins once and for all, the just for the unjust, in order that He might bring us to God" (1 Peter 3:18). That is the wonder of the Gospel—that God loves us! He loves you, in spite of the fact you are a sinner.

Third, repent of your sins. Repentance comes from a Greek word meaning "a change of mind." It means that I admit I am a sinner, and that I feel sorry for the fact I have sinned. But repentance also means I actually turn my back on my sins—I reject them—and determine by God's grace to live as He wants me to live. Jesus said, "unless you repent, you will all likewise perish" (Luke 13:3).

Repentance involves a willingness to leave sin behind, and turn my life over to Jesus Christ as Lord of my life. We see ourselves as God sees us and we pray, "God, be merciful to me, the sinner!" (Luke 18:13).

Fourth, come by faith and trust to Christ. Salvation, the Bible tells us, is a free gift. God has done everything possible to make salvation available to us, but we must respond and make that gift our own. "For the wages of sin is death, but the free gift of God is eternal life in Christ Jesus our Lord" (Romans 6:23).

Feet First, Not Head First

During recent years, I have seen a number of intellectuals respond to the Gospel. Many of them have tried to come head first, and it will not work! There must be a response of the whole man—intellect, will, and emotions—to the saving initiative of God.

Head, Heart, Will

In John there is a description of the hundreds of people who were following Jesus early in His ministry. The Bible says that "many believed in his name when they saw the miracles which he did. But Jesus did not commit himself unto them" (John 2:23-24) because He knew the hearts of all men. Why would Jesus not commit Himself to them? He knew that they believed with their heads and not with their hearts.

There is a vast difference between intellectual belief and the total conversion that saves the soul. To be sure, there must be a change in our thinking and intellectual acceptance of Christ.

There are thousands of people who have had some form of emotional experience that they refer to as conversion but who have never been truly converted to Christ. Christ demands a change in the way you live—and if your life does not conform to your experience, then you have every reason to doubt your experience! Certainly there will be a change in the elements that make up emotion when you come to Christ—hate and love will be involved, because you will begin to hate sin and love righteousness. Your affections will undergo a revolutionary change. Your devotion to Him will know no bounds. Your love for Him cannot be described.

But even if you have an intellectual acceptance of Christ, and an emotional experience—that still is not enough. There must be the conversion of the will! There must be that determination to obey and follow Christ. Your will must be bent to the will of God. Self must be nailed to the cross. . . . Our main desire must be to please Him. It is a total commitment.

In conversion as you stand at the foot of the cross, the Holy Spirit makes you realize that you are a sinner. He directs your faith to the Christ who died in your place. You must open your heart and let Him come in. At that precise moment the Holy Spirit performs the miracle of the new birth. You actually become a new moral creature. There comes the implantation of the divine nature. You become a partaker of God's own life. Jesus Christ, through the Spirit of God, takes up residence in your heart.

Conversion is so simple that the smallest child can be converted, but it is also so profound that theologians throughout history have pondered the depth of its meaning. God has made the way of salvation so plain that "the wayfaring men, though fools, shall not err therein" (Isaiah 35:8). No person will ever be barred from the kingdom of God because he did not have the capacity to understand. The rich and the poor, the sophisticated and the simple—all can be converted.

To sum it up, conversion simply means "to change." When a person is converted he may continue to love objects which he loved before, but there will be a change of reasons for loving them. A converted person may forsake former objects of affection. He may even withdraw from his previous companions, not because he dislikes them, for many of them will be decent and amiable, but because there is more attraction for him in the fellowship of other Christians of like mind.

The converted person will love the good he once hated, and hate the sin he once loved. There will even be a change of heart about God. Where he once may have been careless about God, living in constant fear, dread, and antagonism to God, he now finds himself in a state of complete reverence, confidence, obedience, and devotion. There will be a reverential fear of God, a constant gratitude to God, a dependence upon God, and a new loyalty to Him. Before conversion there may have been gratification of the flesh. Cultural and intellectual pursuits or the making of money may have been of first and supreme importance. Now, righteousness and holiness of heart, and living the Christian life will be placed above all other concerns, for pleasing Christ will be the only goal of real importance. In other words, conversion means a complete change in the life of an individual.

Dynamics of the New Man

In the third century, Cyprian, the Bishop of Carthage, wrote to his friend Donatus: "It is a bad world, Donatus, an incredibly bad world. But I have discovered in the midst of it a quiet and holy people who have learned a great secret. They have found a joy which is a thousand times better than any of the pleasures of our sinful life. They are despised and persecuted, but they care not. They are masters of their souls. They have overcome the world. These people, Donatus, are Christians . . . and I am one of them."

If you have repented of your sins and have received Christ as Savior, then you, too, are one of them.

FORGIVEN AND JUSTIFIED

The moment you were converted to Christ, several dramatic things happened, whether you were aware of them or not. First, your sin was forgiven. "In whom we have redemption through his blood, even the forgiveness of sins" (Colossians 1:14). "Your sins are forgiven you for his name's sake" (1 John 2:12). Throughout the New Testament we are told that the one who receives Christ as Savior also receives immediately, as a gift from God, the forgiveness of sin. The Bible says: "As far as the east is from the west, so far hath he removed our transgressions from us" (Psalm 103:12). The only reason our sins can be forgiven is, of course, because Jesus Christ paid the full penalty for our sins on the cross. He was "delivered for our offenses" (Romans 4:25).

ADOPTED

Second, the new man is adopted. "To redeem them that were under the law, that we might receive the adoption of sons" (Galatians 4:5). The moment we receive Christ as Savior, we receive the divine nature of the sons of God. We are now placed in the position of a joint heir with Jesus Christ. "Having predestinated us unto the adoption of children" (Ephesians 1:5). We have now all the rights of a son. All things in the Kingdom are now ours to enjoy.

SPIRIT OF GOD

Third, the new man is indwelt by the Spirit of God. Before He ascended into Heaven, Jesus Christ said: "And I will pray the Father, and he shall give you another Comforter, that he may abide with you forever; even the

Spirit of truth...ye know him; for he dwelleth with you, and shall be in you" (John 14:16,17). During His lifetime on earth, Christ's presence could be experienced only by a small group of men at any given time. Now Christ dwells through the Spirit in the hearts of all those who have received Him as Savior. The Apostle Paul wrote to the Romans: "But ye are not in the flesh, but in the Spirit, if so be that the Spirit of God dwell in you" (Romans 8:9). Later he wrote to the Corinthians: "Know ye not that ye are the temple of God, and that the Spirit of God dwelleth in you?" (1 Corinthians 3:16).

The Holy Spirit is given to every believer—not for a limited time but forever. Were He to leave us for one moment, we would be in deep trouble.

STRENGTH TO RESIST TEMPTATION

Fourth, the new man has the possibility of victory over temptation and sin. "There hath no temptation taken you but such as is common to man: but God is faithful, who will not suffer you to be tempted above that ye are able; but will with the temptation also make a way to escape, that ye may be able to bear it" (1 Corinthians 10:13).

The Bible teaches that the new man is to "abhor that which is evil" (Romans 12:9) and to "put off concerning the former conversation the old man, which is corrupt according to the deceitful lusts" (Ephesians 4:22). We are told also to "make not provision for the flesh, to fulfill the lusts thereof" (Romans 13:14).

New Man, Not Perfect

There is one problem that Christians face immediately upon conversion. Some people get the idea that they become perfect right away, and then they find themselves tempted, in conflict, and even on occasion yielding to temptation. Many of them become filled with confusion, frustration, and discouragement. They say the Christian life is not what they thought it was going to be. The Bible does teach that we can become mature, but that does not mean that we are ever flawless. Ernest F. Kevan says: "The perfect Christian is the one who, having a sense of his own failure to attain, is minded to press toward the mark" (Philippians 3:14).

The Bible teaches: "For the flesh lusteth against the Spirit, and the Spirit against the flesh: and these are contrary the one to the other: so that ye cannot do the things that ye would" (Galatians 5:17). It teaches that there is a spiritual conflict in the heart of every true believer. It is true that the Christian possesses a new nature, but the old nature is still there. It is now up to us, day by day, to yield to the reign and control of the new nature, which is dominated by Christ. Because we are a new creation for whom all old things have passed away and all things have become new, we no longer practice sin.

We may fall into sin, but we hate it. The new nature commits no sin; but when the Christian sins, it is because the old nature has been yielded to for a moment. And when the Christian sins, he is miserable until the sin is confessed and fellowship with God is restored. This is the difference between the believer and the unbeliever. The unbeliever makes sin a practice, and the believer does not make a practice of sin. He abhors it and rather than live in the former lawlessness, he seeks to abide by the commands of God. Thus Paul says: "Who walk not after the flesh, but after the Spirit" (Romans 8:4). It means that we are to be submissive to the new nature, to the Holy Spirit who indwells us. "Neither yield ye your members as instruments of unrighteousness unto sin: but yield yourselves unto God, as those that are alive from the dead, and your members as instruments of righteousness unto God" (Romans 6:13).

The World Upside Down

The people who followed Jesus were unique in their generation. They turned the world upside down because their hearts had been turned right side up. The world has never been the same. History took a sharp turn for the better. People began to behave like human beings. Dignity, nobility, and honor followed in the wake of Christianity. Art, music, and science—sparked by this new interpretation of life's meaning—began to progress and develop. Mankind began at long last to resemble again the "image of God" in which he was created. Society began to feel the impact of the Christian influence. Injustice, inhumanity, and intolerance were dislodged by the tidal wave of spiritual power which was released by Christ. As F. W. Boreham once said, "The Carpenter of Nazareth has encouraged the goldsmiths of the ages." Virtually every significant social movement in Western Civilization—from the abolition of slavery to child labor laws—owes its origin to the influence of Jesus Christ.

Centuries have rolled by since that initial surge of spiritual life. The stream of Christianity has flowed unceasingly, sometimes at flood tide but more often at ebb tide.

At times the church has been gloriously renewed and used of God. Emboldened by the Holy Spirit, and stirred by the truth of the Word of God, men and women throughout the centuries have continued to turn the world upside down for Christ. At other times, however, man-made tributaries have flowed into it, polluting and adulterating it. Deism, Pantheism, and, of late, Humanism and blatant Naturalism have flowed like muddy currents into the mainstream of Christian thought, so that the world has had difficulty in distinguishing the real from the false. In some parts of the world armies have fought and killed supposedly in the name of Christ—and yet by their actions showing they understood little of His spirit of forgiveness and love.

Yes, Christians are imperfect, and some who have

claimed most loudly to follow Him have been the furthest from His teaching. But don't let that divert you or keep you from Christ Himself. At times people have said to me, "Christians are all hypocrites—I don't want anything to do with Christ!" But that is an excuse to keep from having to face the truth that is in Christ. Instead, understand His teaching and examine His life. And if you know Christ and have committed your life to Him, learn from Him and live a consistent life for Him. Let others see something of Christ—His love, His joy, His peace—in your life.

True Christians are supposed to be happy! Our generation has become well versed in Christian terminology, but is remiss in the actual practice of Christ's principles and teachings. Hence, our greatest need today is not more Christianity but more true Christians.

Balancing the Scales

Let's look at an old pair of country scales for a moment.

On one side is the holiness of God. On the other side is you.

God says the scales must balance. In other words, you must be as holy as God before you can enter Heaven and before the scales can balance.

Let's see what God requires. Have I broken God's commandments? Am I a sinner? Have I sinned against Him?

1. Sin is any transgression of the law in act, in thought, or in implication (1 John 3:4): "Whosoever committeth sin transgresseth also the law: for sin is the transgression of the law."

We may say that the law is summed up in the Ten Commandments. The entire moral law is summarized in these rules of life, which express God's holiness. The ceremonial laws were expressly commended to Jews under the law and to nobody else, but the moral laws are for all.

"Thou shalt have no other gods before me." Perhaps

you have broken that commandment by permitting a heart affection for money or something besides God. If so, you have bowed to another idol. To bow and to worship before a saint of any kind is idolatry, whether that idol be a picture of Christ or an image of the Virgin Mary or a crucifix or the likeness of a saint. If you have bowed before it, you have sinned. You have transgressed the law.

Let's look at another commandment. "Thou shalt not take the name of the Lord thy God in vain." Cursing or using God's name as a byword, saying "Praise the Lord" when we don't mean it from the heart, pretending to praise God in prayer when actually we are thinking more of the people than of God, closing a prayer in "Jesus' Name" when we are not asking the petition for Jesus' sake—these are sin, violation of the third commandment.

Another of the commandments says, "Honor thy father and thy mother." If there has been a time when you have not, you have sinned. You have transgressed if you have failed to provide for your parents' needs when they were old or dependent.

"Thou shalt not kill" is the fourth commandment. Jesus said, "Whosoever hateth his brother is a murderer." You are guilty!

"Thou shalt not commit adultery." Jesus said, "I say unto you, That whosoever looketh on a woman to lust after her hath committed adultery with her already in his heart." In God's eyes lust is adultery.

"Thou shalt not steal." Most of us have broken this commandment. We have pulled a few shady deals. We have gotten the best of bargains.

"Thou shalt not bear false witness against thy neighbor." Even little so-called "white lies" break this commandment. All of us are guilty of transgressing this law.

"Thou shalt not covet." Perhaps we have coveted something that is our neighbor's. If we have kept every one of these commandments and have broken only one, and that only slightly, we are transgressors nevertheless:

"For whosoever shall keep the whole law, and yet offend in one point, he is guilty of all" (James 2:10).

How do you balance?

Today you are being weighed in the balance of God. On one side is God's holiness, summed up in the Ten Commandments. On the other side are you, a lawbreaker, condemned and guilty.

These commandments were summarized by Jesus in Matthew 22: 37–40.

Jesus said unto him, Thou shalt love the Lord thy God with all thy heart, and with all thy soul, and with all thy mind. This is the first and great commandment. And the second is like unto it, Thou shalt love thy neighbor as thyself. On these two commandments hang all the law and the prophets.

Commands to do are simply particular details of the one great command to love. Obedience to God's commandments which doesn't flow simply and naturally out of a heart of love for God and all mankind is not genuine fulfillment of the law. Outwardly you may be perfectly blameless concerning the Ten Commandments, yet you may have violated every one of them in your heart.

2. If you have neglected a known duty, you have sinned (James 4:17): "Therefore to him that knoweth to do good, and doeth it not, to him it is sin." Every time you abstain from what you ought to do, you sin. "And he that doubteth is damned if he eat, because he eateth not of faith: for whatsoever is not of faith is sin" (Romans 14: 23). If you fret or worry, that is sin. Faith is the highest virtue a man can have. Unbelief is the worst sin.

3. Even the thought of foolishness is sin (Proverbs 24:9): "The thought of foolishness is sin: and the scorner is an abomination to men."

4. If you have made a vow to God and not kept it, you have sinned (Deuteronomy 23:21): "When thou shalt vow a vow unto the Lord thy God, thou shalt not slack to pay it: for the Lord thy God will surely require it of thee; and it would be sin in thee." Have you kept all the resolutions

you have made? God's standard is His own standard of perfection and righteousness. You cannot give the excuse "Others are doing it" or "There are hypocrites in the Church."

A Fleeting Shadow

Regularly we read in our newspapers about the budget of this or that nation. We now are used to the term billions. I wonder how many of us really ever stop to think what a billion is. Someone suggested to me, "Before you use the term again, consider what an exaggeration 'Thanks a billion' really is. Just over one billion seconds ago we were in World War II and the atomic bomb had not yet been exploded. Over one billion minutes ago Christ was still on earth. Just over one billion hours ago we were still in the caveman era."

However, in terms of government spending, one billion dollars ago is only a few hours ago because the American government's budget will be about one trillion dollars soon at the present rate of escalation.

Or have you ever stopped to compute how many days you have left? You can do it easily on your small calculator. If you live to be seventy you have lived approximately 25,000 days of life. If you are now thirty-five you have little more than 12,000 days left.

The Bible also teaches that life is like a shadow, like a fleeting cloud moving across the face of the sun. The Psalmist says, "For I dwell with you as an alien, a stranger, as all my fathers were" (Psalm 39:12). The world is not a permanent home, it is only a temporary dwelling. "We are aliens and strangers in your sight, as were all our forefathers. Our days on earth are like a shadow, without hope" (1 Chronicles 29:15).

For every one of us time is slipping away. The late President Kennedy never dreamed on that Friday morning in 1963 as he ate breakfast that by two o'clock in the afternoon he would be in eternity. We never know when our moment is coming. Tragedies such as his death and that of his brother, Bobby, should help us realize the uncertainty of life, the brevity of time, and our need to be ready to meet God at any moment.

The Scripture teaches that God knows the exact moment when each person is to die (Job 14:5). There are appointed bounds beyond which we cannot pass.

I am convinced that when a person is prepared to die, he is also prepared to live. Again, if we knew all that there is to know, we would choose to die at the time God has planned for us to die.

One of the primary goals in life therefore should be to prepare for death. Everything else should be secondary.

11

THE MEANING OF HAPPINESS

Two Kinds of Happiness

Inside us a little voice keeps saying, "We were not meant to be this way—we were meant for better things." We have a mysterious feeling that there is a fountain somewhere that contains the happiness which makes life worthwhile. We keep saying to ourselves that somewhere, sometime we will stumble onto the secret. Sometimes we feel that we have obtained it—only to find it illusive, leaving us disillusioned, bewildered, unhappy, and still searching.

There are, we need to realize, two kinds of happiness.

One kind of happiness comes to us when our circumstances are pleasant and we are relatively free from troubles. The problem, however, is that this kind of happiness is fleeting and superficial. When circumstances change— as they inevitably do—then this kind of happiness evaporates like the early morning fog in the heat of the sun. In addition, even when our outward circumstances are seemingly ideal, we still may be troubled inside by a nagging hunger or longing for something we cannot identify. We say we are "happy"—but down inside we know it is only temporary and shallow at best. Yes, from time to time we may think we have found a degree of happiness, but sooner or later it will vanish. Our search for happiness remains unfulfilled. But there is another kind of happiness—the kind for which we all long.

This second kind of happiness is a lasting, inner joy and peace which survives in any circumstances. It is a happiness which endures no matter what comes our way—and even may grow stronger in adversity. This is the kind of happiness to which Jesus summons us in the Beatitudes. It is happiness which can only come from God. He alone has the answer to our search for lasting happiness.

The happiness which brings enduring worth to life is not the superficial happiness that is dependent on circumstances. It is the happiness and contentment that fills the soul even in the midst of the most distressing of circumstances and the most adverse environment. It is the kind of happiness that survives when things go wrong and smiles through the tears. The happiness for which our souls ache is one undisturbed by success or failure, one which dwells deep within us and gives inward relaxation, peace, and contentment, no matter what the surface problems may be. That kind of happiness stands in need of no outward stimulus.

Sermon on the Mount

I invite you to go with me on a thrilling, adventuresome journey. The object of our search? The secret of happiness. The place? Galilee! Let us roll back the pages of time almost two thousand years.

It's a hot, sultry day with the sweltering wind spinning little dust whirls and carrying them swiftly down the winding road by the Sea of Galilee. There is an air of expectancy in the atmosphere we breathe. The wind skips happily across the surface of the ancient sea. We hear voices raised in an excited, feverish pitch as friend calls a greeting to friend. Along every trail leading to Galilee little groups of people begin to gather. The word has spread abroad that Jesus is returning to Galilee.

Suddenly He and His little band of followers emerge over the brow of a hill on the road to Capernaum, and immediately in their wake follows a vast multitude of people from Galilee, Decapolis, Jerusalem, Judea, and from beyond the Jordan River.

Quickly the word spreads from mouth to mouth: "Jesus is coming!" Other multitudes from Tiberias, Bethsaida, and Capernaum soon appear and join the others. Together they follow thirteen robed men. As they reach the summit of the hill where the gentle winds from the plains sweep over them, affording relief from the sun, Jesus stops and motions for them to sit down and rest.

The air is tense. It is a moment to be captured and held for eternity. The crowd hushes as Jesus climbs atop a large rock and is seated. In the valley on the deserted road, a lone camel rider wends his way along the trail toward Tiberias. A quiet falls upon the multitude as their faces gaze expectantly at Jesus. Then He begins to speak.

What He said there on that Mount of Beatitudes in far away Palestine was to go down in history as the most profound, sublime words ever spoken! There in reverent, measured, simple words He revealed the secret of happiness—not a superficial happiness of time and space, but a happiness which would last forever.

His first word was "happy." Immediately His listeners must have pricked up their ears, as we are prone to do. In the pages to follow it is my prayer that you will do even more: prick up your ears...open your heart...surrender your will. Then you will begin living life with a capital L, find a contentment and joy that crowd the futility and vanity out of the daily walk, and discover the secret of happiness!

Happiness Through Poverty

There is nothing inherently wrong with being rich. I have been privileged to know some very wealthy people across the years who were humble and generous, seeing their wealth as a God-given means to help others. The Bible, however, warns that riches easily overwhelm a person, distorting his values, making him proud and arrogant, and making him think he does not need God. "But they that will be rich fall into temptation and a snare, and into many foolish and hurtful lusts, which drown men in destruction and perdition. For the love of money is the root of all evil" (I Timothy 6:9–10).

For others, wealth only leads to boredom. King Solomon was unquestionably one of the wealthiest men who ever lived. In his search for happiness he tried everything—possessions, music, sex, great building projects, knowledge—but in the end he declared about them, "I have seen all the works that are done under the sun; and, behold, all is vanity and vexation of spirit" (Ecclesiastes 1:14). Only God could satisfy his deepest longings and give him true happiness.

On the other hand, many great people stay poor all their lives, either through choice (such as a missionary or a person who chooses to live modestly and give away money to help others) or through unavoidable circumstances. There are others, however, who go through life filled with resentment, jealousy, and bitterness because they want "just a little bit more." They may have enough to satisfy their legitimate needs, but instead of being thankful for what they have—which would make them unimaginably wealthy in the eyes of those in poorer nations—they are consumed by a desire for riches. They believe the key to happiness would be found in greater wealth.

But Jesus made it plain that happiness and contentment are not found in possessions or money. He stated that material things and riches do not in themselves bring happiness and peace to the soul.

Happy is that person who has learned the secret of being content with whatever life brings him, and has learned to rejoice in the simple and beautiful things around him.

Happiness While Mourning

What did Jesus mean when He said: "Happy are they that mourn"? Certainly He did not mean to imply that a special blessing is promised to "crybabies," "weeping Willies," or the emotionally upset. This verse was not intended to be a comfort for abnormal psychopathic cases, which have somehow become mentally warped and take a morbid view of life. No, it was addressed to normal, average people for the purpose of showing them how to live happier, fuller, richer lives.

Let us begin with the word "mourning" itself. It means "to feel deep sorrow, to show great concern, or to deplore some existing wrong." It implies that if we are to live life on the higher plane then we are to be sensitive, sympathetic, tenderhearted, and alert to the needs of others and the world.

When I mourn it is because my heart has been touched by the suffering and heartache of others—or even by my own heartache. When I do not care and am indifferent, then I do not mourn. The person who mourns is a person with a tender and sensitive heart.

Let's list just six kinds of mourning which I believe were implied in this most significant saying of our Lord. The word here employed by Jesus covers such a wide range of attitudes that five shades of meaning are implied. We should ponder each one of them prayerfully.

First, there is the mourning of inadequacy. Jeremiah, the weeping prophet who mourned not in self-pity but for a wayward, lost world, said: "O Lord, I know that the way of man is not in himself: it is not in man that walketh to direct his steps" (10:23).

Another kind of mourning is the mourning of repentance. Following the consciousness that we are inadequate comes the awareness of the reason for our insufficiency—sin. As individuals, we have no control over the fact of sin in the universe, but as creatures of choice we are responsible for its presence in our lives. Because "all have sinned, and come short of the glory of God" (Romans 3:23), all need to mourn the fact of sin in their lives.

There is, third, the mourning of love. . . . If I would know the measure of my love for God, I must simply observe my love for people around me. My compassion for others is an accurate gauge of my devotion to God. The Bible puts it this way: "Let us love one another: for love is of God; and every one that loveth is born of God, and knoweth God. . . . And this commandment have we from him, That he who loveth God love his brother also" (1 John 4:7, 21).

Another kind of mourning which brings comfort is, fourth, the mourning of soul travail.

This may seem cryptic, but it represents a very real and a profitable kind of mourning. The Bible says: "As soon as Zion travailed, she brought forth her children" (Isaiah 66:8).

We don't use this phrase "soul travail" very often, not as much as our spiritual forefathers a generation or so ago. "Travail" means "toil, painful effort, labor." "Travail of soul" therefore means spiritual toil—not necessarily outward labor which others will see, but that which takes place within the secret recesses of our souls. It refers to the continual flow of prayer which rises out of the Christian heart for a world which is spiritually unborn. And don't be under any illusions: this kind of soul travail is difficult and costly, because we are involved in spiritual warfare against Satan, the Enemy of Souls. "Pray without ceasing," the Bible says (1 Thessalonians 5:17).

Another kind of mourning we shall deal with is, fifth, the mourning of bereavement. Nowhere has God promised anyone, even His children, immunity from sorrow, suffering, and pain. This world is a "vale of tears," and disappointment and heartache are as inevitable as clouds and shadows. Suffering is often the crucible in which our faith is tested. Those who successfully come through the "furnace of affliction" are the ones who emerge "like gold tried in the fire." The Bible teaches unmistakably that we can triumph over bereavement. The Psalmist said: "Weeping may endure for a night, but joy cometh in the morning" (Psalm 30:5).

Lastly, there is the mourning of blank despair. "I could not think about my own death," says one young AIDS patient. "I wanted to live forever." The tragedy of AIDS is obvious. But as C. S. Lewis said of war, "War does not increase death. Death is total in every generation." So it could be said of AIDS; it does not increase death; death is total in every generation. However, in this present grim situation, a merciful God has given people time. A short time perhaps, torn with frustration, anger, bitterness and fear—but still time. Time to think of God, His love for a world gone wrong, the sending of His Son to bear in His own body on the cross, all the sins of mankind. Time to come to Him in childlike repentance and to discover the love of Jesus, His transforming power, and the life everlasting that He promises and has gone to prepare for us.

HAPPINESS THROUGH MEEKNESS

To most people today, the word "meek" brings to mind a picture of someone who is a weak personality, someone who allows everyone to walk over him. Meekness, in fact, in the popular mind is not seen as a desirable personality trait. Our society says, "Get ahead by intimidation" or "Look out for Number One." In the eyes of many people the only way to get ahead is to disregard other people and shove them out of the way. "I want to climb the ladder of success," one woman was quoted as saying, "and I don't care whose fingers I step on as I climb up the rungs."

But what does Jesus mean when He speaks of meekness? Does He, for example, mean that we are to be cringing before God, fearful of Him and slavishly yielding to His will because of fear of what He might do to us if we fail?

Could it be that Christ wanted His followers to be like the subdued puppy that comes crawling into its master's presence whipped and beaten? Is happiness the result of forced submission? Certainly not!

Jesus is not trying to convey the thought that God is an autocrat whose ego can be satisfied only by coerced yielding. Nothing could be further from the truth. There is no happiness in being compelled to do what you do not wish to do. No employees are more miserable than those who constantly resent their position in life. It would be against God's nature, as well as against man's free moral agency, to demand an allegiance which is not freely offered.

God conducts Himself in keeping with His righteousness. He will never violate our freedom to choose between eternal life and spiritual death, good and evil, right and wrong. His ultimate goal is not only to glorify Himself but also to make a happy relationship with His crowning creation—man. Never will He make any demands which encroach upon our freedom to choose.

HAPPINESS THROUGH HUNGER

A hungry person is a normal person. Those who are sick and abnormally upset refuse nourishment, but the normal person craves food. In that sense there is a blessedness in hunger. It is a natural reaction.

The normal person also possesses a spiritual hunger—although he may not label it as such. He may think he has filled it, but apart from God there is no lasting quenching of his spiritual hunger and thirst. David said: "As the hart panteth after the water brooks, so panteth my soul after thee, O God" (Psalm 42:1). Isaiah said: "With my soul have I desired thee in the night; yea, with my spirit within me will I seek thee early: for when thy judgments are in the earth, the inhabitants of the earth will learn righteousness" (Isaiah 26:9).

HAPPINESS THROUGH MERCY

To paraphrase this Beatitude we might say, "They which have obtained mercy from God are so happy that they are merciful to others." Our attitude toward our fellow men is a more accurate gauge of our religion than all of our religious rantings.

Alexander Pope prayed:

Teach me to feel another's woe,
To hide the fault I see;
That mercy I to others show,
That mercy show to me.

Emerson must have been reading the gauge of human mercy when he said: "What you are speaks so loud that I cannot hear what you say." Jesus summed up the whole matter of genuine Christianity when He said: "If any man thirst, let him come unto me, and drink. He that believeth in me, as the Scripture hath said, out of his inmost soul flow rivers of living water" (John 7:37, 38).

HAPPINESS IN PURITY

Purity of heart has both a negative and a positive side. On one hand, our hearts are to be emptied of sin and its dominion over us. On the other hand, we are to be pure in our actions and filled with all that is pure. The Bible illustrates these negative and positive sides to purity: "Put to death therefore what is earthly in you: fornication, impurity, passion, evil desire, and covetousness. . . . put them all away: anger, wrath, malice, slander, and foul talk. . . . Put on then, as God's chosen ones, holy and beloved, compassion, kindness, lowliness, meekness, and patience. . . . And above all these, put on love" (Colossians 3:5, 8, 12, 14, RSV).

HAPPINESS THROUGH PEACEMAKING

There are many areas of our lives where we can be peacemakers. There is no part of our lives which is not affected by this peace of God which we are to share with others. . . .

We can be peacemakers in the home. . . . With the continual clash of personalities in a domestic pattern, there must be an integrating force, and the Living God is that Force! He can give love where there has been hate or indifference. He can make a husband sensitive to the needs of his wife, and the wife sensitive to the needs of her husband instead of two people constantly clamoring and demanding only to have their own needs met. True self-giving love—the kind God has for us, and the kind He can give us for others—is like a beautiful diamond which sends out flashes of light from its many facets. The Bible gives the most profound and concise summary of love's facets in all of literature: "Love is patient and kind; love is not jealous or boastful; it is not arrogant or rude. Love does not insist on its own way; it is not irritable or resentful; it does not rejoice at wrong, but rejoices in the right. Loves bears all things, believes all things, hopes all things, endures all things" (1 Corinthians 13:4–7, RSV).

HAPPINESS IN SPITE OF PERSECUTION

Jesus Christ spoke frankly to His disciples concerning the future. He hid nothing from them. No one could ever accuse Him of deception. No one could accuse Him of securing allegiance by making false promises.

In unmistakable language He told them that discipleship meant a life of self-denial, and the bearing of a cross. He asked them to count the cost carefully, lest they should turn back when they met with suffering and privation.

Jesus told His followers that the world would hate them. They would be "as sheep in the midst of wolves."

They would be arrested, scourged, and brought before governors and kings. Even their loved ones would persecute them. As the world hated and persecuted Him, so they would treat His servants. He warned further, "They will put you out of the synagogue: indeed, the hour is coming when whoever kills you will think he is offering service to God" (John 16:2, RSV).

Many of Christ's followers were disappointed in Him, for in spite of His warning they expected Him to subdue their enemies and to set up a world political kingdom. When they came face-to-face with reality, they "drew back and no longer went about with him" (John 6:66, RSV). But the true disciples of Jesus all suffered for their faith.

Tacitus, a Roman historian, writing of the early Christian martyrs, said, "Mockery of every sort was added to their deaths. Covered with the skins of beasts, they were torn by dogs and perished, or were nailed to crosses, or were doomed to the flames and burnt, to serve as nightly illumination, when daylight had expired. Nero offered his gardens for the spectacle." How true were the words of Paul to the early Christians. "Through many tribulations we must enter the kingdom of God" (Acts 14:22, RSV).

12

THE POWER OF PRAYER

Power of Prayer

In our modern age we have learned to harness the power of the mighty Niagara and turn its force to beneficial use. We have learned to hold steam captive in boilers and release its tremendous energy to turn our machines and pull our trains. We have learned to contain gasoline vapors in a cylinder and explode them at the appointed second to move our automobiles and trucks along our highways. We have even discovered the secret of releasing energy in the atom, which is capable of lighting cities, operating great industries, or of destroying entire cities and civilizations.

But very few of us have learned how to fully develop the power of prayer.

Effectual prayer is offered in faith. Jesus said, "I tell you, whatever you ask for in prayer, believe that you have received it, and it will be yours" (Mark 11:24). James wrote: "If any of you lacks wisdom, he should ask God, who gives generously to all without finding fault, and it will be given to him. But when he asks, he must believe and not doubt, because he who doubts is like a wave of the sea, blown and tossed by the wind" (James 1:5, 6). If our prayers are aimless, meaningless, and mingled with doubt, they will be unanswered. Prayer is more than a wish turned heavenward: it is the voice of faith directed Godward.

What a privilege is yours—the privilege of prayer! In the light of coming events, examine your heart, re-consecrate your life, yield yourself to God unreservedly, for only those who pray through a clean heart will be heard of Him. The Bible says, "The prayer of a righteous man is powerful and effective" (James 5:16).

We are to pray not only for our own needs but for the needs of others. We are to pray in times of adversity, lest we become faithless and unbelieving. We are to pray in times of prosperity, lest we become boastful and proud. We are to pray in times of danger, lest we become fearful and doubting. We need to pray in times of security, lest we become careless and self-sufficient.

"More things are wrought by prayer than this world dreams of." Tennyson's well-known words are no mere cliche. They state a sober truth. Bible teaching, church history, Christian experience, all confirm that prayer does work. But as we relate this matter of prayer specifically to the subject of suffering, we need to keep in mind several things which we have already stated and which we now summarize.

For one thing, we must always remember that prayer does not work automatically, nor is it a piece of spiritual magic. It's not like pressing an electric button and expecting an immediate response. We can't manipulate God or dictate to Him. He is sovereign, and we must recognize His sovereign rights.

This means, as we have stressed all along, that our prayers are subject to His will. And we should be glad of that. It takes the burden off ourselves and places it on the Lord. To say "Thy will be done" is not a sigh, but a song because His will is always what is best—both for us and those for whom we pray. As Dante said, "in His will is our peace." As believers we cannot find true peace outside the will of God.

Again, we may be sure that God is true to His Word and answers all sincere prayer offered in the name of the Lord Jesus Christ. But His answer is not always the same. As is so often pointed out, His answer may not necessarily be "Yes." It may be "No"—or it may be "Wait." If it is "No" or "Wait," we have no right to say that God has not answered our prayer. It simply means that the answer is different from what we expected. We must get rid of the idea that if only we pray hard and long enough, God will always give us what we ask for in the end.

As we have seen, when we pray for help in trouble or for healing in sickness or for deliverance in persecution, God may not give us what we ask for, for that may not be His wise and loving will for us. But He will answer our prayer in His own way. He will not let us down in our hour of need. He will give us the patience, courage and strength to endure our suffering, the ability to rise above it, and the assurance of His presence in all that we are called to pass through.

In any case, let us never forget that prayer is not just asking God for things. It's far bigger and better than that. At its deepest level, prayer is fellowship with God: enjoying His company, waiting upon His will, thanking Him for His mercies, committing our lives to Him, talking to Him about other people as well as ourselves, and listening in the silence for what He has to say to us.

This is what makes prayer so real and precious a thing, especially in times of stress and strain. When we come to the end of ourselves, we come to the beginning of God. As it has been said, our little things are all big to God's love; our big things are all small to His power.

You are denying yourself a marvelous privilege if you don't pray. The path of prayer is always open, whatever your need. Take it to the Lord in prayer!

More than Wish

Few of us have learned how to develop the power of prayer. We have not yet learned that a man has more strength when he is at prayer than when he is in control of the most powerful military weapons ever developed.... Effective prayer is offered in faith. From one end of the Bible to the other, we find the record of people whose prayers have been answered—people who turned the tide of history by prayer, men who prayed fervently and whom God answered.

David gave some powerful prayer patterns in his Psalms for those who are going through difficult times.

When you are distressed: "Answer me when I call to you, O my righteous God. Give me relief from my distress; be merciful to me and hear my prayer" (Psalm 4:1).

When you need mercy: "The Lord has heard my cry for mercy; the Lord accepts my prayer" (Psalm 6:9).

When you need help: "O Lord my God, I called to you for help and you healed me!" (Psalm 30:2).

Prayer is powerful, but if our prayers are aimless, meaningless, and mingled with doubt, they will be of little hope to us. Prayer is more than a wish; it is the voice of faith directed to God. One of my favorite verses is: "If any of you lacks wisdom, he should ask God, who gives generously to all without finding fault, and it will be given to him. But when he asks, he must believe and not doubt, because he who doubts is like a wave of the sea, blown and tossed by the wind" (James 1:5–6).

The Bible says, "The prayer of a righteous man is powerful and effective" (James 5:16). Jesus said, "I tell you, whatever you ask for in prayer, believe that you have received it, and it will be yours" (Mark 11:24).

Are Prayers Answered?

Christians in desperate situations search the Scriptures for the many wonderful promises of God. One of our favorites is the statement made by Jesus that "You may ask me for anything in my name, and I will do it" (John 14:14). We claim that promise and ask the Lord to heal our loved one. But what happens if healing doesn't come? It's easy for Christians to feel guilty or believe our faith is weak if we pray for healing, and it doesn't take place.

Believers throughout the ages have had to face the fact that God does not heal everyone who prays for healing. But our lack of faith does not determine God's decision on healing. If that were so, He would have to apologize to all of His great servants in the Hebrews 11 Hall of Fame. Look at that cast of characters: Abel, Enoch, Noah, Abraham, Sarah, Isaac, Jacob, Joseph, Moses, Rahab, Gideon, Barak, Samson, Jephtah, David, Samuel, and all the prophets! All of these received great deliverance from God and endured incredible hardships through faith. What happened to them? "Some faced jeers and flogging, while still others were chained and put in prison. They were stoned; they were sawed in two; they were put to death by the sword. They went about in sheepskins and goatskins, destitute, persecuted and mistreated" (Hebrews 11:36–37).

Even though God was pleased because of their faith, they didn't receive much of the world's pleasures. Why? Because God had a better destination, a heavenly city, waiting for them. It was not because of lack of faith or as a punishment for sin that these men and women of God were not delivered from suffering and death. We have the faith to believe that God has a special glory for those who suffer and die for the sake of Christ.

Answered Prayers

From one end of the Bible to the other there is the record of those whose prayers have been answered—people who turned the tide of history by prayer, men who prayed fervently and God answered.

Elijah prayed when challenged by his enemies, and fire was sent from heaven to consume the offering on the altar he had built in the presence of God's enemies.

Elisha prayed, and the son of the Shunammite woman was raised from the dead.

David prayed, and some of his psalms could serve as "pattern prayers" for others who are going through difficulty or as examples of how to praise the Lord in the midst of trouble: "Answer me when I call to you, O my righteous God. Give me relief from my distress; be merciful to me and hear my prayer" (Psalm 4:1).

"The Lord has heard my cry for mercy; the Lord accepts my prayer" (Psalm 6:9).

"In my distress I called to the Lord; I cried to my God for help. From his temple he heard my voice; my cry came before him, into his ears" (Psalm 18:6).

"O Lord my God, I called to you for help and you healed me" (Psalm 30:2).

"In you, O Lord, I have taken refuge; let me never be put to shame; deliver me in your righteousness. Turn your ear to me, come quickly to my rescue; be my rock of refuge, a strong fortress to save me" (Psalm 31:1, 2).

Daniel prayed, and the secret of God was made known to him for the saving of his and his companions' lives, and the changing of the course of history.

Jesus prayed at the tomb of Lazarus, and the one who had been dead for four days came forth. He prayed in the Garden of Gethsemane and found strength to endure His suffering.

The thief prayed on a cross, and Jesus assured him that on that same day he would be with Him in paradise.

The early church prayed, and Peter was miraculously released from prison.

Peter prayed, and Dorcas was raised to life to have added years of service for Jesus Christ.

When the disciples came to Jesus and asked, "Lord, teach us to pray," the Savior answered their request by giving them "The Lord's Prayer" as a model petition. The Lord's Prayer, however, was only the beginning of His teaching on this subject. In scores of passages Christ offered further guidance, and because He practiced what He preached, His whole life was a series of lessons on how prayer prevails in every aspect of life.

Thy Will Be Done

As we face problems and personal suffering, we must not forget that our prayers are subject to His will. This takes the burden off of us and gives it to the Lord. His will is always best. The difficulty most of us face is knowing the will of God. As believers, we cannot find true peace outside the will of God.

In our computerized society, many people have learned the value of using these amazing machines. A computer, however, has no worth unless it is programmed. When the proper data is put into it, it will do more work accurately than many people. The believer has tremendous potential, but that potential cannot be used until he is programmed with the Word of God.

J. Grant Howard said: "God has given every believer a handbook with many of the basic rules and regulations for life. If and when a believer follows these rules, he is in the will of God. When he consciously violates them, he is out of the will of God. Therefore, I must know the precepts taught in the Word if I am going to do the will of God."

Prayers that are selfish, vengeful, or mean are not in the will of God. However, we may be sure that God is true to

His word and answers all sincere prayers offered in the name of the Lord Jesus Christ. His answer may be yes, or it may be no, or it may be "Wait." If it is no or "Wait," we cannot say that God has not answered our prayer. It simply means that the answer is different from what we expected.

When we pray for help in trouble, or for healing in sickness, or for deliverance in persecution, God may not give us what we ask for because that may not be His wise and loving will for us. He will answer our prayer in His own way, and He will not let us down in our hour of need.

True prayer is a way of life, not just for use in cases of emergency. Make it a habit, and when the need arises, you will be in practice.

Praying Through the Pain

Jesus is the supreme model of a person devoted to prayer. He was constantly in an attitude of prayer, and never more urgently than in the face of suffering. One of the most amazing things in all the Scriptures is how much time Jesus spent in prayer. He had only three years of public ministry, but He was never too hurried to spend hours in prayer. He prayed before every difficult task and at every crisis in His ministry. No day began or closed in which He was not in communion with His Father.

When He was arrested in the Garden of Gethsemane, He was praying. He had taken the disciples with Him, and sensing the magnitude of what was ahead, He asked Peter, James, and John to stay with Him and keep watch. He went into the garden and fell with His face to the ground, praying, "My Father, if it is possible, may this cup be taken from me. Yet not as I will, but as you will" (Matthew 26:39).

We pray so haphazardly. Snatches of memorized verses are hastily spoken in the morning. Then we say goodbye to God for the rest of the day, until we sleepily push through a few closing petitions at night, like leaving a wake-up call at the hotel switchboard. That is not the example of prayer that Jesus gave. He prayed long and repeatedly. He spent at least one entire night in prayer (Luke 6:12).

He prayed briefly when He was in a crowd; He prayed a little longer when He was with His disciples; and He prayed all night when He was alone. Today, many in the ministry tend to reverse that process.

The Scriptures say, "Pray without ceasing" (1 Thessalonians 5:17 KJV). This should be the motto of every true follower of Jesus. No matter how dark and hopeless a situation might seem, never stop praying. It's not only to resolve our problems that we should pray, but to share in the strength of God's friendship. For us, prayer should be not merely an act, but an attitude of life.

Pattern for Prayer

Jesus frequently prayed alone, separating Himself from every earthly distraction. I would strongly urge you to select a place, a room or corner in your home, place of work, or in your yard or garden—where you can regularly meet God alone. This does not contradict "Pray without ceasing" (1 Thessalonians 5:17), but expands it.

Jesus prayed with great earnestness. At Gethsemane, in the earnestness of His praying, He fell to the ground and agonized with God until His sweat became "like drops of blood" (Luke 22:44). The force of His prayers was increased during times of extreme suffering.

When we see the need of someone else, pray. When we know someone is in pain, pray. Let someone know you have prayed for them, and ask others to pray for you.

We are to plead for our enemies, asking God to lead them to Christ and for His sake to forgive them.

Persecution, whether it is physical, social, or mental, is one of the worst types of pain, but those who persecute us are to be the objects of our prayers.

In His first words uttered from the cross after the nails had been hammered through His hands and feet, Jesus said "Father, forgive them, for they do not know what they are doing" (Luke 23:34). I have often thought that because of His prayer we will see the men who nailed Jesus to the cross in Heaven. No prayer that Jesus ever prayed to the Father went unanswered.

Christian teachers through the ages have urged the importance of prayer in the lives of believers. One wise man said, "If Christians spent as much time praying as they do grumbling, they would soon have nothing to grumble about."

Someone said, "If there are any tears in Heaven, they will be over the fact that we prayed so little." Cameron Thompson said, "Heaven must be full of answers for which no one ever bothered to ask."

13

ANGELS AND DEVILS

Angels

Isn't talking about angels merely adding to the speculation about supernatural phenomena? What possible value is there in such a discussion? Didn't the fascination with angels vanish with the Middle Ages?

Because all the powers of the evil world system seem to be preying on the minds of people already disturbed and frustrated in our generation, I believe the time has come to focus on the positives of the Christian faith. John the Apostle said, "greater is he that is in you, than he that is in the world" (1 John 4:4). Satan is indeed capable of doing supernatural things—but he acts only by the permissive will of God; he is on a leash. It is God who is all-powerful. It is God who is omnipotent. God has provided Christians with both offensive and defensive weapons. We are not to be fearful; we are not to be distressed; we are not to be deceived; nor are we to be intimidated. Rather, we are to be on our guard, calm and alert "lest Satan should get an advantage of us, for we are not ignorant of his devices" (2 Corinthians 2:11).

One of Satan's sly devices is to divert our minds from the help God offers us in our struggles against the forces of evil. However, the Bible testifies that God has provided assistance for us in our spiritual conflicts. We are not alone in this world! The Bible teaches us that God's Holy Spirit has been given to empower us and guide us. In addition, the Bible—in nearly three hundred different places—also teaches that God has countless angels at His command. Furthermore, God has commissioned these angels to aid His children in their struggles against Satan. The Bible does not give as much information about them as we might like, but what it does say should be a source of comfort and strength for us in every circumstance.

I am convinced that these heavenly beings exist and that they provide unseen aid on our behalf. I do not believe in angels because someone has told me about a dramatic visitation from an angel, impressive as such rare testimonies may be. I do not believe in angels because UFOs are astonishingly angel-like in some of their reported appearances. I do not believe in angels because ESP experts are making the realm of the spirit world seem more and more plausible. I do not believe in angels because of the sudden worldwide emphasis on the reality of Satan and demons. I do not believe in angels because I have ever seen one—because I haven't.

I believe in angels because the Bible says there are angels; and I believe the Bible to be the true Word of God.

I also believe in angels because I have sensed their presence in my life on special occasions.

CREATED BEINGS

The Bible states that angels, like men, were created by God. At one time no angels existed; indeed there was nothing but the Triune God: Father, Son and Holy Spirit. Paul, in Colossians 1:16, says, "For by him were all things created, that are in Heaven, and that are in earth, visible and invisible." Angels indeed are among the invisible things made by God, for "all things were created by him, and for him." This Creator, Jesus, "is before all things, and by him all things consist" (Colossians 1:17), so that even angels would cease to exist if Jesus, who is Almighty God, did not sustain them by His power.

It seems that angels have the ability to change their appearance and shuttle in a flash from the capital glory of Heaven to earth and back again. Although some interpreters have said that the phrase "sons of God" in Genesis 6:2 refers to angels, the Bible frequently makes it clear that angels are non-material; Hebrews 1:14 calls them ministering "spirits." Intrinsically, they do not possess physical bodies, although they may take on physical bodies when God appoints them to special tasks. Further, God has given them no ability to reproduce, and they neither marry nor are given in marriage (Mark 12:25).

VISIBLE OR INVISIBLE

In Daniel 6:22 we read, "My God hath sent his angel, and hath shut the lions' mouths." In the den, Daniel's sight evidently perceived the angelic presence, and the lions' strength more than met its match in the power of the angel. In most instances, angels, when appearing visibly, are so glorious and impressively beautiful as to stun and amaze men who witness their presence.

Can you imagine a being, white and dazzling as lightning? General William Booth, founder of the Salvation Army, describes a vision of angelic beings, stating that every angel was surrounded with an aurora of rainbow light so brilliant that were it not withheld, no human being could stand the sight of it.

Who can measure the brilliance of the lightning flash that illuminates the countryside for miles around? The angel who rolled away the stone from the tomb of Jesus was not only dressed in white, but shone as a flash of lightning with dazzling brilliance (Matthew 28:3). The keepers of the tomb shook and became as dead men. Incidentally, that stone weighed several times more than a single man could move, yet the physical power of the angel was not taxed in rolling it aside.

Abraham, Lot, Jacob and others had no difficulty recognizing angels when God allowed them to manifest themselves in physical form. Note, for example, Jacob's instant recognition of angels in Genesis 32:1, 2. "And Jacob went on his way, and the angels of God met him. And when Jacob saw them, he said, This is God's host: and he called the name of that place Mahanaim." Further, both Daniel and John described the glories of the angels (Daniel 10:6 and Revelation 10:1) visibly descending from Heaven with unmeasurable beauty and brilliance, shining like the sun. Who has not thrilled to read the account of the three Hebrew children, Shadrach, Meshach, and Abednego? They refused to fall in tune with the music of obeisance and worship to the king of Babylon. They learned that the angel presence can be observed on occasion by people in the unbelieving world on the outside. After they had refused to bow, the angel preserved them from being burned alive or even having the smell of smoke on their garments from the seven-times-hotter fire. The angel came to them in the midst of the flame without harm and was seen by the king who said, "I see four men . . . in the midst of the fire" (Daniel 3:25).

On the other hand, the Bible indicates angels are more often invisible to human eyes. Whether visible or invisible, however, God causes His angels to go before us, to be with us, and to follow after us. All of this can be fully understood only by believers who know that angelic presences are in control of the battlefield about us, so that we may stand (Isaiah 26:3) with complete confidence in the midst of the fight. "If God be for us who can be against us?"

WORSHIPING OR NOT WORSHIPING

Unquestionably, angels ascribe honor and glory to the Lamb of God. But angels do not spend all their time in

Heaven. They are not omnipresent (everywhere present at the same time), so they can be in only one place at a given time. Yet as God's messengers, they are busy around the world carrying out God's orders. Is it not, therefore, obvious that when they are engaged in their ministry here, they cannot stand before God's throne? But when angels do stand before the throne of God, indeed they worship and adore their creator.

We can look for that future day when angels will have finished their earthly ministry. Then they will gather with all the redeemed before the throne of God in Heaven. There they will offer their praise and sing their songs. In that day the angels who veiled their faces and stood mute when Jesus hung on the cross will then ascribe glory to the Lamb whose work is finished and whose kingdom has come. The angels may also stop to listen as the redeemed children of God express their own thanksgiving for salvation. It may well be true as the hymn writer has said in verse 3 of the song, "Holy, Holy Is What the Angels Sing,"

> Then the angels stand and listen,
> For they cannot join that song,
> Like the sound of many waters,
> By that happy, blood-washed throng.

But the children of God will also stop to listen to the angels. They have their own reasons for singing, ones that differ from ours. They have given themselves to the service of God Almighty. They have had a part in bringing in the kingdom of God. They have helped the children of God in difficult circumstances. So theirs shall be a shout and a song of victory. The cause they represent has been victorious; the fight they fought is finished; the enemy they met has been conquered; their wicked companion angels who fell shall vex them no more. The angels sing a different song. But they sing; my, how they sing! And I believe that angels and those of us who have been redeemed will compete with each other for the endless ages of eternity to see who can best ascribe glory and praise to our wonderful God!

The Angelic War

The greatest catastrophe in the history of the universal creation was Lucifer's defiance of God and the consequent fall of perhaps one third of the angels who joined him in his wickedness.

When did it happen? Sometime between the dawn of creation and the intrusion of Satan into the Garden of Eden. The poet Dante reckoned that the fall of the rebel angels took place within twenty seconds of their creation and originated in the pride that made Lucifer unwilling to await the time when he would have perfect knowledge. Others, like Milton, put the angelic creation and fall immediately prior to the temptation of Adam and Eve in the Garden of Eden.

But the important question is not, "When were angels created?" but, "When did they fall?" It is difficult to suppose that their fall occurred before God placed Adam and Eve in the Garden. We know for a fact that God rested on the seventh day, or at the end of all creation, and pronounced everything to be good. By implication, up to this time even the angelic creation was good. We might then ask, "How long were Adam and Eve in the Garden before the angels fell and before Satan tempted the first man and woman?" This question must remain unanswered. All we can say positively is that Satan, who had fallen before he tempted Adam and Eve, was the agent and bears a greater guilt because there was no one to tempt him when he sinned; on the other hand Adam and Eve were faced with a tempter.

Thus, we pick up the story where it began. It all started mysteriously with Lucifer. He was the most brilliant and most beautiful of all created beings in Heaven. He was probably the ruling prince of the universe under God, against whom he rebelled. The result was insurrection and war in heaven! He began a war that has been raging in heaven from the moment he sinned and was brought to earth shortly after the dawn of human history. It sounds like a modern world crisis!

Isaiah 14:12–14 records the conflict's origin. Prior to his rebellion, Lucifer, an angel of light, is described in scintillating terms in Ezekiel 28:12–17 (NASB): "You had the seal of perfection, full of wisdom and perfect in beauty.... You were the anointed cherub who covers, and I placed you there. You were on the holy mountain of God. You walked in the midst of the stones of fire. You were blameless in your ways from the day you were created, until unrighteousness was found in you. ... Your heart was lifted up because of your beauty; you corrupted your wisdom by reason of your splendor." When the angel Lucifer rebelled against God and His works, some have estimated that as many as one third of the angelic hosts of the universe may have joined him in his rebellion. Thus, the war that started in Heaven continues on earth and will see its climax at Armageddon with Christ and His angelic army victorious.

Lucifer's Rebellion

Lucifer, the son of the morning, was created, as were all angels, for the purpose of glorifying God. However, instead of serving God and praising Him forever, Satan desired to rule over Heaven and creation in the place of God. He wanted supreme authority! Lucifer said (Isaiah 14),

"I will ascend into Heaven.
"I will exalt my throne above the stars of God.
"I will sit also upon the mount of the congregation.
"I will ascend above the heights of the clouds.
"I will be like the most high."

I...I...I...I...I.
Lucifer was not satisfied with being subordinated to his creator. He wanted to usurp God's throne. He exulted at the thought of being the center of power throughout the universe—he wanted to be the Caesar, the Napoleon, the Hitler of the entire universe. The "I will" spirit is the spirit of rebellion. His was a bold act to dethrone the Lord Most High. Here was a wicked schemer who saw himself occupying the superlative position of power and glory. He wanted to be worshiped, not to worship.

Satan's desire to replace God as ruler of the universe may have been rooted in a basic sin that leads to the sin of pride I have already mentioned. Underneath Satan's pride lurked the deadliest of all sins, the sin of covetousness. He wanted what did not belong to him. Virtually every war ever fought began because of covetousness. The warfare in Heaven and on earth between God and the devil certainly sprang from the same desire—the lust for what belonged to God alone.

Where Sin Began

The puzzling question is where did evil and sin originate, and why did God allow it? The Bible teaches that sin did not originate with man, but with the angel whom we have come to know as Satan. Yet exactly how sin originated is not fully known. It is one of those mysteries the Bible does not fully reveal. We catch glimpses now and again in the Bible of the answer to this riddle.

For example, in the twenty-eighth chapter of Ezekiel there is a description of a great and glorious being of whom the prophet said: "Thou art the anointed cherub that covereth; and I have set thee so: thou wast upon the holy mountain of God . . . thou wast perfect in thy ways from the day that thou wast created, till iniquity was found in thee" (Ezekiel 28:14,15).

Here we find a glimpse of where it all started. In some unknown past, iniquity was found in the heart of one of the most magnificent creatures of heaven. How this iniquity got there we are not told. For some reason it has not pleased God to reveal the full answer to the mystery of where iniquity began. It is enough for us to know that it is in the world and that man has fallen under its power.

In the book of Isaiah we have another hint of the origin of evil: "How art thou fallen from heaven, O Lucifer, son of the morning! How art thou cut down to the ground, which didst weaken the nations! For thou hast said in thine heart, I will ascend into Heaven, I will exalt my throne above the stars of God: I will sit also upon the mount of the congregation, in the sides of the north: I will ascend above the heights of the clouds; I will be like the most High. Yet thou shalt be brought down to Hell, to the sides of the pit" (Isaiah. 14:12–15). Here we have a picture of Lucifer's sin. It is a description of the iniquity that was found in his heart, but there is no explanation as to how it got there.

From these references we learn that he fell and became Satan because of his undue ambition. The New Testament gives us a glimpse concerning the sin of pride: "Lest being lifted up with pride he fall into the condemnation of the devil" (1 Timothy 3:6). Here the Apostle Paul affirms that the basic sin of Lucifer was pride.

Crafty and Clever Camouflage

The underlying principle of all Satan's tactics is deception. He is a crafty and clever camouflager. For Satan's deceptions to be successful they must be so cunningly devised that his real purpose is concealed by wiles. Therefore, he works subtly and secretly. No Christian, however spiritual, is beyond the seductive assaults of Satan. His deception began in the Garden of Eden. "The woman said, The serpent beguiled me, and I did eat" (Genesis 3:13). From that time to this, Satan has been seducing and beguiling. "But evil men and seducers," Paul warned Timothy, "shall wax worse and worse, deceiving, and being deceived" (2 Timothy 3:13). He also warned the church at Ephesus: "Let no man deceive you with vain words" (Ephesians 5:6); and again: "That we henceforth be no more children, tossed to and fro, and carried about with every wind of doctrine, by the sleight of men, and cunning craftiness, whereby they lie in wait to deceive" (Ephesians 4:14). Yes, there will be more and more false teachers and preachers, as the age draws toward its end. As the Apostle Peter said: "There shall be false teachers among you, who privily shall bring in damnable heresies, even denying the Lord that brought them, and bring upon themselves swift destruction. And many shall follow their pernicious ways; by reason of whom the way of truth shall be evil spoken of. And through covetousness shall they with feigned words make merchandise of you: whose judgment now of a long time lingereth not, and their damnation slumbereth not" (2 Peter 2:1–3).

Satan does not build a church and call it The First Church of Satan. He is far too clever for that. He invades the Sunday school, the Bible class, and even the pulpit. He even invades the church under cover of an orthodox vocabulary, emptying sacred terms of their biblical sense. Paul warned that many will follow false teachers, not knowing that in gulping down and feeding upon what these apostates say, they are taking the devil's poison into their own lives. Thousands of uninstructed Christians are being deceived today. False teachers use high-sounding words that seem like the epitome of scholarship and culture. They are intellectually clever and crafty in their sophistry. They are adept at beguiling thoughtless, untaught men and women. Of them the Apostle Paul wrote: "Now the Spirit speaketh expressly, that in the latter times some shall depart from the faith, giving heed to seducing spirits, and doctrines of devils; speaking lies in hypocrisy" (1 Timothy 4:1, 2). These false teachers have departed from the faith God revealed in the Scriptures. The Bible states plainly that the reason for their turning away is that they gave heed to Satan's lies and deliberately chose to accept the doctrines of devils rather than the truth of God. So they themselves became the mouthpiece of Satan, speaking lies.

Angels as Messengers

While God has delegated angels to make special pronouncements for Him, He has not given them the privilege of proclaiming the Gospel message. Why this is so, Scripture does not say. Perhaps spirit-beings who have never experienced the effects of separation from fellowship with God because of sin would be unable to preach with understanding.

But notice what the writer says in "Holy, Holy Is What the Angels Sing":

> Holy, Holy is what the angels sing,
> And I expect to help them make the
> courts of heaven ring.
> And when I sing redemption's story,
> They will fold their wings,
> For angels never felt the joy
> that our salvation brings.

Down through the ages man's heart has remained unchanged. Whatever the color of his skin, whatever his cultural or ethnic background, he needs the Gospel of Christ. But who has God ordained to bring that Gospel to fallen men? Fallen angels cannot do it; they cannot even be saved from their own sins. Yet unfallen angels cannot preach the Gospel either. Presumably they do not hear the Gospel the way we do; in their purity they have escaped the effects of sin and are unable to comprehend what it means to be lost.

Rather, God has commanded the Church to preach. This great task is reserved to believers. God has no other means. Only man can speak salvation's experience to man.

God has, however, assigned angels to assist those who preach. Their assistance includes the use of miraculous and corroborating signs. Missionaries of the eighteenth and nineteenth centuries have reported many wonderful incidents where angels seemed to help them proclaim the gospel. My wife, whose parents were missionaries to China, can remember many instances in her life where angels must have intervened in the ministry of her father and his fellow missionaries.

At any rate, you and I have the privilege of conveying a message to men from God in Heaven, a message that angels cannot speak. Think of that! The story is told of a question asked of God: "In the event that men fail to preach the gospel as you have commanded, what other plan have you in mind?" "I have no other plan," He said.

No angel can be an evangelist. No angel can pastor a church, although angels watch over particular churches. No angel can do counseling. No angel can enjoy sonship in Jesus or be partaker of the divine nature or become a joint heir with Jesus in His kingdom. You and I are a unique and royal priesthood in the universe, and we have privileges that even angels cannot experience.

Shadowed by Angels

Every true believer in Christ should be encouraged and strengthened! Angels are watching; they mark your path. They superintend the events of your life and protect the interest of the Lord God, always working to promote His plans and to bring about His highest will for you. Angels are interested spectators and mark all you do, "for we are made a spectacle unto the world, and to angels, and to men" (1 Corinthians 4:9). God assigns angelic powers to watch over you.

Hagar, Sarah's maid, had fled from the tents of Abraham. It is ironic that Abraham, after having scaled such glorious heights of faith, should have capitulated to his wife's conniving and scolding, and to the custom of that day, to father a child by Hagar. And it is ironic that Sarah his wife should have been so jealous that when their own son, Isaac, was born years later, she wanted to get rid of both Hagar and the earlier child, Ishmael. So Abraham's self-indulgence led to sorrow and he thrust Hagar out of his home.

Nonetheless, God sent His angel to minister to Hagar. "And the angel of the Lord found her by a fountain of water in the wilderness, by the fountain in the way to Shur" (Genesis 16:7). The angel spoke as an oracle of God, turning her mind away from the injury of the past with a promise of what she might expect if she placed her faith in God. This God is the God not only of Israel but the God of the Arab as well (for the Arabs come from the stock of Ishmael). The very name of her son, Ishmael, meaning "God hears," was a sustaining one. God promised that the seed of Ishmael would multiply, and that his destiny would be great on the earth as he now undertook the restless pilgrimage that was to characterize his descendants. The angel of the Lord revealed himself as the protector of Hagar and Ishmael. Hagar in awe exclaimed, "Thou God seest me" (Genesis 16:13), or as may be better translated, "I have seen Thou who seest all and who sees me."

Psalm 34:7 underscores the teaching that angels protect and deliver us, "The angel of the Lord encampeth round about those who fear him, and delivereth them." We also find this idea reflected in one of Charles Wesley's songs:

Angels, where ere we go,
Attend our steps whate'er betide.
With watchful care their charge
attend,
And evil turn aside.

The great majority of Christians can recall some incident in which their lives, in times of critical danger, have been miraculously preserved—an almost plane crash, a near car wreck, a fierce temptation. Though they may have seen no angels, their presence could explain why tragedy was averted. We should always be grateful for the goodness of God, who uses these wonderful friends called angels to protect us. Evidence from Scripture as well as personal experience confirms to us that individual guardian, guiding angels attend at least some of our ways and hover protectively over our lives.

The Scriptures are full of dramatic evidences of the protective care of angels in their earthly service to the people of God. Paul admonished Christians to put on all the armor of God that they may stand firmly in the face of evil (Ephesians 6:10–12). Our struggle is not against flesh and blood (physical powers alone), but against the spiritual (superhuman) forces of wickedness in heavenly spheres. Satan, the prince of the power of the air, promotes a "religion" but not true faith; he promotes false prophets. So the powers of light and darkness are locked in intense conflict. Thank God for the angelic forces that fight off the works of darkness. Angels never minister selfishly; they serve so that all glory may be given to God as believers are strengthened.

Angels in Jesus' Life

It would take an entire book to spell out in detail how the life of Jesus was intertwined with the attending ministry of angels. Before He was here, they followed His orders. And since He ascended into Heaven, they have worshiped Him before the throne of God as the Lamb slain for our salvation.

To prepare for the coming of Jesus an angel appeared to Zacharias to inform him that his wife would be the mother of John the Baptist (Luke 1:13). Gabriel, one of the mighty angels of God, announced to Mary that she would give birth to the Messiah. An angel and a multitude of the heavenly host spread the good news of Jesus' coming to the shepherds in the field (Luke 2:9). These angelic incidents preceded and accompanied His birth, but when Jesus began His public ministry angels were intimately involved in His life as well.

Angels in the Wilderness

Perhaps the most difficult period in the life of Jesus before His crucifixion was His temptation by the devil in the wilderness. After He had fasted forty days and nights, Satan tried to break Him down. In Christ's weakened human condition, Satan began his attack, seeing this as his greatest opportunity to defeat the program of God in the world since his victory in the Garden of Eden. He was out to shipwreck the hope of the human race. Wishing to prevent the salvation of sinners, he struck at the moment when Christ's physical weakness made Him most susceptible to temptation. Satan always directs his sharpest attack at his victim's weakest point. He knows where the Achilles' heel may be, and he does not fail to strike at the opportune time.

Three times Satan attempted to defeat Jesus. Three times Jesus quoted Scripture, and three times Satan went down to defeat. Then the Bible declares that "he [Satan] departed from him [Jesus] for a season" (Luke 4:13). It was at this point that angels came to His assistance—not to help Him resist Satan as they help us, for He did that by Himself, but to help Him after the battle was won. The angels "ministered" to Jesus. . . . "Behold, angels came and ministered unto him" (Matthew 4:11). Angelic ambassadors supported, strengthened and sustained Him in that trying hour. From that moment on our Lord Jesus Christ, who was in all points tempted as we are, could sympathize and help Christian believers for the ages to come, and lead them to victory in their hour of temptation.

Angels in the Garden

The night before His crucifixion Jesus was in the Garden of Gethsemane. Only a short time later He was to be seized by the soldiers, betrayed by Judas Iscariot, set before the rulers, beaten and at last crucified. Before He was hung on the cross He went through the terrible agony in the Garden which made Him sweat, as it were, drops of blood. It was in this situation that the Son of man needed inner strength to face what no other being in Heaven, Hell or earth had ever known. In fact, He was to face what no created being could have faced and gone through in victory. He was about to take upon Himself the sins of men. He was to become sin for us.

Jesus had taken Peter, James, and John with Him to the Garden. They could have provided Him with reinforcement and encouragement, but instead they fell asleep. The Son of man was all alone. He prayed, "Father, if thou be willing, remove this cup from me: nevertheless not my will, but thine, be done" (Luke 22:42). Then it was at that crucial moment that the angel came to assist Him, "strengthening Him". . . . Where the disciples of the Lord Jesus had failed to share His agony, as they slept the angel came to help.

Angels at the Cross

The tragedy of sin reached its crescendo when God in Christ became sin. At this point He was offering Himself as the sacrifice required by the justice of God if man was to be redeemed. At this moment Satan was ready to try his master stroke. If he could get Christ to come down from the cross, and if Christ allowed the mockery of the crowd to shame or anger Him, then the plan of salvation would be jeopardized. Again and again they shouted, "If thou be the Son of God, come down from the cross" (Matthew 27:40). He knew He could come down if He chose; He knew He could get help from more than twelve legions of angels who hovered about with drawn swords.

Yet for our salvation He stayed there. The angels would have come to the cross to rescue the King of kings, but because of His love for the human race and because He knew it was only through His death that they could be saved, He refused to call for their help. The angels were under orders not to intervene at this terrible, holy moment. Even the angels could not minister to the Son of God at Calvary. He died alone in order to take the full death penalty you and I deserved.

We can never plumb the depths of sin, or sense how terrible human sin is, until we go to the cross and see that it was "sin" that caused the Son of God to be crucified. The ravages of war, the tragedy of suicide, the agony of the poverty-stricken, the suffering and irony of the rejected of our society, the blood of the accident victim, the terror of rape and mug victims of our generation—these all speak as with a single voice of the degradation that besets the human race at this hour. But no sin has been committed in past history, nor is any being committed in the world today that can compare with the full cup of the universe's sin that brought Jesus to the cross. The question hurled toward Heaven throughout the ages has been, "Who is He and why does He die?" The answer comes back, This is my only begotten Son, dying not only for your sins but for the sins of the whole world. To you sin may be a small thing; to God it is a great and awful thing. It is the second largest thing in the world; only the love of God is greater.

When we comprehend the great price God was willing to pay for the redemption of man, we only then begin to see that something is horribly wrong with the human race. It must have a Savior, or it is doomed! Sin cost God His very best. Is it any wonder that the angels veiled their faces, that they were silent in their consternation as they witnessed the outworking of God's plan? How inconceivable it must have seemed to them, when they considered the fearful depravity of sin, that Jesus should shoulder it all. But they were soon to unveil their faces and offer their praises again. A light was kindled that day at Calvary. The cross blazed with the glory of God as the most terrible darkness was shattered by the light of salvation. Satan's depraved legions were defeated and they could no longer keep all men in darkness and defeat.

Angels as Executors

The writer of Hebrews speaks of angelic forces as executors of God's judgments: "Who maketh his angels spirits, and his ministers a flame of fire" (Hebrews 1:7). The flaming fire suggests how awful are the judgments of God and how burning is the power of the angels who carry out God's decisions. Angels administer judgment in accord with God's principles of righteousness.

Unknown to men they have undoubtedly in the past helped destroy evil systems like Nazism, because those governments came to the place where God could no longer withhold His hand. These same angels will carry out fearful judgments in the future, some of which the book of Revelation vividly describes.

We often get false notions about angels from plays given by Sunday school children at Christmas. It is true that angels are ministering spirits sent to help the heirs of salvation. But just as they fulfill God's will in salvation for believers in Jesus Christ, so they are also "avengers" who use their great power to fulfill God's will in judgment. God has empowered them to separate the sheep from the goats, the wheat from the chaff, and one of them will blow the trumpet that announces impending judgment when God summons the nations to stand before Him in the last great judgment.

Know Your Enemy

Know your enemy—Satan. "Be sober, be vigilant; because your adversary the devil, as a roaring lion, walketh about, seeking whom he may devour" (1 Peter 5:8). Military personnel soon learn that one of the most serious errors that a military leader can make is to underestimate the ability and the power of the enemy. To underrate the skill of an opposing team is to lose the game.

When in doubt about what to do in any given circumstance, ask yourself these questions. "Does it glorify the Lord Jesus Christ? Will it make me a stronger Christian? Will it offend someone else?" You may think that something is "all right," but if there are other Christians around you who feel it is questionable, you should not "put a stumbling block or an occasion to fall" (Romans 14:13) in your brother's way. Paul said that if eating meat were to make his brother to offend, he would "eat no flesh while the world standeth" (1 Corinthians 8:13) lest he should make his brother to offend.

Form the habit of bringing everything to the Lord Jesus. Make victory even more habitual than were your defeats.

Never go any place where you cannot take Christ with you. "And whatsoever ye do in word or deed, do all in the name of the Lord Jesus, giving thanks to God and the Father by him" (Colossians 3:17).

God and a Christian are always a majority. Paul said, "I can do all things through Christ which strengtheneth me" (Philippians 4:13). Notice that it is through Christ that he could do all things, not within himself. Here is where many fail. They have the desire to do right and to resist temptation, but they are not fully surrendered to Christ. Consequently, they are not able to do what they know is God's will for them. If only we would fully surrender to Christ, we could do the "all things" which are within His blessed will. The deeper our separation from the world and unto Christ is, the more powerful and fruitful are we in our appeal to those who are dead in sin. Human endurance in divine things and in extraordinary trials will not suffice. We cannot endure in our own strength. "The arm of flesh will fail you, ye dare not trust your own." Jesus said, "My grace is sufficient for thee: for my strength is made perfect in weakness" (2 Corinthians 12:9).

We can endure every fiery trial, every persecution, every temptation and every attempt of Satan to hurt us only if we stay close to the Lord Jesus Christ. You were saved by faith, simply by trusting Christ. Live the same way! Trust Him for deliverance in times of temptation. Don't wait until you sin and then turn to God for forgiveness, even though He will forgive, but turn to Him at the moment of temptation. "Lord Jesus, help me now," can mean the difference between victory and defeat in your life. It can mean the difference between joy and unhappiness, between peace and unrest.

But if you do fail, if you do sin—don't give up! Don't brood over the sin. Confess it immediately; forget it and pass on. "If we confess our sins, He is faithful and just to forgive us our sins, and to cleanse us from all unrighteousness" (1 John 1:9).

Three Enemies

We have already seen that the Devil is a mighty being who opposes God and tempts God's people. We have found that even though he was beaten at the cross by Christ he still has power to influence men for evil. The Bible calls him "the wicked one," "the devil," "a murderer," "a liar, and the father of lies," "an adversary" who seeks to devour, "that old serpent" and "accuser of our brethren" (Matthew 13:19; Luke 4:33; John 8:44; 1 Peter 5:8; Revelation 12:9–10).

The moment you made your decision for Christ, Satan suffered a tremendous defeat. He is angry now. From now on he is going to tempt you and try to lead you into sin. Don't be alarmed. He cannot rob you of your salvation, and he need not rob you of your assurance and victory. He will do everything in his power to sow seeds of doubt in your mind as to whether your conversion is a reality or not. You cannot argue with him for he is the greatest debater of all time.

Your second enemy is the world. The world means the cosmos, this world system. The world has a tendency to lead us into sin, evil companions, pleasures, fashions, opinions, and aims.

You will find in your born-again experience that your pleasures have been lifted into an entirely new and glorious realm. Many non-Christians have accused the Christian life as being a set of rules, taboos, vetoes, and prohibitions. This is another lie of the devil. It is not a series of "don'ts," but a series of "dos." You become so busy in the work of Christ and so completely satisfied with the things of Christ that you do not have time for the things of the world.

The Bible says, "Love not the world, neither the things that are in the world" (1 John 2:15). The Bible also warns that the world and the "lust thereof" shall pass away, "but he that doeth the will of God abideth forever" (1 John 2:17).

The third enemy that you will face immediately is the lust of the flesh. The flesh is that evil tendency of your inward self. Even after you are converted, sometimes your old, sinful cravings will return. You become startled and wonder where they come from. The Bible teaches that the old nature, with all its corruption, is still there and that these evil temptations come from nowhere else. In other words, "a traitor is living within." "That wretched bent toward sin is ever present to drag you down." War has been declared! You now have two natures in conflict, and each one is striving for dominance.

The Bible teaches "the flesh lusteth against the Spirit, and the Spirit against the flesh" (Galatians 5:17). It is the battle of the self-life and the Christ-life. This old nature cannot please God. It cannot be converted, or even patched up. Thank God, when Jesus died He took you with Him, and the old nature can be made inoperative and you can "reckon ye also yourselves to be dead indeed unto sin" (Romans 6:11). This is done by faith.

14

HEAVEN AND HELL

Whatever Happened to Heaven?

What about Heaven? In the Gallup survey, 66 percent of the general population said they believe in "a Heaven where people who have led good lives are eternally rewarded." More people are confident that there is a Heaven than are concerned about Hell. I was especially interested that those who believed in Heaven were asked a further question, "How would you describe your own chances of going to Heaven—excellent, good, fair, or poor?"

Among the Protestant denominations, only 26 percent of the Baptists, 20 percent of the Lutherans, and 16 percent of the Methodists thought their chances of attaining heaven were excellent. The survey further revealed that while only 24 percent of the Protestants said they were sure of a place in Heaven, 41 percent of the Catholics had this assurance.

Why did members of organized churches, or those professing to be either Protestant or Catholic, have such a low assurance of Heaven? Could it be that in our descriptions of Heaven we have failed to mention the horrors of its alternative? Have we overreacted to the old "hellfire and brimstone" preaching by discarding or at least watering down the clear teaching of the Bible? Jesus spoke of Hell as "darkness, where there will be weeping and gnashing of teeth" (Matthew 8:12). Or have we even neglected the whole question of life after death by emphasizing only this life?

Heaven, a Home

Not only is Heaven a place, but the Bible teaches that Heaven is going to be Home. The Bible says that those of us who know Christ—the moment you accept Christ, you become a citizen of Heaven. Now we are citizens of two worlds. I am a citizen of this earth, but I'm a citizen of another world. I am a citizen of Heaven because of what Christ did on the Cross. And in this world with its secularism and its materialism and all of its hostile forces, I'm living for God, I'm a stranger and a pilgrim.

The Bible refers to that in several places. We are strangers and we are pilgrims. "They were strangers and pilgrims on the earth," says Hebrews 11. 1 Peter 2 says, "I beseech you as strangers and pilgrims." Our citizenship is in Heaven.

Now as good citizens of this earth we ought to vote. As good citizens we ought to be interested in our community. As good citizens we ought to help every good project in our community. As good citizens we ought to be interested in all the social problems that we face. As good citizens we ought to do what we can to make this a better place in which to live. But we are citizens of two worlds . . . this world and the future world. We are citizens of Heaven.

Now in Heaven there is not going to be any racial discrimination. There is not going to be any poverty. There is not going to be any war. The policemen won't have anything to do. Oh, what a glorious world it is going to be— Heaven! Everything that word means, everything that you ever dreamed of—the Utopia that we dreamed of and thought that maybe we could build on this earth, and have failed, is going to be in Heaven.

And then Heaven is going to be a place of service. Now you're not just going to go there and sit under a palm tree and have a pretty girl waving a palm branch over you. Lots of people have the idea that is what Heaven is like. One of the great religions of the world teaches that. It says, "You're going to have a thousand girls to wait on you." No, that's not what the Bible says. It says we are going to work. I imagine that is going to be hard on some. But we are going to work, because it says in Revelation 22:3, "His servants shall serve him."

And Heaven is going to be a place where all mysteries are going to be cleared up. Why did we have a certain amount of suffering down here? Why were loved ones taken at a particular moment when they were? We are going to understand something of the enormity of sin. We are going to understand the problem of evil. We are going to understand what the devil was all about, and why God allowed him to exist as long as he did. We'll know something of the price that Christ paid on the Cross that we cannot know now. When He said, "My God, My God, why hast thou forsaken me?"—none of us can understand what went on at that moment, but on that Day, we will understand.

We will know why there is a Hell. We will understand why God moves in a mysterious way His wonders to perform. You know there are ten thousand questions I want to ask the Lord as soon as I get there . . . because they are just mysteries in the Bible that we don't know all the answers to. We must take them by faith.

And you know Heaven is going to be the place of the final coronation of the King of Kings. What a day that is going to be! The Bible says, "There will be written on Him, King of Kings, and Lord of Lords." You and I are going to be present at the coronation of Jesus Christ when He is crowned King of the Universe. I am looking forward to that day. My seat is reserved. It was bought not with my silver and gold. It was bought with the blood of Christ on the Cross. What a time that is going to be!

Citizens of Heaven

No exemption is granted the Christian from the common lot of the human race. We are born to trouble even as others and have tribulation like the rest. When depression comes, we may be out of work. When war rages, we are in danger. We are exposed to the same diseases and many of the same psychological problems as others. Thus we must take an interest in the present world. We must do all we can to help our neighbors with whom we dwell, be they believers or not.

However, it is true that even in this world the Christian has certain privileges as he anticipates Heaven. As Charles Spurgeon used to say: "All the legions of Hell cannot compel us to do the devil's work." The prince of this world may make his servants serve him, but he cannot raise a conscription among us "aliens." The true child of God claims an immunity from all the commands of Satan. In actuality, we are the only ones who are completely free. There are those today who say that we must do as others do, that we must conform to our world, that we must swim with the tide, that we must move with the crowd. But the believer says: "No, do not expect me to fall in with the evil customs and ways of this world. I am in Rome, but I will not do as Rome does. I am an alien, a stranger, and a foreigner. My citizenship is in Heaven."

We are tuned to a different world. The Scripture says: "If any man love the world, the love of the Father is not in him" (1 John 2:15). Be willing rather to be sneered at than to be approved, counting the cross of Christ greater riches than all the treasures of Washington, London, Paris, or Moscow.

To aliens, the treasures of this world will not be attractive. Our treasure is in Heaven "where neither moth nor rust doth corrupt, and where thieves do not break through nor steal" (Matthew 6:20). Neither the American dollar, the British pound, nor the German mark can be spent in

Heaven. When we get to Heaven we shall wish that we had laid up more treasure in its banks. I would far rather be rich toward God than before men.

As citizens of Heaven, we also share in Heaven's glory. The Bible teaches that even the angels are our servants. The great saints of the past are our companions. Christ is our Brother. God is our Father. And we will receive immortality. "Beloved, now are we the sons of God, and it doth not yet appear what we shall be: but we know that, when he shall appear, we shall be like him; for we shall see him as he is" (1 John 3:2).

Speaking from Heaven

How does God speak from Heaven?

First, He speaks through the Bible, His written Word. This is why I use the phrase "the Bible says." I would not have the authority to say what I do during crusades or in sermons unless it was based upon the Word of God. "All Scripture is God-breathed and is useful for teaching, rebuking, correcting, and training in righteousness" (2 Timothy 3:16). The authors of the Old Testament, for example, make it clear that God was speaking to them and through them. More than 3,000 times they said, "Thus saith the Lord," or the equivalent. And that's good enough for me!

God also speaks in nature. When He created the heavens and the earth, He gave us the most incredible, complex, beautiful, orderly universe. He has spoken in such a way that men and women are without excuse if they do not hear and understand the Psalmist's praise in saying, "The heavens declare the glory of God; and the firmament showeth his handiwork" (Psalm 19:1 KJV). Because of the clarity of the message, we can also agree with his statement that "The fool says in his heart, 'There is no God'" (Psalm 14:1). As the Bible declares, "For since the creation of the world God's invisible qualities—his eternal power and divine nature—have been clearly seen, being understood from what has been made, so that men are without excuse" (Romans 1:20).

God speaks most clearly and completely through His Son, Jesus Christ, who is revealed for us in the pages of the Bible and is the Word of God incarnate. When God, the Son, stepped out of Heaven onto earth in the form of man, He accomplished what God intended Him to do from eternity past. "In the past God spoke to our forefathers through the prophets at many times and in various ways, but in these last days he has spoken to us by his Son, whom he appointed heir of all things, and through whom he made the universe" (Hebrews 1:1–2).

God also speaks to us through our consciences. This may be a "still, small voice" that will not let us go until we do what we know is right, or it may be a loud, clear indication that God wants us on the path. We might even think of it as a searchlight revealing the way in which we should go, beamed from Heaven itself. Proverbs says, "The lamp of the Lord searches the spirit of a man; it searches out his inmost being" (Proverbs 20:27). We must never silence that inner voice—although we must check what we think it is saying against the Scriptures, to be sure that inner voice is not simply our self-will or our emotions.

When God speaks through His Word, we may receive it clearly, or because of our human frailty it may be distorted, something like a scrambled TV signal coming in over the satellite. Sometimes our receivers are tuned. At other times we may have to wait until we can more clearly hear or "receive" the picture. . . .

God speaks to us from Heaven when we pray. Sometimes the answers are clear; sometimes they are vague; sometimes they say "wait." However, we know that someday we will be with Him in His home, and communications will be crystal clear, because we will be with

Him. "Now we see but a poor reflection; then we shall see face to face. Now I know in part; then I shall know fully, even as I am fully known" (1 Corinthians 13:12).

Paid Ticket to Heaven

Why do some people believe they have a paid ticket to Heaven? They give many answers, but most can be classified within three basic attitudes.

The first is, "Just look at what I've done on earth. My record is pretty good, compared to some. I'll be in Heaven because I lived such a good life."

That person is in trouble. The Bible says "for all have sinned and fall short of the glory of God" (Romans 3:23). So if we're placing our good deeds on a scale of 1 to 10, even a perfect 10 wouldn't make it. No one can ever live a life that is "good enough." The Bible says, "For whoever keeps the whole law and yet stumbles at just one point is guilty of breaking all of it" (James 2:10).

The second answer might be, "I really don't know, and I'm not sure that I care. I gave it some thought for a while, but there were so many other things that seemed more important."

As mothers say, "Excuses will get you nowhere." The Bible says, "For since the creation of the world God's invisible qualities—his eternal power and divine nature—have been clearly seen, being understood from what has been made, so that men are without excuse" (Romans 1:20).

Only one answer will give a person the certain privilege, the joy, of entering Heaven. "Because I have believed in Jesus Christ and accepted Him as my Savior. He is the One sitting at the right hand of God and interceding for me." No one can deny that Christian his entrance into Heaven.

What Won't Be in Heaven

In Heaven there will be no sectarian worship, no denominational differences, no church creeds. There will be no temple worship, for God and His Son, Jesus Christ, will be the centers of worship (Revelation 21:22). . . . God did not invent denominations, man did. When we go to His home, He will invite us in, but will not ask us for our church or Sunday school credentials. Only one question will be asked: "What did you do on earth with My Son, Jesus?"

In Heaven we won't get secondhand knowledge. On earth we listen to pastors, teachers, philosophers, parents, and writers, and sometimes we don't know whom to believe. . . .

In Heaven there will be no fear. We won't need locks on the doors, bars at the windows, or alarm systems. Everything that causes fear will be eliminated. We will walk the golden streets with no concern for danger lurking in doorways.

In Heaven there will be no night. On earth we equate night with darkness and ignorance; we say, "I was really left in the dark." Light is a symbol of understanding; we may nod our heads as a problem is clarified and say, "Now I see the light!" "The Lord is my light and my salvation—whom shall I fear?" (Psalm 27:1).

Finally, in Heaven there will be no more suffering or death. Think of it! "And I heard a loud voice from the throne saying, 'Now the dwelling of God is with men, and he will live with them. They will be his people, and God himself will be with them and be their God. He will wipe every tear from their eyes. There will be no more death or mourning or crying or pain, for the old order of things has passed away.' He who was seated on the throne said, 'I am making everything new!' Then he said, 'Write this down, for these words are trustworthy and true'" (Revelation 21:3–5).

Whatever Happened to Hell?

As attitudes toward death and dying changed, another significant shift began to take place within the human family. The reality of Satan was ignored increasingly or discarded as a myth. Even many who believed in a personal devil were not allowed to acknowledge his power in this world, nor did they believe in Hell.

Hell, in the eyes of unbelievers and even some believers, was abandoned. Or it was relegated to some vague concept of "evil in the world." Even some theologians chose to reject the Bible's clear teaching on Hell.

Certainly war, hunger, terrorism, greed, and hatred are Hell on earth, but, except for the Bible believer, a future Hell became part of the ash heap of ancient history. As Hell was becoming for many no more than a swear word, sin was also an accepted way of life. People began to look to science, education, and social and moral programs as possible solutions to the growing chaos of an insane world. If people can ignore what the Bible calls sin, then they can quite logically discount what it says about the reality of Hell.

Whoever chooses to deny that there is a Hell must then face certain questions. "Where do I go when I die?" "Who goes to Heaven and who doesn't?" And, "If I don't go to Heaven, what is the alternative?"

In contemporary society Hell is not a popular subject. George Gallup made a survey on Hell, and there were some interesting results. In his national poll 53 percent of the general population of the United States said they believe in Hell. The percentage goes down dramatically among people with a college education and those with high incomes. Simply stated, the Gallup poll showed that the more education and money people had, the less likely they were to believe in Hell.

The Reality of Hell

Hell has been cloaked in folklore and disguised in fiction for so long, many people deny the reality of such a place. Some think it is merely a myth. This is understandable. Our minds revolt against ugliness and suffering. However, the concept of Hell is not exclusive to the Christian faith.

Centuries before Christ, the Babylonians believed in "The Land of No-Return." The Hebrews wrote about going down to the realm of Sheol, or the place of corruption; the Greeks spoke of the "Unseen Land." Classical Buddhism recognizes seven "hot hells," and the Hindu *Rig Veda* speaks of the deep abyss reserved for false men and faithless women. Islam recognizes seven hells.

Jesus specifically states that nonbelievers will not be able to escape the condemnation of Hell (Matthew 23:33). He told His disciples, "Do not be afraid of those who kill the body and after that can do no more. But I will show you whom you should fear: Fear him who, after the killing of the body, has power to throw you into hell" (Luke 12:4, 5).

Bible's Description of Hell

Let's consider the Bible's description of Hell. Let's find out how God's Holy Word describes this awful place.

Revelation 20:15—The lake of fire.
Psalm 11:6—A horrible tempest.
Psalm 18:5—A place of sorrows.
Matthew 13:42—A place of wailing.
Matthew 8:12—A place of weeping.
Matthew 13:41-42—A furnace of fire.
Luke 16:23—A place of torment.
Revelation 20:11-12—A place of filthiness.
Revelation 16:11—A place of cursing.
Matthew 8:12—A place of outer darkness.

Revelation 14:11—A place of unrest.

Luke 16:27—A place where people pray.

Luke 16:24—A place where people scream for mercy.

Matthew 25:46—A place of everlasting punishment.

Matthew 25:41—A place prepared for the devil and his angels.

Luke 16:2—A place where one begs for a drop of water.

Isaiah 33: 11—A place where one's breath is flame.

Luke 16:2—A place where one is tormented with fire.

Revelation 21:8—A place where one is tormented with brimstone.

Luke 16:25—A place of memory.

We need not add to or take away from this description.

The Bells of Hell

In World War I, British soldiers had a popular song that went like this:

> Oh Death, where is thy sting-a-ling-a-ling,
> Oh Grave, thy victoree?
> The bells of Hell go ting-a-ling-a-ling
> For you but not for me.

A lot of people talk about Hell, use it to tell others where to go, but do not want to be confronted with the thought that it might be their destination. Hell, for them, is only where the Hitlers and Stalins should end up, along with murderers, rapists, or child pornographers. But most think that "Good People" who mind their own business, pay their taxes, and put a few dollars in the collection plate will have some "eternal rewards."

However, if the Bible is true, we know there is abundant life after death for the followers of Christ. Those who have accepted His grace and been saved will be with Him in Heaven. And what about the others? "Surely a loving

God would not punish good people!" says the humanitarian or the religious person who wants to ignore the uncomfortable and unpopular descriptions of Hell in the Bible. Yes, they are right in some ways, for a loving God does not want anyone to perish. The Lord is not slow in keeping His promise, as some understand slowness. "He is patient with you, not wanting anyone to perish, but everyone to come to repentance" (2 Peter 3:9).

However, the Scriptures are very clear. Jesus told His disciples not to fear the killers of men, because they only cause physical death. He did not mean, of course, that we are not to be concerned about murderers, but His point was a warning of something more serious than the death of our bodies. Jesus said, "But I will show you whom you should fear: Fear him who, after the killing of the body, has power to throw you into Hell" (Luke 12:5).

Paradise Lost

Hell is probably the hardest of all Christian teachings to accept.

Some teach "universalism"—that eventually everybody will be saved and the God of love will never send anyone to Hell. They believe the words "eternal" or "everlasting" do not actually mean forever. However, the same word which speaks of eternal banishment from God is also used for the eternity of Heaven.

Others teach that those who refuse to accept Jesus Christ as Savior are simply annihilated, they no longer exist. I've searched the Bible and have never found convincing evidence to support this view. The Bible teaches, whether we are saved or lost, there is an everlasting existence of the soul.

Some believe God gives a second chance. But the Bible says, "Now is the day of salvation" (2 Corinthians 6:2). At our crusades I invite people to accept Christ right then, for we do not know when we will pass into eternity.

The Bible teaches there is Hell for every person who willingly and knowingly rejects Christ as Lord and Savior. Many passages could be quoted to support that fact.

"But anyone who says, 'you fool!' will be in danger of the fire of Hell" (Matthew 5:22).

"The Son of Man will send out his angels, and they will weed out of his kingdom everything that causes sin and all who do evil. They will throw them into the fiery furnace, where there will be weeping and gnashing of teeth" (Matthew 13:41, 42).

"Then death and Hades were thrown into the lake of fire. The lake of fire is the second death. If anyone's name was not found written in the book of life, he was thrown into the lake of fire" (Revelation 20:14,15).

In the Sermon on the Mount, Jesus said, "It is better for you to lose one part of your body than for your body to be thrown into Hell" (Matthew 5:29).

Will a loving God send a man to hell? The answer from Jesus and the teachings of the Bible is, clearly, "Yes!" He does not send man willingly, but man condemns himself to eternal Hell because in his blindness, stubbornness, egotism, and love of sinful pleasure, he refuses God's way of salvation and the hope of eternal life with Him.

Suppose a person is sick and goes to a doctor. The doctor diagnoses the problem and prescribes medicine. However, the advice is ignored and in a few days the person stumbles back into the doctor's office and says, "It's your fault that I'm worse. Do something."

God has prescribed the remedy for the spiritual sickness of the human race. The solution is personal faith and commitment to Jesus Christ. Since the remedy is to be born again, if we deliberately refuse it, we must suffer the horrible consequences.

Yes, there is an alternative to Heaven. No matter what your conception of it may be, we know it will be separation from God and all that is holy and good. John Milton described it in *Paradise Lost*:

> A dungeon horrible on all sides round,
> As one great furnace, flamed; yet from those flames
> No light, but rather darkness visible
> Serv'd only to discover sights of woe,
> Regions of sorrow, doleful shades, where peace
> And rest can never dwell, hope never comes
> That comes to all; but torture without end.

15

PAIN AND SUFFERING

The Many Faces of Pain

Pain has many faces. One can suffer physically, mentally, emotionally, psychologically, and spiritually. Our difficulties are rarely confined to only one of these areas; they tend to overlap in human experiences. Some of the most intensive suffering can be psychologically induced and frequently lead to complications in the physical realm.

There are as many invisible hurts as there are visible hurts, and there can be difficulty in diagnosing them. We know that the unseen part of man is often the victim of the most debilitating of pains. In certain circumstances, a man can endure excruciating physical pain; and yet he can be felled by one unkind word. When we hear the story of the torture inflicted upon a P.O.W., we are astounded by his personal fortitude and the resiliency of the human body. But that same man's life can be devastated by a single viciously perpetrated act or word.

Scripture has much to say about the power of the tongue to inflict cruelty. The Psalmist says that bitter words are like deadly arrows. James wrote: "The tongue is a small part of the body, but it makes great boasts. Consider what a great forest is set on fire by a small spark. The tongue also is a fire, a world of evil among the parts of the body" (James 3:5, 6).

Man is capable of great victories and susceptible to great defeats. Man is both strong and sensitive. As the Psalmist exclaimed, "I praise you because I am fearfully and wonderfully made" (Psalm 139:14).

In earnest we must endeavor to apply this sensitivity when dealing with the matter of suffering, especially as we consider the sufferings of others. We cannot feel someone else's pain. We can see the anguish in his face and try to empathize. But we do not have his nerve endings. We cannot fully know the magnitude of his anguish. We must never minimize the suffering of another. Scripture's mandate to us is, "Weep with them that weep" (Romans 12:15, KJV).

Our physical sufferings express a great truth. As C. S. Lewis cogently penned, "Pain...plants the flag of truth within the fortress of a rebel soul." The truth is this— man's body is mortal, temporal. Man must look beyond himself to find immortality.

Suffering is one of God's ways of speaking to us, of awakening us to our need of Him, and calling us to Himself. To quote C. S. Lewis again: "God whispers to us in our pleasures, speaks in our conscience, but shouts in our pains: it is His megaphone to rouse a deaf world." If our suffering leads us to God, it has become a blessed and precious friend.

Elimination of Suffering

We must bear in mind that God has acted on our behalf to rid the world of suffering. And the astounding fact is that He did it by suffering Himself. He is a Father who witnessed the torture and death of His own Son. God, who loves His Son, allowed Him to suffer so that you and I might be released from suffering. By virtue of Christ's passion and death, those who have accepted Him as their

Savior will be freed from the most intense suffering imaginable—eternal separation from God.

It is in God's own suffering that we see His great love. We must not try to evaluate God's character and judge whether or not He is a loving God by looking at our own sufferings. It is by looking at the Cross that we come to know and experience the depth of God's love for us.

Thus we see that God has a plan for the elimination of suffering.

But why doesn't God remove all suffering from our world now? He has the power; why doesn't He use it for the good of mankind now?

First, if God were to eradicate all evil from this planet, He would have to eradicate all evil men. Who would be exempt? "For all have sinned and fall short of the glory of God" (Romans 3:23). God would rather transform the evil man than eradicate him.

Second, if God were to remove all evil from our world (but somehow leave man on the planet), it would mean that the essence of "humanness" would be destroyed. Man would become a robot.

Let me explain what I mean by this. If God eliminated evil by programming man to perform only good acts, man would lose his distinguishing mark—the ability to make choices. He would no longer be a free moral agent. He would be reduced to the status of a robot.

Let's take this a step further. Robots do not love. God created man with the capacity to love. Love is based upon one's right to choose to love. We cannot force others to love us. We can make them serve us or obey us. But true love is founded upon one's freedom to choose to respond. Man could be programmed to do good, but the element of love would be lost. If man were forced to do good, suffering would be eliminated—and so would love. What would it be like to live in a world without love?

Thus we can see that God's use of His power to eliminate evil would not prove to be a positive solution to the problem of suffering. The results of such action would create greater dilemmas. Either man would be reduced to the status of a robot in a loveless world or he would be annihilated.

It is really God's love for man which restrains Him from removing evil from our world by a display of His power. God's plan is to remove evil by a display of His love—the love that He demonstrated at Calvary.

It is in God's love that we find the key to the ultimate solution of the problem of suffering. The answer to the age-old question of suffering rests in an understanding and appreciation of the character of God.

The Supreme Sufferer

Do we look at ourselves, our trials, our problems, when we are suffering? Do we live under the circumstances, instead of above the circumstances? Or do we look at the One who knew more suffering than we are able to conceive?

In *Table Talk* Martin Luther said, "Our suffering is not worthy the name of suffering. When I consider my crosses, tribulations, and temptations, I shame myself almost to death, thinking what are they in comparison of the sufferings of my blessed Savior Jesus Christ."

There are several things about the life of Christ that reveal His role as the "suffering servant" Messiah. We cannot begin to trace every aspect of this search through His life, but consider these truths.

In Isaiah 53 the sufferings of the Savior are so minutely pictured that one might well read it as the record of an eyewitness, rather than the prediction of a man who wrote eight hundred years before the event.

Observe that Jesus' life began in the midst of persecution and peril. He came on a mission of love and mercy, sent by the Father. An angel announced His conception and gave Him His name. The heavenly host sang a glorious anthem at His birth. By the extraordinary "star" or meteor, the very heavens indicated His coming. In Himself He was the most illustrious child ever born—the holy child of Mary, the divine Son of God. Yet no sooner did He enter our world than Herod decreed His death and labored to accomplish it.

Notice, too, that He assumed a role of deep abasement. The Son of the eternal Father, He became the infant of days and was made in the likeness of man. He assumed our human nature with all its infirmities, and weakness, and capacity for suffering. He came as a child of the poorest parents. His entire life was one voluntary humiliation. He came to be a servant and to minister rather than to be ministered unto.

Another aspect of His suffering is the vile suspicions and bitter misrepresentations He had to bear. "He came to that which was his own, but his own did not receive him" (John 1:11). Rather they scorned Him and treated Him with contempt. He was "despised and rejected" by most of them. They treated Him as a transgressor of God's law, a Sabbath breaker, an unholy person—a winebibber and drunkard, one who associated with outcasts and notorious sinners.

Notice also that He was constantly exposed to personal violence. At the beginning of His ministry, His own townsfolk at Nazareth tried to hurl Him down from the brow of the hill (Luke 4:29). The religious and political leaders often conspired to seize Him and kill Him. At length He was arrested and brought to trial before Pilate and Herod. Even though He was guiltless of the accusations, He was denounced as an enemy of God and man, and not worthy to live.

The sufferings of Jesus also included the fierce temptations of the devil. The account of this transaction is given in graphic form in Matthew 4:1, "Then Jesus was led by the Spirit into the desert to be tempted by the devil."

Remember, too, that He knew in advance what was

coming, and this enhanced His suffering. He knew the contents of the cup He had to drink; He knew the path of suffering He should tread. He could distinctly foresee the baptism of blood that awaited Him. He spoke plainly to His disciples of His coming death by crucifixion.

Jesus, the supreme sufferer, came to suffer for our sins. As a result of His sufferings, our redemption was secured.

What does the divine sufferer demand from us? Only our faith, our love, our grateful praise, our consecrated hearts and lives. Is that too much to ask?

Christ living in us will enable us to live above our circumstances, however painful they are. Perhaps you who read these words find yourself almost crushed by the circumstances which you are now facing. You wonder how much more you can stand. But don't despair! God's grace is sufficient for you and will enable you to rise above your trials. Let this be your confidence: "Who shall separate us from the love of Christ? Shall trouble or hardship or persecution or famine or nakedness or danger or sword? . . . No, in all these things we are more than conquerors through him who loved us" (Romans 8:35–37).

Grief Happens

Grief comes with many losses. It may be the loss of a job or a friend, a pet or a possession. The loss of a marriage relationship may cause grief as wrenching as death. Whatever its cause, grief will come to all of us.

Grief which is not dealt with properly can cause us to lose our perspective on life. A friend told me about his mother who mourned the death of her husband so keenly that seventeen years after he died, she would cry every time he was mentioned. My friend's wife told her husband, "Honey, I love you very much, but I will never grieve for you for seventeen years!"

Edna St. Vincent Millay expressed the type of hopelessness that many feel in facing a loss. In her poem "Lament," she wrote:

> Life must go on,
> and the dead be forgotten;
> Life must go on,
> Though good men die;
> Anne, eat your breakfast;
> Dan, take your medicine;
> Life must go on;
> I forget just why.

Jesus was no stranger to grief. Isaiah 53:3, 4 foretold that Christ would be "despised and forsaken of men, a man of sorrows, and acquainted with grief" (NASB).

Happiness is a choice, but grief is a certainty. When Jacob thought that Joseph had been torn apart by wild beasts, the Bible says he "tore his clothes and mourned for his son many days." When King David heard that his son had been killed, he expressed his grief in words which have echoed throughout the ages: "O my son Absalom, my son, my son Absalom! Would God I had died for thee, O Absalom, my son, my son!" (2 Samuel 18:33 KJV).

When death separates us from someone we love, there is a time when we think no one has suffered as we have. But grief is universal. The method of handling grief is personal and vital.

16

DEATH

The Threefold Death

Because all men have sinned, all are under the penalty of death. Not only does man suffer as a result of sin in this life, but he must face the judgment to come. As it was with Adam, so it is with all people. God punishes sin with a threefold death—physical, spiritual, and eternal.

First, there is physical death. The Bible says: "It is appointed unto men once to die" (Hebrews 9:27). The Bible teaches that there is "a time to be born and a time to die" (Ecclesiastes 3:2). As Psalm 89:48 asks: "What man is he that liveth, and shall not see death?" Thus the Bible states clearly that God has already made an appointment for each person with death. There is for each man a day, an hour, a minute. The Bible talks in many places about the brevity of life. We are told that our physical lives are "a tale that is told"—"a weaver's shuttle"—a "flower that fades"—"grass that withers." One generation passes and another comes. If God had not given the judgment of physical death on the human race, men would have continued in their sins until the earth would have become hell itself. Each generation has a fresh new start. Thus although death is a penalty for sin, divinely imposed on individuals, when it comes to successive generations of mankind, death is a blessing.

Because of the brevity of life, the Bible warns that we should be prepared to meet God at all times. "Seeing his days are determined, the number of his months are with thee, thou has appointed his bounds that he cannot pass" (Job 14:5).

The Bible exhorts us: "Prepare to meet thy God" (Amos 4:12). Caesar Borgia said in his last moments: "I have provided in the course of my life for everything except death; and now alas! I am to die entirely unprepared."

Second, there is spiritual death. There are millions of persons here and now who are suffering spiritual death. Almost any day you can pick up a newspaper and read of those whose lives testify that they are empty or lost. They were made for fellowship with God, and they are separated from their Maker. This is spiritual death. It is the separation of the soul from God, the separation of man from the One who said: "I am . . . the life." It is spoken of in Scripture as being "dead in trespasses and sins" (Ephesians 2:1).

Third, there is eternal death. The Bible has a great deal to say about Hell. No one spoke more about Hell than Jesus did, and the Hell He came to save men from was not only a Hell on earth. It was not only some condition in which men are now living. It was something to come. Jesus never once taught that anyone on earth was living in Hell now. He always warned of a Hell to come. Whatever He meant by Hell, essentially it is the separation of the soul from God as the culmination of man's spiritual death. There are many mysteries here, and we dare not go beyond the teaching of Scripture. It is enough to warn men that Jesus said: "And these shall go away into everlasting punishment" (Matthew 25:46). Jesus also said: "The Son of man shall send forth his angels, and they shall gather out of his kingdom all things that offend and them which do iniquity; and shall cast them into a furnace of fire: there shall be wailing and gnashing of teeth" (Matthew 13:41–42).

Before We Die

Before we die, two basic issues must be resolved.

The first is, "Am I ready?" Have you confessed your sins and asked Jesus Christ to come into your heart, to take possession of your life? Millions of Christians throughout the world are assured "That if you confess with your mouth, 'Jesus is Lord,' and believe in your heart that God raised him from the dead, you will be saved" (Romans 10:9).

But the Christian life doesn't end there! The next basic issue is "How then do I live?" This is to say, before you die, what service will you render to God and man? Are you investing your life in those things that will last for eternity? "So we make it our goal to please him, whether we are at home in the body or away from it. For we must all appear before the judgment seat of Christ, that each one may receive what is due him for the things done while in the body, whether good or bad" (2 Corinthians 5:9–10).

The Bible says we will all have to give account to Jesus someday (1 Peter 4:5). We will stand before the Judgment Seat of Christ (Romans 14:10). On that day, what we have done on earth will be past. Our chances to speak to the neighbor about the love of Christ, to give to missions, to help evangelism, will be over. Opportunities to share our earthly goods with the starving will be gone. Whatever gifts we were given will be worthless if we hoarded them on earth.

Death is Perennial

Death tolls in wars and epidemics, and the news we read of famine in foreign lands, draw our attention to the fatal aspects of the world around us. Reports from Africa and South America tell of millions of affected citizens, thousands of casualties, miles of affected territory, months and years of suffering, and all the tragedy that can be summed up in statistical fashion. But statistics, and the ways they are fed to us by the media, can be misleading. Death is perennial. During World War II, C. S. Lewis pointed out that war does not increase death; death is total in every generation. It takes every one of us. George Bernard Shaw wryly wrote, "The statistics on death are quite impressive. One out of one people die."

Death, Enemy of God

"But, Lord, I don't want to die." And the Lord, as it were, answers: I didn't plan the world that way, but some day, even this enemy will be destroyed. God reminds us of that through the apostle Paul. "For he must reign until he has put all his enemies under his feet. The last enemy to be destroyed is death" (1 Corinthians 15:25, 26).

Why is death an enemy of God? Because it destroys life, in contrast to God, the creator and author of life. In fact, the Bible tells us that neither sin nor pain, disease nor death were part of God's original plan for man. Death was the penalty for sin, and Adam and Eve made the choice of their own free wills. When they did not obey God, He told the first man and woman if they ate from the fruit of the tree of the knowledge of good and evil, they would die. But Satan scoffed at God's warning and told them they surely would not die. Adam and Eve chose to ignore God's warning and to believe Satan's lie. "For the wages of sin is death, but the gift of God is eternal life in Christ Jesus our Lord" (Romans 6:23).

Death is the common lot of every human being and of every other living thing—both plants and animals. Sin and death, the Bible tells us, have afflicted the whole of God's creation, including the natural world, and only when Christ comes in His glory at the end of the present era will sin be eradicated and creation be restored to God's original plan. "The creation waits in eager expectation for the sons of God to be revealed. For the creation was subjected to frustration, not by its own choice, but by the will of the one who subjected it, in hope that the creation itself will be liberated from its bondage to decay and brought into the glorious freedom of the children of God" (Romans 8:1–21).

Death, Our Mortal Enemy

The Bible stresses that death is an enemy, not a friend—both of God and of us.

Why is death our enemy? I'm not thinking of the death which is a release from pain, debilitating disease, or advanced age, but death the enemy who snatches a child before he learns to play in the sunshine. It is the enemy who takes the young couple before they can be married, stops the youth who wants to be a pilot, or kills the young father and leaves orphaned children and a destitute wife. As you read this sentence, one person will die. Death, like an unfinished symphony, leaves fragments of many promising careers and lives.

Death for the Christian

Most of us know what it means to be stunned by the sudden passing of a dedicated friend, a godly pastor, a devout missionary, or a saintly mother. We have stood at the open grave with hot tears coursing down our cheeks and have asked in utter bewilderment, "Why, O God, why?"

The death of the righteous is no accident. Do you think that the God whose watchful vigil notes the sparrow's fall and who knows the number of hairs on our heads would turn His back on one of His children in the hour of peril? With Him there are no accidents, no tragedies, and no catastrophes as far as His children are concerned.

Paul, who lived most of his Christian life on the brink of death, expressed triumphant certainty about life. He testified, "To me, to live is Christ and to die is gain" (Philippians 1:21). His strong, unshakable faith took trouble, persecution, pain, thwarted plans, and broken dreams in stride.

He never bristled in questioning cynicism and asked, "Why, Lord?" He knew beyond the shadow of a doubt that his life was being fashioned into the image and likeness of his Savior; and despite the discomfort, he never flinched in the process.

Death of a Child

When a child or young person dies, parents sometimes elevate him or her to a pedestal never attained in life. The one who is gone may become the most perfect son or daughter who ever lived, at least in the memory of mother and father. One woman told me of resenting her dead sister all her life, because her mother always talked about "little Lucille" as if she had been a saint.

It is unfair to attribute virtues beyond a person's true character. On the other hand, it can be healing to blot out the bitter memories and grasp the happy ones.

A family either comes closer together as a result of death, or is driven farther apart. Nothing ever seems to remain the same. The death of a child, especially a firstborn or an only child, can place severe strains on a marriage.

But there is help. C. S. Lewis says, "God whispers to us in our pleasures, speaks in our conscience, but shouts in our pains: it is His megaphone to rouse a deaf world."

No one likes to be shouted at, and yet God loves us so much that when troubles come, He is there to call us closer to Him.

Children may be the little trumpet players who bring us to our senses, and to our knees. "Jesus said, 'Let the little children come to me, and do not hinder them, for the kingdom of Heaven belongs to such as these'" (Matthew 19:14).

Preparation for the Journey

But how do we prepare for that *last day*? What if the old childhood bedtime prayer, "If I should die before I wake," becomes a reality? Before we embark on our final trip, have we left an earthly home in a state of chaos or a condition of order?

The first step in preparation is to accept the fact that we *are* going to die. Unless we are willing to talk openly about this fact, we will never be motivated to follow through on any of the remaining steps.

It has been said that someone found St. Francis working in his garden and asked him, "What would you do if you knew that you would die in ten minutes?" St. Francis replied, "I'd try to finish this row."

Most of us are not that ready. We might need ten days instead of ten minutes!

After accepting our mortality, the next step is to put our material affairs in order. Dr. Bell taught me a great lesson about that. When I was a very young man, he urged me to make a will. When he died, his papers were found to be perfectly categorized and numbered in file folders, and there was no confusion about how he wanted his earthly estate to be dispersed.

From that I learned the value of writing down instructions and leaving vital information where it could be found. This includes providing information about where bank books are kept, how insurance papers are filed, and where the key is to your safe deposit box. Our treasures may be laid up in Heaven, but those things we leave on earth will mean a great deal more to those we leave behind. Many Christians today seek to include their church and other ministries in their will.

[Third,] plan your own funeral. Did you make plans for your own wedding? Did you ever have a special party, an anniversary or birthday celebration, where you planned in advance what you would do? Then what's so strange about planning your own funeral?

Why give instructions for your own funeral? Certainly not because you will be concerned about them. You won't attend your own funeral. However, your spouse, your children, your friends and business associates may all be there. The survivors would want to know your wishes. Where will you be buried? Have you left instructions about cremation or a burial plot? What hymns would you want to be sung? Are there any words of assurance you would want to be said to your loved ones and friends? Are there any requests about an open or closed casket?

How often the survivors of the deceased have to struggle with those decisions when they are in no condition to be making such plans, and when it would have been so much easier to have the plans already made and settled.

If we plan our own funeral, we should keep in mind family traditions or customs in the part of the country where we live. For instance, in many places viewing the body is an important part of the grief process, which allows the survivors to say farewell to the physical part of the person they loved. It gives a certain finality to the death process.

Comforting His People

My wife says that the ones who comforted her mother the most after her father died, were the widows who came to the house, put their arms around Mother Bell, and wept with her. They didn't need to say a thing.

But how can we have a ministry of comfort if we have never experienced deep sorrow ourselves? What could we say to the girl whose mother, father, brother, and grandmother were all killed in an automobile accident? What comfort could we offer the parents who have spent two years with a dying child? How could we understand the emotions of a mother and father whose only daughter was a victim of rape-murder by the Hillside Strangler? They are beyond our ability to understand. And yet God does not suggest, He commands us to "Comfort my people" (Isaiah 40:1). However, allow me to make some general observations and suggestions for those who want to obey that command and be a source of support and comfort for the grief-stricken.

The first suggestion is to ask God to give us a tender heart. David asked the Lord, "Create in me a pure heart" (Psalm 51:10). We could add, an understanding heart, an aching heart, a considerate heart. "Finally, all of you, live in harmony with one another; be sympathetic, love as brothers, be compassionate and humble" (1 Peter 3:8).

Second, use the gift of listening. Somehow this is very difficult for all of us. We talk, many times, because we think we need to say something. Listening is hard. The sound of our own voices may be therapy for us, but it is not necessarily healing for the wounded griever. During a time of shock, people need to repeat their story over and over again. You may think they would grow weary of giving details, or telling what happened, but that isn't the case at all.

Third, we shouldn't be shocked by whatever the grief-stricken person may say. Death can be a nightmare, and while visitors are there, life and reality may be distorted. A perfectly rational person may say irrational things. One man returned to his home from the hospital where his daughter had died, and saw his best friend sitting in his kitchen, wearing a worn sweater the friend had taken from the closet. The distraught father snapped at his friend, "Why are you wearing that? It's my fishing sweater."

The understanding friend took off the sweater without

a word. Did the father make an issue over a trivial matter? Of course he did, but in later years he remembered
every detail of that night and thanked his friend for being
there when he needed him.

Fourth, let the bereaved one decide if he or she wants
Bible reading or prayer. "Would you like to have me pray
with you?" is a simple request. But keep it simple and
short, for a mind in agony cannot grasp lengthy prayers
that circle the globe.

Fifth, anticipate needs without being told. Be the one
who asks, "May I answer the phone for you?" Or "I
would like to drive you to the funeral home to make the
arrangements." Or, "Don't worry about anything in the
kitchen, I'll handle it."

One of the worst things to say is, "Call me if you need
anything."

Finally, don't stop being a comforter when the wounds
seem to be healed. A wedding anniversary, a birthday,
holidays, the anniversary of a death, these are hard times
to grope through. Remembering those times with an invitation to dinner, a phone call, or a little note, will provide
thoughtful comfort.

17

JUDGMENT

The Final Judgment

Consider what happened in John's vision. It is a picture of the absolute horror of the final judgment. Carefully, the Lamb opened the sixth seal (Revelation 6:12–17). Suddenly, chaos gripped the universe. An earthquake that no Richter scale could measure shakes the entire world. The sun is eclipsed completely. In fact, reports John, "the sun turned black . . . the whole moon turned blood red, and the stars in the sky fell to earth, as late figs drop from a fig tree when shaken by a strong wind" (Revelation 6:12–13).

Here is a storm of apocalyptic proportions. The world trembles with terror. The great cities collapse. John sees kings, princes, generals, the rich, the mighty, slaves, the free, every human being left on the earth running to escape the horror of God's final judgment. They flee to mountain caves. They cower behind rocks and boulders. But there is no escape. Desperately they cry out, "Hide us from the face of Him who sits on the throne and from the wrath of the Lamb! For the great day of their wrath has come, and who can stand?" (Revelation 6:16–17).

There will be a day of reckoning when God closes His books on time and judges every creature, living and dead.

This vision of the judgments leading to the final judgment permeates the sixty-six books of the Holy Scripture. Before John's vision it was called the "day of wrath" (Zephaniah 1:15; Romans 2:5). Amos called it "the day of the Lord" (Amos 5:18), as did Jesus' own disciple, Peter (2 Peter 3:10). Paul, again and again, called it "the day of our Lord Jesus Christ" (1 Corinthians 1:8; Philippians 1:6). It is often referred to as the Great Tribulation.

All through history there have been days of judgment. The first judgment of God fell on Adam and Eve at the beginning of time (Genesis 3:16–19). Their original sin brought God's day of wrath and a permanent curse on all who followed. God judged Cain. God judged the descendants of Cain with the flood that Noah escaped. Other judgments include the confusing of tongues at Babel, the fiery destruction of Sodom and Gomorrah, and the captivity and dispersion of the Israelites.

A Compassionate Warning

Before the storm of judgment comes, however, God always warns the people. He warned the people of Noah's day before destruction came. He warned the people of Sodom before destruction came. He warned the people of Nineveh before judgment came. He warned the people of Jerusalem before destruction came.

What happened in Noah's day will be repeated at the end of history. We have the word of Jesus who said, "As it was in the days of Noah, so it will be at the coming of the Son of Man" (Matthew 24:37). The two experiences will run parallel in many important aspects, not only in the vast extent of lawlessness and the universality of catastrophe, but also in the earnestness of warning and the provision of a way of escape. At God's bidding, Noah preached for 120 years. During that time he warned the people to repent of their sins and turn to God, but the people laughed and sneered. Then, as time ran out, astonishing things began to happen. Clouds appeared in the sky for the first time. Animals began to gather. The rain came. Jesus said, "The flood came and destroyed them all" (Luke 17:27).

The apostle Peter wrote, "In the last days mockers will undoubtedly come—men whose only guide in life is what they want for themselves—and they will say: 'What has happened to his promised coming? Since the first Christians fell asleep, everything remains exactly as it was since the beginning of creation!'" (2 Peter 3:3–4 PHIL).

But Peter warned, "The day of the Lord will come as suddenly and unexpectedly as a thief. In that day the heavens will disappear in a terrific tearing blast; the very elements will disintegrate in heat and the earth and all that is in it will be burned up to nothing" (verse 10).

Before all of these terrifying things take place, the Bible indicates there will be a turning away from the true faith on the part of many who profess Christ, and much social and political unrest all over the world.

Time's Final Drama

Imagine that the time has come when the Judge is speaking. The angels and archangels are in attendance. Time's final drama is about to take place. Skyscrapers have fallen and the wheels of industry have ceased turning; the places of amusement are empty; the cocktail bars are vacant; the theaters have no one in them—all the places of the world are deserted. Motor cars are at a standstill, and the beaches are empty.

Then God calls for the dead to be brought forth. From the ocean depths where ships were sunk long ago, from graveyards long since forgotten, from the battlefields of the world they come—millions and millions and millions of people. They are crying for the rocks to fall on them, they are crying for the caves to open up and give them a place to hide, but there is no hiding from Him Who sits on the throne. They come before the Lord and they say, "But, Lord, we cast out demons in Your name."

"Depart from Me, ye cursed, I never knew you."

"But, Lord, we were members of the First Church."

"Depart from me, ye cursed, I never knew you."

"But, Lord, I lived a good life."

"Depart from me, ye cursed, I never knew you."

"But, Lord, I paid my debts and led a good, respectable life."

"Depart from me, ye cursed, I never knew you."

The Bible says there will be only one question in that day—what did you do with Jesus? You don't go to Hell for drinking liquor, you don't go to Hell for using profanity—you go to Hell for rejecting Christ! Are you certain that you are saved? If there is the slightest doubt in you mind, you can make sure.

God says, "Prepare to meet God." How do you prepare? "If we confess with our mouths the Lord Jesus and believe in our hearts that God hath raised him from the dead, we shall be saved," the Bible tell us. "But as many as received him, to them gave He power to become the sons of God, even to them that believe on his name" (John 1:12). God says, "Believe on My Son and you will live; and when you die, you will go to Heaven."

Certainty of Punishment

The Bible says so.

"I am tormented in this flame" (Luke 16:24). "Whosoever shall say, Thou fool, shall be in danger of hell fire" (Matthew 5:22).

"The Son of man shall send forth his angels, and they shall gather out of his kingdom all things that offend, and them which do iniquity; and shall cast them into a furnace of fire: there shall be wailing and gnashing of teeth" (Matthew 13: 41–42).

All peoples have believed in it.

Throughout my college days I emphasized the subject of scientific anthropology. We studied the history, the culture, the physical characteristics and the religions of peoples the world over. We did not find one group of people who did not believe that somehow, somewhere, they would pay for their sins and errors against their God. Innate in the heart and mind of man is the belief that when he breaks the moral laws of the universe he must suffer. I make bold to say further that man believes innately that after death there will be some form of punishment for the wicked, wayward life he led in his sojourn here.

18

RESSURECTION

Resurrection as History

There is a basis of historical fact for our belief in the bodily resurrection of Christ. It rests on more evidence than any event that took the place in that time.

THE ACTUAL DEATH OF JESUS

There are those who say that Jesus did not actually die, but that He only fainted. A resurrection presupposes a death. In order to be raised from the dead, Jesus had to die. This is a self-evident fact deduced from the crucifixion. The soldiers were certain that Jesus was dead and that they did not need to induce death by shock by breaking His legs, as in the cases of the two thieves. It was the enemies, not the friends of Jesus, who attested his death, and they made certain when they thrust a spear into His heart.

THE PHYSICAL BURIAL OF JESUS

The body of Jesus was wrapped in fine linen with spices, according to the local custom. An actual tomb was involved, which required the placing of a body. Moreover, a stone was rolled against the face of the tomb, a seal was placed upon it, and a Roman guard set before it. This burial of the body of Jesus presupposes the impossibility of burying a spirit. Spirits are immaterial and cannot be buried. The body of Jesus was physical and material.

It was not only buried so that it occupied space in a tomb, but it was buried for three days. This could not have been true of a spirit, for spirits occupy neither time nor space.

THE EMPTY TOMB

When the disciples saw the tomb in which they had previously buried the body of Jesus, it was empty. The burial garments were in such shape and place to indicate their abandonment by the orderly departure of the body of Jesus. When Jesus later appeared to His disciples, it was in a body, for He said: "A spirit hath not flesh and bones, as ye see me have" (Luke 24:39). His resurrection body occupied spatial conditions and performed the functions of movement, appearance, and the eating of food. He talked and heard. He occupied a room but did not need a door for access. It was the same body in its glorified spiritual form that Jesus took from the tomb, leaving it empty and without occupant.

THE BODILY RESURRECTION

There were thirteen different appearances of Jesus under every conceivable condition and circumstance. Unlike hallucinations, which can continue to deceive, the appearances of Jesus ceased, for they ended with His ascension.

Any notion that seeks to disprove the bodily resurrection of Jesus is confronted with these appearances of Jesus in His own body. It was a body both similar and dissimilar to that which was nailed to the tree. It was so similar that Mary mistook Him for the caretaker of the garden. It was so similar that it could receive food, engage in conversation, and occupy a room.

The dissimilarity was in its properties. It combined both material and immaterial properties. It could pass through closed doors or vanish. When viewed scientifically, this would not seem to be incredible.

Who Hasn't Risen

Turn back in history for a few moments. I want you to see several leaders who have lived and played their part in life. They died, never to rise again.

Remember for a moment Pharaoh Shishak who lived two thousand, eight hundred years ago. He was mentioned in the Old Testament; the lord of two Egypts, the founder of a new dynasty, a very boastful and arrogant man. His tomb was opened a few months ago [1950], verifying the Scriptures. They found only a dried and shriveled mummy, for he died and never rose again. Go to the Great Pyramid built thousands of years ago. It has more than two million three hundred thousand blocks of limestone, and took a hundred thousand workers twenty years to build. But it marks nothing except the failure of a selfish Pharaoh. Today that Pharaoh is still there, never rising from the grave.

Charlemagne, who controlled the far-flung Holy Roman Empire, who was crowned king of the Holy Roman Empire on Christmas day 800, is today only a jumble of moldy bones, buried in the dust of his tomb, for he never rose again from the grave.

Go to the Taj Mahal in India, the most beautiful tomb in all the world, but all that remains of the Mongol emperor and his wife are moldy bones. They died and never rose again.

Go to Mt. Vernon and see the grave of the father of our country, George Washington. Stand there at attention, with your hat off, and the tears streaming down your cheeks, honor his memory, but know that George Washington lies in the grave. George Washington, though a great man and father of his country, lies buried in a tomb and has never risen from the grave.

Or go to Russia to see the body of Lenin. They say that he was embalmed with a fluid that would never let his body decay, and they say that he looks as though he were breathing. There are many people who think that Lenin is the Antichrist and is going to be raised up and will be Satan incarnate. I do not know, but this one thing I do know—Lenin is still in the grave and he has never been raised from the grave.

Go to India and see Mahatma Gandhi's burial place. He was one of the greatest men that ever lived, a leader to the masses of India. When Gandhi was shot... he died and has never risen from the grave.

Every tomb, every burial place of man, whether it be massive as the pyramid or simple as your family plot, speaks of death. Every burial place, every cemetery, every gravestone, every casket, every hearse, are all testimonies of human failure—all prove the Scriptural fact that it "is appointed unto man once to die."

The Truth of the Resurrection

What does the resurrection of Jesus Christ mean to you and me?

First of all, it means that Jesus Christ is what He claimed to be. That Jesus Christ was deity. That Jesus Christ was God incarnate. That Jesus Christ spoke the truth when He said, "I and my father are one" (John 10:30). And then the Lord Jesus Christ said He came to save us from sin. If we believe on Christ, we shall be saved. He meant what He said, and there is no other way of salvation except through Him.

Secondly, the resurrection means that God has accepted Christ's atoning work. Listen to this: "Who was delivered for our offenses and raised again for our justification." God accepted Abel's sacrifice, but He rejected Cain's sacrifice. What would He do with the sacrifice of Jesus Christ upon the cross of Calvary? Would He accept it? Can we be saved through the sacrifice of Christ upon the cross of Calvary? How can we know? God said, "This is my Son in whom I am well pleased."

God turned His back and the Lord Jesus was separated from God for a space of time on the cross of Calvary, going to Hell for our sins, suffering spiritually and physically, yet on the third day the Father loved the Son and because the Father also loved you and me, He accepted the finished work on the cross of Calvary. He raised up the Lord Jesus. When Jesus rose from the dead, it was a living proof that anyone can be saved by the blood of Jesus Christ; by believing on the Lord Jesus Christ, accepting Him as your Lord and Savior. Scripture says that you can be born again by accepting Christ as your Savior.

The Bible tells us that if we confess with our mouths the Lord Jesus and believe in our hearts that God has raised Him from the dead, we shall be saved. But you cannot be saved without believing in the resurrection of Jesus Christ. Unless He rose again, His death would mean no more than the death of any human martyr.

You know why the apostles and the early Christians were persecuted and beaten, stoned and thrown into the lion's den? Not for preaching the teaching of Jesus, nor the virgin birth. It was not for preaching His coming again, but for preaching the resurrection. Unbelievers couldn't stand the truth of the resurrection because if Satan can win the battle of the resurrection, he's won everything. Thanks be unto God, Satan never won the battle. It was won by the Lord Jesus when He died and was raised up by God from the grave.

Meaning of the Resurrection

The presence of the living Christ. Christ is the living companion of every person who puts his trust in Him. He said: "Lo, I am with you always, even unto the end of the world" (Matthew 28:20). He is the guarantee that life has a new meaning. After the crucifixion, the beleaguered disciples despaired and said: "We had hoped that he was the one to redeem Israel" (Luke 24:21, RSV). There was anguish, despair, and tragedy in their midst. Life had lost its meaning and purpose. But when the resurrection became apparent, life took on a new meaning. It had purpose and reason. . . .

The prayers of the living Christ. The Scripture says: "It is Christ that died, yea rather, that is risen again, who is even at the right hand of God, who also maketh intercession for us" (Romans 8:34). In other words, there is a Man at the right hand of God the Father. He is living in a body that still has the nail prints in His hands. He is interceding for us with God the Father as our great High Priest.

The power of the living Christ. The resurrection made it possible for Christ to be identified with all Christians in all ages and to give them power to serve Him. "Verily, verily, I say unto you, He that believeth on me, the works that I do shall he do also; and greater works than these shall he do; because I go unto my Father" (John 14:12). Paul even prayed: "That I may know him, and the power of his resurrection" (Philippians 3:10). His resurrection presence gives us strength and power for each day's task.

The pattern of our new bodies. The resurrected body of Jesus Christ is the pattern of what our bodies will be when we too are raised from the dead. "For our conversation is in Heaven; from whence also we look for the Savior, the Lord Jesus Christ: who shall change our vile body, that it may be fashioned like unto his glorious body, according to the working whereby he is able even to subdue things unto himself" (Philippians 3:20, 21).

The promise of a returning Redeemer. The entire plan for the future has its key in the resurrection. Unless Christ is raised from the dead, there can be no kingdom and no returning King. When the disciples stood at the place of the ascension, they were given angelic assurance that the Christ of resurrection would be the Christ of returning glory. "Ye men of Galilee, why stand ye gazing up into Heaven? This same Jesus, which is taken up from you into Heaven, shall so come in like manner as ye have seen him go into heaven" (Acts 1:11). Thus the resurrection is an event that was both preparatory for and confirmative of a future event even of His second coming.

Yes, our leader Jesus Christ is alive.

19

THE END TIMES

Signs of the Times

We sometimes wonder where God is during the storms of life, in all the troubles of the world. Where is God? Why doesn't He stop the evil? The Bible assures us that God will abolish evil when Christ returns. Someday Christ will come with the shout of acclamation, and there will be a dramatic reunion of all those who have trusted in Him.

No wonder Scripture tells us that at that time "every knee should bow, in heaven and on earth and under the earth, and every tongue confess that Jesus Christ is Lord" (Philippians 2:10–11). If you do not receive Christ as Savior and bow to Him now as Lord of your life, the day is coming when you will bow before Him as Judge.

Jesus did not tell us when He is coming back. He said we were not to speculate. "No one knows about that day or hour, not even the angels in Heaven, nor the Son, but only the Father" (Matthew 24:36). The sixth chapter of Revelation gives a strikingly detailed portrait of the end times, but no one knows when these things will be except the Father in Heaven. Not even the angels know. But Jesus also said that there would be certain signs that we could watch for. They are called the "signs of the times," and they are given in detail in chapters 24 and 25 of the

Gospel of Matthew—the first book of the New Testament.

Both passages from Matthew and Revelation, taken together, give us a graphic storm warning of events yet to come and provide clearly identifiable signs of the end times. Jesus' own narrative reveals specific details of the fall of Jerusalem and the persecution that would follow. Then in the chapters that follow, Matthew records His triumphal entry into Jerusalem when the crowds hailed Him with palm branches and hosannahs as Messiah. Matthew relates the heartbreaking events of the trials before the Sanhedrin and Pilate, the beatings, the crucifixion, and the thrilling account of Christ's rising from the grave. He provides intimate details of the forty days Jesus spent with the disciples in His glorified body, teaching and challenging them before returning to the throne of Heaven.

But one portion of this story deserves to be examined in greater detail. For when Jesus came up to Jerusalem for that final Passover, He wept over the ancient city. He cried, "O Jerusalem, Jerusalem! The one who kills the prophets and stones those who are sent to her! How often I wanted to gather your children together, as a hen gathers her chicks under her wings, but you were not willing!" (Matthew 23:37 NKJV).

Jesus tried to prepare the disciples for the humiliation He was about to endure—the floggings, the cursings, the mockery, and the shameful death on a cross among thieves—but they did not understand. When He told them He must die and rise again in three days, they were mystified. Surely He was speaking in parables; no man could die and rise again by his own command—unless he were God.

As they passed through the city walls, the people with Him marveled at the size and grandeur of the temple buildings. But Jesus told them that soon these walls, this temple, and all the grand palaces and structures in Jerusalem would be flattened, and "not one stone here will be left on another" (Matthew 24:2). They were astonished that Jesus would even suggest such a thing. These were just simple fishermen, tax collectors, and tradesmen from the remote northern region of Galilee, but they could see that Jerusalem was a beautiful, grand city. It was the city hailed by the prophets. How could such towering buildings ever be flattened? What army, what force, could do such a thing? So a group of disciples came to Jesus privately and asked Him, "Tell us, when will these things be? And what will be the sign of Your coming, and of the end of the age?"

The Very Headlines of Our Day

Jesus warned that the price of believing in Him would be high. Mockery, laughter, persecution, even death would be common, but many would refuse to pay such prices. "Then they will deliver you up to tribulation and kill you," He said, "and you will be hated by all nations for My name's sake. And then many will be offended, will betray one another, and will hate one another. Then many false prophets will rise up and deceive many. And because lawlessness will abound, the love of many will grow cold. But he who endures to the end shall be saved."

I believe this is a realistic portrait of our times. Our confidence has been shocked by scandals in the church, in government, in education, and at every level of authority. We have seen graphic images of police officers beating citizens; we have seen top officials of government and business convicted of cheating, lying, and fraud.

We have seen moral and religious leaders, men who claim to be followers of Jesus, fall into disgrace in the eyes of God and man. And worst of all, we have seen the gospel of Jesus Christ twisted and distorted by false teachers to accommodate the destructive morals and secular behavior of these times. These warnings from the Book of Matthew are not parables or myths; they are the very headlines of our day. They are the evidence of Christ's prophecy fulfilled before our eyes.

The World's Last War

There is coming a time in the future—whether near or far I do not know (especially since Jesus warned us not to speculate on dates)—when a counterfeit world system or ruler will establish a false utopia for an extremely short time. The economic and political problems of the world will seem to be solved. But after a brief rule the whole thing will come apart. During this demonic reign tensions will mount, and once again the world will begin to explode with a ferocity involving conflict on an unparalleled scale. Even the grip of the world leaders will be unable to prevent it. This massive upheaval will be the world's last war, the battle of Armageddon. According to secular and scientific writers, there is an inevitability to humanity's date with Armageddon.

Two Mighty Trinities

We know that the Antichrist will appear and try to ensnare the minds and hearts of men. The time draws close, the stage is set; confusion, panic, and fear are abroad. The signs of the False Prophet are everywhere at hand, and many may be the living witnesses of the awesome moment when the final act of this age-old drama begins. It may well come in our time, for the tempo is speeding up, events move more swiftly, and on every side we see men and women consciously or unconsciously choosing up sides— aligning themselves with the devil or with God.

It will be a battle to the death, in the truest meaning of that word—a battle that will give no quarter, that will make no allowances or exceptions. The human phase of this battle started in the Garden of Eden when the devil seduced mankind from God, making it possible for there to be billions of warring wills, every man turning to his own way. "All we like sheep have gone astray; we have turned every one to his own way; and the Lord hath laid on him [Christ] the iniquity of us all" (Isaiah 53:6). It will continue until the end of time, until one or the other of these two mighty forces—the force of good or evil—triumphs and places the True King or the false king on the throne.

At this moment in history, two mighty trinities stand face to face: the Trinity of God (the Father, Son, and Holy Ghost) and the false trinity that Satan would have us worship in its place. The trinity of evil (the Devil, Antichrist, and False Prophet) is described in the Book of Revelation: "And I saw three unclean spirits like frogs come out of the dragon, and out of the mouth of the beast, and out of the mouth of the false prophet" (Revelation 16:13).

Never for a second of your waking or sleeping life are you without the influence of these two powerful forces, never is there a moment when you cannot deliberately choose to go with one or the other. Always the devil is standing at your side tempting, coaxing, threatening, cajoling. And always on your other side stands Jesus, the all-loving, the all-forgiving, waiting for you to turn to Him and ask His aid, waiting to give you supernatural power to resist the Evil one. You belong to one or the other. There isn't a no-man's land in between where you can hide.

In moments of your greatest fear and anxiety, in moments when you feel yourself helpless in the grip of events you cannot control, when despair and disappointment overwhelm you—in these moments many times it is the devil who is trying to catch you at your weakest point and push you further along the path that Adam took.

In these perilous moments remember that Christ has not deserted you. He has not left you defenseless. As He triumphed over Satan in His hour of temptation and trial, so He has promised that you, too, can have daily victory over the Tempter. Remember: "Ye are of God . . . and have overcome them: because greater is he that is in you, than he that is in the world" (1 John 4:4).

The Four Horsemen

Picture John somewhere above Patmos caught up in his vision to the very throne of God. The Lamb is about to open God's book. The four creatures bow in silence. The twenty-four elders tremble in anticipation. The choir of ten thousand times ten thousand angels stops its singing and stands on tiptoe waiting to see what happens next. Then, as John, an eyewitness on the scene, reports in Revelation, "the Lamb opened the first of the seven seals" (Revelation 6:1).

What should happen then is obvious. A page of writing should appear peeled back from the leather scroll, and John and the creatures and the elders should all crowd around to read that page. But this is no ordinary book! This is an illustrated, God-inspired volume whose pictures leap full-blown from the pages and thunder across their vision. Apparently, there is a brief moment between that time when the Lamb breaks open the seal and the time when the four horsemen of the Apocalypse can ride. In that instant they await God's command like racehorses poised at the gate. The four horsemen cannot ride at their own command because of God's sovereign control; they pause for God's order to begin their journey.

In that pause, as the riders await God's command to ride, we learn several great lessons about these judgments.

First, we learn that the judgment of the four horsemen is in part conditional.

As I have written . . . I have pondered repeatedly a very basic question about these judgments. It is this. Are these judgments which John foresees inevitable? Will they definitely happen? Or can these judgments somehow be delayed or even completely averted? In other words, are they unconditional—definitely going to take place no matter what happens? Or are they conditional—able to be diverted if certain conditions are met, such as our repentance and faith?

This is not an easy question to answer, and I am aware sincere students of the Bible may not all agree. However, after careful study I have come to the conclusion that the answer is—both! At some time in the future—a time unknown to us—the terrible hooves of the four horsemen will finally trample across the stage of human history with an unprecedented intensity, bringing in their wake deception, war, hunger, and death on a scale which staggers the imagination. God will use those four horsemen in an awesome act of judgment on the earth, and like a tremendous tidal wave smashing on the shore, nothing will be able to prevent it. Some day, the Bible says, judgment is certainly coming. "For he has set a day when he will judge the world with justice by the man he has appointed" (Acts 17:31).

Until this time that God has appointed, however, there are many occasions when God seemingly delays or averts His hand of judgment for a period of time because men have repented and turned to Him in faith and obedience. Throughout the centuries the hoofbeats of the four horsemen have echoed and re-echoed across the pages of history: deception, war, hunger and death have haunted the human race to one degree or another since the day Adam and Eve chose to rebel against God. At times those hoofbeats have hammered loudly, bringing suffering and death on a massive scale. At times they have become much fainter. Why? I believe it is because there are times when God delays His judgments, possibly even for several generations, because many have listened to His message of warning and turned to Him in repentance and faith.

Second, we learn that the judgment of the four horsemen is correctional.

God's judgment in some ways is similar to pain in our

physical bodies. Some of you reading this have had the experience of realizing one day that you had a vague pain some place in your body. Perhaps you ignored it at first, but as time went by it became more and more intense until at last you could dismiss its insistent voice no longer. You realized that the only intelligent thing to do was to go to a doctor and find out the reason for your pain. For some of you the doctor's examination revealed a potentially deadly cancer eating away at your body. Only surgery could remove it—but once it was removed, your health returned, and you were well again. The pain had been like an alarm clanging in the night, warning of impending disaster. The purpose of that pain was collective—to let you know something was wrong so you would take action to correct the underlying problem.

In the same way, God's judgments are meant to be corrective. They are meant to remind us forcefully of our need of God and the demand to follow His principles for living. God can use trials and difficulties (even if they sometimes are not His direct judgments on us) to teach us and make us into better persons for His glory. "My son, do not make light of the Lord's discipline, and do not lose heart when he rebukes you, because the Lord disciplines those he loves. . . . No discipline seems pleasant at the time, but painful. Later on, however, it produces a harvest of righteousness and peace for those who have been trained by it" (Hebrews 12:5, 6, 11). The four horsemen of the Apocalypse point inevitably to deeper moral and spiritual problems which affect our lives. May God use their warning to make us face these problems and turn to God, who alone can bring us forgiveness and the strength of the Holy Spirit to live a new life.

THE WHITE HORSEMAN

Who is this rider on the white horse? Is this rider on the white horse Christ, as some have suggested? For centuries biblical scholars and commentators have argued about the identity of this rider. You will note that he is wearing a crown of victory and carrying a bow of great destruction in his hand. In Revelation 19 Christ is pictured on a white horse wearing many crowns, and this has led some to believe that the rider on the white horse here in Revelation 6 is also Christ.

However, after careful study I do not believe this to be the case. In the Greek language the crown worn by the rider of Revelation 6 is called *stephanos*, which was the crown of victory worn by a conqueror. The crowns Christ wears in Revelation 19, on the other hand, are *diadema*, or the crowns of royalty. Furthermore, although the rider on the white horse bears a resemblance to Christ, the appearance is actually deceptive because a deeper look reveals his true nature. He is "a conqueror bent on conquest," greedily riding roughshod over all who stand in his way in his lust for power.

Who, therefore, is the rider on the white horse? He is not Christ, but a deceiver who seeks to capture the hearts and souls of men and women. He is one who seeks to have people acknowledge him as Lord instead of the true Christ.

The rider who deceives has been at work in the world since the dawn of human history. He was at work in the Garden of Eden when Satan accosted Adam and Eve and by his diabolical power of deception convinced them to turn their backs on God and disobey His clear command. As a result of that action the human race fell from its sinless glory, bringing death and despair in its wake.

THE RED HORSEMAN

Again, somewhere above Patmos, John stands trembling before God's eternal throne. The white horse bearing the rider who deceives has galloped from the scroll and down the parapets of Heaven to wreak havoc on the earth. Again the celestial servant of God shouts the command of the Almighty: "Come!" Immediately a second horseman charges from the scroll and reins in before the throne. Does God speak to the rider? All John reports is this: The second rider "was given power to take peace from the earth and to make men slay each other" (Revelation 6:4). Does God Himself hand the rider a Roman sword? John states simply, "To him was given a large sword" (Revelation 6:4). Does the rider lift the sword in salute or simply spur the great heaving flanks of the horse red as blood and plunge from their sight toward the world below?

Remember, God is not the cause of war. God had a far greater plan for His creation—and at first that plan was a reality, with no hint of war or conflict to stain His perfect creation. But man, created free, chose not to obey God, and his resulting fallen nature turned to making war, not peace. This heavenly vision is God's way of showing us our folly and warning us of its consequences. Mankind throughout history has refused to listen to the warnings of God. I have often wondered, while the hoofbeats of that fiery red horse still rang in John's ear, whether he heard other sounds—the clanking of sword against sword, the sound of heavy iron spears piercing flesh and crunching bone, the sound of women screaming and children crying, the groans of the wounded and the gasps of the dying?

Listen! The distant sounds of those same hoofbeats can be heard closing in on the place you now sit reading. Above those noisy hoofbeats arise other sounds—the metallic thud of machine guns, the whistle of flamethrowers and mortar rounds, the crackle of burning schools, homes and churches, the high-pitched shriek of missiles zeroing in with their nuclear warheads, the explosion of fifty-megaton bombs over our cities, the scream of terror and death. . . and the silence of a scorched and desolate earth.

The two scenes I've described above, one ancient and one modern, are no exaggeration. For John the Apostle was well aware of the roar and horror of warfare. Just before John's life and ministry, from 67 to 37 B.C., Palestine had been besieged and bloodied by revolution. Without the aid of news teams and television body counts, ancient historians reckoned 100,000 deaths from the conflict. And just before John's exile, in A.D. 61, the Romans crushed another rebellion by Queen Boadicea in the northern empire, with a loss of over 150,000 soldiers and civilians. In the long year between A.D. 68 and 69, Rome had been ruled by four different Caesars. Each brought with him his own unique bloodbath.

War, anarchy, brother against brother, neighbor against neighbor—the complete breakdown of sane human relationships has characterized human history. The rider on the red horse has ridden from the beginning of time, and John's vision was sent as a harbinger of that final holocaust when the Messiah Himself will intervene and crush the allies of evil at Armageddon. Jesus forecast that worst of woes and wars as "unequaled from the beginning of the world until now—and never to be equaled again. If those days had not been cut short, no one would survive" (Matthew 24:21,22).

THE BLACK HORSEMAN

The Lamb carefully pries open the third seal. The leather scroll gently unrolls. At the same moment, the third of God's servant creatures steps to the center stage of John's vision and gives out God's command, "Come!" (Revelation 6:5). Again into the presence of the Lamb of God, the twenty-four elders and the host of angelic witnesses emerge a horse and rider. This black horse and rider bear yet a third warning to the peoples of our planet—a warning of massive hunger and starvation. "Its rider was holding a pair of scales in his hand. Then I heard what sounded like a voice among the four living creatures, saying, 'A quart of wheat for a day's wages, and three quarts of barley for a day's wages, and do not damage the oil and the wine!'" (Revelation 6:5,6).

In New York City's Museum of Modern Art, Umberto Boccioni's "The City Rises" depicts the four horsemen of the Apocalypse in a contemporary, urban setting. This huge six-by-nine-foot oil on canvas captures the horror of the third horse and its rider. Boccioni's black horse rises like a tornado, whirling above the other horsemen.

We read in Lamentations 4:8 and 9 where the blackness of famine haunts the land and kills its victims.

For an instant the black horse and rider stand on parade before John and, through John, before all of us. Just before the rider whirls away on his destructive journey to the earth, we see him in all his prophetic terror. It is easy to picture the horse—black as tar, hooves pounding, flanks heaving, eyes flashing. The rider holds up a balance scale in his hand. Then, John reports, a voice comes from amidst the four apocalyptical beings, announcing: "A quart of wheat for a day's wages" (Revelation 6:6).

Holding up his scale to weigh the tiny amount of grain that will be available to the average working man, the rider on the black horse is a symbol of the desperate plight of the world after the first two horsemen have ridden.

With the advent of this third rider, Jesus is indicating that deception and false religion lead to war, and that war in turn leads to famine and pestilence. Following the white and red horses, famine will prevail upon the earth. Millions will die of hunger. Millions more will suffer malnutrition, and with inadequate diet comes disease, mental and emotional illness, despair and death. The black horse and rider are God's warning of the human suffering that lies ahead if man refuses to obey His commands.

The voice calls out one more instruction to the third horseman, who rides the black horse and carries the scale of judgment. "Do not damage the oil and the wine!" he says (Revelation 6:6). This is a picture of famine coexisting with luxury. Jesus told Peter, Andrew, James and John that, prior to His return, famine would stalk the earth and starve whole peoples in various parts of the world (Matthew 24:7; Mark 13:8; Luke 21:11). But He characterized those in other parts of the world as eating and drinking, apparently to gross excess, implying they could coexist in the same country. He said, "As it was in the days of Noah, so it will be at the coming of the Son of Man. For in the days before the flood, people were eating and drinking, marrying and giving in marriage, up to the day Noah entered the ark" (Matthew 24:37, 38). These two disparate conditions would be parallel and simultaneous. John the Apostle later prophesied that there would be societies leading a Babylonian existence—living in the lap of luxury. These are pictures of people surfeiting themselves to the hilt.

The rider of the black horse carries a pair of scales that say a worker will work an entire day just to keep himself alive. He will have nothing left to divide with his family. He will watch his children die. (The average parent passing through such an experience would rather be dead himself.)

Then the writer in Revelation adds, don't hurt the oil and the wine. He is stating that alongside the famine-stricken poor, there would be the rich who do not suffer famine and pestilence. One of the great problems in our world today is that too often the poor become poorer and the rich become richer. This is one of the basic causes of social unrest in Central America and other parts of the world. And in the future the rich will become fewer in number and the numbers of the poor will increase. The disparity between starvation and riches side by side in the world today will be dwarfed in comparison to that which has been predicted for the future. There is an incomparably blacker day coming.

THE PALE HORSEMAN

Three horses had galloped into John's vision and, bearing their riders of judgment, had ridden toward the earth.

Again, the Lamb moved to break a fourth seal holding the pages of God's great scroll in place. As before, one of God's appointed emissaries stepped forward to command. "Come!" he exclaimed. And another page was thrown back to reveal a fourth horse and rider.

What did John see in that flashing moment? And what did it mean to him and through him to all of us? In the biblical text John writes, "I looked, and there before me was a pale horse!" (Revelation 6:8). The word in Greek is *chloros*. The horse trembling there, rearing high in anger, was the yellow-green color of sickly grass. Goodspeed translates *chloros* as the "color of ashes." Barclay calls it the color of a face "blanched with terror." Moffatt paints the horse as livid, the bloodless color of a corpse. We use the root of that ancient Greek word when we describe the color of chlorine gas that seeps from a wrecked tanker car and mists its poisonous way across the landscape, lethally levelling all life—plants and people alike—in its wake.

At that moment John's eyes were confronted with a consummately terrifying sight. Seated on the pale horse was a rider "named Death, and Hades was following close behind him" (Revelation 6:8). In the Victoria and Albert Museum in London, there is a painted reproduction of a series of seven tapestries woven in the fourteenth century. Some 472 feet long, it depicts John's vision of the Apocalypse. Six hundred years ago the artists-weavers read the sixth chapter of Revelation and artistically interpreted the rider as a skull wrapped in graveclothes sitting upon the pale horse and carrying the Roman broadsword in preparation for the carnage he would inflict.

In the fifteenth century, Albrecht Durer depicted John's vision in fifteen large, carefully cut wood blocks. Death rides the pale horse in the more traditional form of Father Time, an emaciated, bearded harbinger of judgment carrying a three-pronged spear and riding at full gallop toward men whose faces are upturned in defenseless horror.

Of all the dozens of artistic interpretations of the four

horsemen the most graphic for me is the nightmare vision of a modern Japanese artist, Fujita, who painted the fourth horseman as a full skeleton grinning fiendishly, riding on the full skeleton of a horse across a battlefield strewn with skeletons. The entire charnel scene is framed in a chlorine green cloud of death. With Hiroshima and Nagasaki being etched into the Japanese psyche, who could better portray the pale horse than a Fujita?

THE FIFTH HORSEMAN

The little phrase, "and Hades was following close behind him," has puzzled scholars over the centuries. Was there a second rider on the pale horse riding tandem with Death? Or was there a fifth horseman of the Apocalypse? Hades is the place where departed spirits reside between death and the resurrection, the transitional abode of the dead. This is the place that for a time swallows up the spirits of those who die outside of Christ. In the vision, John sees Death and Hades in all too ordinary terms of a man cleaning up refuse along a public road, spearing a bit of trash and dumping it into the trash bag he lugs along.

Two Judgments

The first is the judgment of sin that took place on the cross of Calvary more than 1900 years ago. Now when Christ died on the cross of Calvary, you as a Christian in God's reckoning, and in God's sight, died with Christ. Paul said, "I am crucified with Christ: nevertheless I live." And Paul also said to reckon ourselves dead indeed unto sin. On the cross of Calvary, the Lord Jesus Christ died in our stead as a substitute for our sins. Scripture says about the one who had his sins judged at Calvary, "hath everlasting life, and shall not come into condemnation; but is passed from death unto life" (John 5:24). I believe that Scripture teaches that Christians will not appear at the great White Throne Judgment.

I shall never be there, thanks be unto God. There is therefore now no judgment to them that are in Christ Jesus, because the Lord Jesus Christ was judged, of His own will, sin in our stead. My sins were borne by Christ at Calvary, and I'll never have to face them again. Satan may point his finger at me and say, "There's Billy Graham. Why, Billy Graham is a sinner! Look at the kind of life he leads. Look at all the lies he's told. Look at all the things he did when he was a boy."

But God says, "But the blood of Jesus Christ has cleansed Billy from every sin." You'll never be able to work your way into that position before God. You can't buy it. It's a free gift from God, the Father, through the Lord Jesus Christ.

When the Lord Jesus Christ said, "It is finished," that guaranteed to every believing child of God that the plan of salvation was completed. I can never work for it, I can never buy it, but I can receive it through belief in Christ.

The most awful, horrible, terrible judgment of all time took place at Calvary. The Lord Jesus suffered more when God turned away from Him than all the people in the world can ever suffer. When God judged the Lord Jesus Christ in your stead and in my stead, that judgment was so awful that Jesus said, "My God, my God, why has thou forsaken me?"

Then the second judgment is the judgment of self. I just want to mention it in passing. Unless we judge ourselves, God has to chasten us. Now notice in Scripture that God has two weapons, the first is the rod and the second is a sword. The Christian will never suffer the judgment of the sword. That is to be for the unrepentant sinner alone. God used the sword on Cain. That is the sword that He is going to use on the unbeliever. But God does use the rod on Christians. Do you know why God has to use the rod on us and spank us? Because we don't judge ourselves. We don't confess our sins; we go on backsliding and grieving the Holy Spirit. Then God has to take the rod and paddle us, and when God punishes us, it's not just a little light stroke, it hurts. Sometimes He leaves a bruise by His hand.

White Throne Judgment

I want you to see that awful scene. The angels and archangels stand in attendance. At a place designated by Almighty God, Jesus Christ sits upon the throne. The angels are standing at attention. The heralds blow their horns and as the horns and the trumpets sound, the gates open and Hades releases all of the sinners who had been there. Here they come crying for the rocks to fall on them. Crying for the caves to open up and give them a place of hiding, for the mountains to shelter them, but there is no shelter, there is no hiding from Him that sits on the throne. From battlefields long since forgotten they come. Graveyards have given up the dead which lay there for hundreds of years. From the ocean depths where ships were sunken long ago they come. Millions and millions of them, the earth's great and little who played their parts upon the stage of life. They all come to stand before God at the great White Throne Judgment. If you are outside of Christ, if you've never taken Him as your Savior, you'll be in that group. You'll be there and this is God's description and God's Word. Who's going to be the judge?

"The Father judgeth no man, [God is not going to judge] but hath committed all judgment unto the Son" (John 5:22).

Look at Him, as He sits on the throne. That can't be Jesus. Look at the fire coming from His eyes. Look at the sword coming from His mouth. That can't be my Lord Jesus, but I look closer and I see the scars in His hands and I see the place where they put the spear in His side and I

see the scars in His feet, and I say, "That's Jesus! I knew
Him as Savior down yonder, but now He is judge and He
sits on the judicial throne of the universe—not in mercy
nor love, but in judgment. His holiness is flaming against
the sins of the world."

Inside the Apocalypse

During my study of the Scripture spanning more than
fifty years now, I have often been intrigued, inspired, and
informed by the words of this dramatic book written
under divine inspiration by John on the island of Patmos.
Sitting in my study at home in North Carolina, I have read
literally thousands of pages from articles and scholarly
works on the book. In my personal devotions I have thoroughly immersed myself in the sound and fury of John's
language, listening to the voice of God speaking through
the apostle. But as I consider all that I have learned about
this work, its sinister images, and the actual structure of
the Revelation, I am constantly humbled by it. Many great
minds have grappled with the meaning of John's visions
over the centuries, but in light of the storm I am convinced
is coming, I feel compelled to take another look into it to
discover its meaning for our age. Perhaps it is because I,
like John, am growing older and have a longer perspective
on the events of our time. There is something ominous in
the air, and I am intrigued by both the horror and hope of
what lies just ahead. Of course, John wrote nearly two
thousand years ago. His culture and ours are light years
apart, but his message has a signal importance for our
time. His visions, dreams, and nightmares were not meant
to confound or confuse us. The very word, *apocalypse*, is a
Greek word combining the verb *calypto* ("to veil," "to
cover," or "to conceal") and the preposition *apo* ("from").
Thus, apocalypse means "to remove the veil," "to uncov-
er," "to reveal," and "to make clear." John's storm warn-

ings were clear to Christians in the first century, and they should be even clearer in the climate of today.

Understanding John's Vision

To understand John and the Book of Revelation we need to remember several important things about this remarkable man.

First, John was an apocalyptist. That is, he wrote Revelation in a certain type of poetic language known as apocalyptic language. An apocalyptic writer such as John was one who used vivid imagery and symbolism to speak about God's judgment and the end of the world. Among the Jewish people in biblical times writers often used an apocalyptic style. Some parts of the Old Testament (such as portions of Daniel and Ezekiel) make use of apocalyptic language.

The difficulty, of course, is that this style of writing, using vivid word pictures and symbols, is quite foreign to us today. Undoubtedly most of John's first readers had little difficulty understanding what his symbols stood for and which of them were symbols and which were not. It takes careful study for us today to understand some of the more obscure parts of his message (much of it quoted from the Old Testament), and some of them we may never understand fully.

As an apocalyptist John concentrated on one overpowering theme: the end of human history as we know it and the dawn of the glorious messianic age. As such, his message is always one of both warning and hope—warning of the coming judgment and hope of Christ's inevitable triumph over evil and the establishment of His eternal kingdom.

Second, John was also a prophet. The apocalyptists despaired of the present and looked to the future expectantly. The prophets, on the other hand, often held out hope for the present—hope that God's judgment could be delayed if people would repent and turn to God in faith and obedience. That does not mean that the prophets offered an easy way out of all difficulties, as if somehow all problems would vanish if people would just profess their faith in God. Instead, like Winston Churchill standing amidst the bombed ruins of London, the prophets offered "blood, sweat, and tears" for those who would follow God. It would not be easy to serve God and fight against the evil of this present dark and sinful world, and yet the prophets knew that God would be victorious in the end and His people would share in that victory.

Third, John was also an evangelist. John's concern was not with a sterile message having no power to influence lives. John was concerned about people. He was concerned with the daily problems they faced as they sought to be faithful to God. He was concerned with the pressures and persecutions many of them encountered as Christians. He was concerned about people because he knew God loved them and had sent His Son to die for them.

The word "evangelist" comes from a Greek word meaning "one who announces good news"—in this case, the good news of the Gospel. To some, John's message of the future may have sounded gloomy and depressing. John knew, however, that the worst thing he could do would be to assure people that everything was all right and that there was no need to be concerned about the evil in the world or God's judgment. But John's message is ultimately a message of the good news of salvation in Jesus Christ.

The Price We Must Pay

Our chaotic, confused world has no greater need than to hear the Gospel of Jesus. John's message in Revelation focuses not just on events that will happen in the future, but on what can happen now when Jesus Christ becomes Lord and Savior of our individual lives. John's message focuses supremely on Jesus, the Son of God, who died for our sins and rose again from the dead to give us eternal life. What John declared at the end of his Gospel could also have been applied with equal force to his words in Revelation: "But these are written that you may believe that Jesus is the Christ, the Son of God, and that by believing you may have life in his name" (John 20:31).

John was also a pastor. Revelation was the apostle's last letter to the people he knew and loved best. He began the letter with seven personal notes, one to each of the seven groups of Christians scattered across Asia Minor. As you read through the personal notes, see how well John knew his people and how deeply he loved them. Try to feel his fear for them and for us as well. It is easy to picture how those first-century Christians began their life in Christ. I have preached in more than eighty nations of the world. I have seen thousands of people listening to the good news of Jesus' life, death, and resurrection. I have watched many literally run to accept Christ as Savior and Lord of their lives. I have witnessed their enthusiasm and been thrilled by their early and rapid growth. Then, just as John did, I have watched first love die. I have seen men and women eagerly embrace the faith, then slowly abandon it, giving in again to immorality, idolatry, and self-destruction. I have witnessed others who accepted Christ and remained faithful to the end but found terrible suffering and sacrifice along the way.

I look back on my many years as an evangelist, and I wonder, Have I made the Christian faith look too easy? Even before I heard the expression, I have constantly borne in mind what Dietrich Bonhoeffer called "cheap grace." Of course it is "by grace you have been saved, through faith...not by works, so that no one can boast" (Ephesians 2:8–9). Of course our salvation was a result of what Christ has done for us in His life, death, and resurrection, not what we must do for ourselves. Of course we can trust Him to complete in us what He has begun. But in my eagerness to give away God's great gift, have I been honest about the price He paid in His war with evil? Have I adequately explained the price we must pay in our own war against the evil at work in and around our lives?

That Distant Thunder

John worried about his flock as he wrote out his vision of this world (where evil reigns) and of the world to come (where God will restore righteousness and peace again). He wrote of the war between the worlds and of the men and women who fight and die on the battlefield in that war. At the center of his vision, he wrote of Jesus, the Lord of the world to come, who has entered this world to rescue humankind (wherever they find themselves on the battlefield), to guide them through enemy lines, and to deliver them safely home again.

Revelation is not an academic paper produced for some scholarly professional meeting. It is not a poem created by a gifted genius to entertain and divert. It is not the diary of a senile old man driven to wild hallucinations by his isolation and loneliness. Revelation is a pastor's letter to his floundering flock, an urgent telegram bearing a brilliant battle plan for a people at war. It reflects all the realistic horror and heartbreak of a battlefield strewn with the dead. It is frank and it is frightening, but it is a plan for victory—if not for every battle, certainly for the war.

Like John, I have heard that distant thunder. I have seen lightning striking in many places of our world; thus, I know that the coming storm could engulf the whole world. I have seen the storm clouds mounting in the lowering sky. I am still an evangelist whose one goal is to proclaim new life in Christ, but there is serious trouble ahead for our world and for all of us who live in it. In the images of the Apocalypse there is both a storm warning and message of hope for the troubled times yet to come.

Jesus or Caesar

Most citizens of the empire were glad to pay tribute to the emperor and to the empire that had brought them this period of peace. But for Christians, another loyalty oath was at the center of their faith: "Jesus is Lord," not Caesar. In spite of their gratitude to the empire and to the emperor, in spite of the admonitions of Paul and Peter to worship God and honor the emperor, this act of Caesar worship was impossible. Because of their refusal to put Caesar before Christ, Christians began to be persecuted.

William Barclay writes, "This worship [of Caesar] was never intended to...wipe out other religions. Rome was essentially tolerant. A man might worship Caesar *and* his own god. But more and more Caesar worship became a test of political loyalty; it became...the recognition of the dominion of Caesar over a man's life, and...soul" (The Revelation of John, 1:21–22). Imagine a village in the suburbs of Ephesus or Laodicea. Christian believers are at work tanning leather, dyeing cloth, harvesting crops, raising families, studying math and history—at worship, at work, or at play. Then, suddenly, hoofbeats are heard clattering up the nearby cobbled streets. The horses are reined in by a Roman centurion and his honor guard. A leather camp table is unfolded. An incense burner is placed upon the table. A flame is lit. Heralds sound the trumpets. There is no place to hide, no time to decide.

Believers must join their neighbors in that line. Just ahead the village mayor tosses his incense into the flames and exclaims proudly, "Caesar is Lord." Others follow. The line ahead grows shorter. The moment of decision draws near. Will the Christians avoid the conflict and protect their lives and security with the simple act of obedience? Will they mutter "Caesar is Lord" and sneak back home to safety? Or will they recognize that act as a symbol of a wider disobedience, refuse the incense, proclaim "Jesus is Lord" and pay the price for their disloyalty to the state?

Did John wander up and down the beach at Patmos that Sabbath remembering the centurion, the incense, and the terrible decision of ultimate loyalty each believer had to make? Who knows? Perhaps it was in just such a line, surrounded by his neighbors and friends, that John himself failed the emperor's test and, as punishment, was exiled to the island prison. We don't know the charges leveled against the apostle that led to his exile, but we do know why John said he was there: "I, John, your brother and companion in the suffering and kingdom and patient endurance that are ours in Jesus, was on the island of Patmos because of the Word of God and the testimony of Jesus" (Revelation 1:9).

It was not easy to be a Christian then. It is not easy now. Late in the first century, during the time of John's exile, the persecutions of the Christian church by the Roman Empire had begun in earnest. It was difficult to keep the faith then. It is now. There are grand and awful moments before a centurion's blazing fire. There are little, awful moments almost daily when one longs to give in to the values of this world, to give up the high standards of our Lord, to give way to the various temptations that pressure every man, woman, or young person who believes. Even Christians are tempted to surrender to the passions or the pleasures that pursue us all.

Seer of the Unseen World

When the Spirit of the risen Christ came to John in his barren cell, the aging apostle must have been in awe, for the unseen world burst upon him with fearsome reality. As a Roman prisoner, half-starved, sometimes beaten, constantly harassed and abused, his life on that barren, rock-strewn island in the Aegean Sea was as real and unmysterious as the cold ground upon which he slept, as real as bread and water. The life he lived was as physical and tangible as the pain in his aching joints and the burns and blisters on his hands and feet.

Tradition tells us that John's face was wrinkled and blackened by the sun. His arms were lean and muscular, and his hands were rough with calluses. As a political prisoner, exiled to a rock off the coast of what is now modern Turkey, John was forced to carry stones chipped from granite cliffs above the sea to a cargo dock below the Roman citadel. The fortress guarded the narrow isthmus between the Bay of Scala and the Bay of Merika. The gravel John carried on his back was used to build the foundations for the temples and palaces of the Emperor Domitian and to pave Roman roads, which always led to Rome.

We can imagine that John, stumbling under the loaded straw basket strapped to his forehead, used both hands to grasp his staff and pick his way painfully down the treacherous path. Even the Roman guards must have wondered at the determination of this gray-bearded Christian Jew who worked alongside the other prisoners by day and then spent his evenings writing stories no one could understand.

But John was not doing what he wanted to do; he was under the compulsion of a mystery. He was writing at the direction of the Holy Spirit of God, who came to him in waking dreams and vision. At the beginning of his book, John wrote, "On the Lord's Day I was in the Spirit, and I heard behind me a loud voice like a trumpet, which said: 'Write on a scroll what you see and send it to the seven churches: to Ephesus, Smyrna, Pergamum, Thyatira, Sardis, Philadelphia and Laodicea'" (Revelation 1:10–11).

So, in his cavelike prison cell, John, the seer of the unseen world, spent every free moment recording the seismographic warnings of a world bulging and buckling just beneath the surface. I often have the feeling that in many ways John's ancient world was much like our own.

20

PEACE AND HOPE

The Promise of Peace

The world we live in is like a hurricane—ever-changing, ever changeable, always unpredictable, and frequently destructive—but there are some things that never change: The love of God. His matchless grace and mercy. His boundless forgiveness. Until that day when Christ shall come "with shout of acclamation," there is still hope for the human race. While there is yet time, we must earnestly seek Him.

The more I learn of the realities of the Book of Revelation, the more I realize there are still many mysteries, ambiguities, and complex uncertainties which cannot yet be fully understood. But we are not without understanding. From the truth we have already learned of God, we have proof of His love and provision for humanity. From the unfailing accuracy of biblical prophecy, we have evidence of the faithfulness of Scripture and its often stunning relevance to the circumstances and events of our lives. Thus we know His Word is true.

Paul wrote to Timothy, "All Scripture is given by inspiration of God, and is profitable for doctrine, for reproof, for correction, for instruction in righteousness, that the man of God may be complete, thoroughly equipped for every good work" (2 Timothy 3:16–17 NKJV). With that assurance, we study this Word and discover how its truth can be applied to our individual lives and needs.

Paul also understood the implications of his message. He writes: "I charge you therefore before God and the Lord Jesus Christ, who will judge the living and the dead at His appearing and His kingdom: Preach the word! Be ready in season and out of season. Convince, rebuke, exhort, with all longsuffering and teaching" (2 Timothy 4:1–2 NKJV).

I do not fully understand everything that will happen . . . but I also realize we do not have the complete picture yet. God reveals to each age what His children are able to understand. I am prepared to rest in that knowledge until God opens up the next chapter in this incredible adventure.

Three Kinds of Peace

There are three kinds of peace described in the Bible.

First, peace with God. "Therefore being justified by faith, we have peace with God through our Lord Jesus Christ" (Romans 5:1). "Having made peace through the blood of his cross . . ." (Colossians 1:20). There is a peace that you can have immediately—peace *with* God.

The second peace spoken of in the Bible is the peace *of* God. Everyone who knows the Lord Jesus Christ can go through any problem, and face death, and still have the peace of God in his heart. When your spouse dies, or your children get sick, or you lose your job, you can have a peace that you don't understand. You may have tears at a graveside, but you can have an abiding peace, a quietness.

The third peace the Scriptures mention is future peace. The Bible promises that there will be a time when the whole world is going to have peace. It seems that the world is heading toward Armageddon. In Revelation 6:4

John the beloved apostle says there's a red horse, "and power was given to him that sat thereon to take peace from the earth." We're not going to have peace—permanent peace—until the Prince of Peace comes.

A Word for the World

Jesus, however, also said another interesting thing that I have already elaborated on: "This gospel of the kingdom will be preached in the whole world as a testimony to all nations, and then the end will come" (Matthew 24:14). Today, for the first time in history, we are witnessing the preaching of the gospel on a global scale such as the world has never known, using radio, the printed page, and television. It's one of the signs that we are to look for as we approach the end of history. The Bible teaches that there is deliverance from the things that are about to come upon the world for those who put their faith and trust in Jesus Christ. Not by chemicals, but by Christ. Not by smoking crack cocaine or injecting heroin, but by bringing minds and hearts into harmony with God through submission to His will and accepting His forgiveness as offered from the cross. In Christ alone there is deliverance from the world's tortured thoughts, healing for weakened minds and bodies, and freedom from the sordid, destructive, and immoral habits that are destroying so many today.

But more important, there is hope for the future. The Bible teaches that God has planned utopia. There *is* a glorious new social order coming, but it is going to be brought by Jesus Christ Himself when He returns. I believe the time is short; we must each tell that good news however we can. Listen for the voice of Jesus above the storm, saying, "So you also must be ready, because the Son of Man will come at an hour when you do not expect him" (Matthew 24:44). Are you ready?

The Secret of Joy

When Jesus Christ is the source of joy, there are no words that can describe it. It is a joy "inexpressible and glorious" (1 Peter 1:8). Christ is the answer to the sadness and discouragement, the discord and division in our world.

Christ can take discouragement and despondency out of our lives. Optimism and cheerfulness are products of knowing Him.

The Bible says, "A cheerful heart is good medicine, but a crushed spirit dries up the bones" (Proverbs 17:22).

If the heart has been attuned to God through faith in Christ, then its overflow will be joyous optimism and good cheer.

Out West an old sheepherder had a violin, but it was out of tune. He had no way of tuning it, so in desperation he wrote to one of the radio stations and asked them at a certain hour on a certain day to strike the tone "A." The officials of the station decided they would accommodate the old fellow, and on that particular day the true tone of "A" was broadcast. His fiddle was thus tuned, and once more his cabin echoed with joyful music.

We have to be tuned to God. We will never be free from discouragement and despondency until we know and walk with the very fountainhead of joy.

Christ Himself is the Christian's secret of joy: "Though you have not seen him, you love him; and even though you do not see him now, you believe in him and are filled with an inexpressible and glorious joy" (1 Peter 1:8).

Promise of the Future

Whenever you look closely at the prophecies of the end times, you will inevitably raise dark specters and enigmas that trouble the soul. That is as it should be, and that is why God has given us such pronounced warnings of this coming storm. But let me also remind you of God's promise. For in the midst of the pessimism, gloom, and frustration, there is a marvelous hope, and in this present hour of concern there is still the overarching hope, the promise made by Christ: "If I go and prepare a place for you, I will come back" (John 14:3). He died on the cross for our sins. He was raised again. He ascended to Heaven. The Bible says that He's going to return in triumph.

One day after His resurrection, He was talking to His disciples. "They asked him, 'Lord, are you at this time going to restore the kingdom to Israel?' He said to them: 'It is not for you to know the times or dates the Father has set by his own authority. But you will receive power when the Holy Spirit comes on you; and you will be my witnesses in Jerusalem, and in all Judea and Samaria, and to the ends of the earth'" (Acts 1:6–8). After He had said that, He was taken up from them. They watched His ascent and a cloud enveloped Him beyond their sight.

The faith of the disciples was still small, and some of them probably had nagging doubts that they would ever see Him again in spite of His promises. They must have been looking intently into the sky, with a sense of loss and sadness as He was ascending. Then there appeared beside them two men dressed in white. "'Men of Galilee,' they said, 'why do you stand here looking into the sky? This same Jesus, who has been taken from you into Heaven, will come back in the same way you have seen him go into Heaven'" (Acts 1:11).

The time of His return, Jesus had assured them, was a secret known only to His Father. However, indications as to when it will happen are foretold in various books of the Bible. In the ninth chapter of Daniel we are told that an angel brought the word to the prophet that God had appointed seventy weeks to His people and their holy city. There have been scores of books written about these seventy weeks, and I do not intend to spend time here discussing what they mean. I can only meditate, think, and interpret as best I can. There are some things I believe we can know for certain about this and other prophetic passages; there are other passages where we must be more cautious, and sincere Bible scholars may disagree on some details where God has chosen not to speak as clearly concerning the future. But virtually everything has been fulfilled that was prophesied in the Scriptures leading up to the coming of Christ. We know His coming is near!

What needs to be noted here is that the angel did say something to Daniel that relates to the four horsemen: "War will continue until the end, and desolations have been decreed" (Daniel 9:26). This gives us a clear clue to the whole history not only of the Middle East, but of the past several thousand years of the human race. It has been a great battleground and a scene of unfulfilled dreams, dashed hopes, broken hearts, mutilated bodies across thousands of battlefields on which hundreds of millions have died.

The Hope of His Coming

The great creeds of the church teach that Christ is coming back. The Nicene Creed states, "He shall come again with glory to judge both the living and the dead." Charles Wesley wrote seven thousand hymns, and in five thousand he mentioned the Second Coming of Christ. When Queen Elizabeth II was crowned by the Archbishop of Canterbury, he laid the crown on her head with the sure pronouncement, "I give thee, O sovereign lady, this crown to wear until He who reserves the right to wear it shall return."

But till that time, one of America's best-known columnists summed it up when he said, "For us all, the world is disorderly and dangerous; ungoverned, and apparently ungovernable." The question arises: Who will restore order? Who can counter the danger of the nuclear holocaust? Who can bring an end to AIDS and the other epidemics of our time? Who alone can govern the world? The answer is Jesus Christ!

The Psalmist asked centuries earlier: "Why do the nations conspire and the peoples plot in vain? The kings of the earth take their stand and the rulers gather together against the LORD and against his Anointed One. 'Let us break their chains,' they say, 'and throw off their fetters.' The One enthroned in Heaven laughs; the Lord scoffs at them. Then he rebukes them in his anger and terrifies them in his wrath, saying, 'I have installed my King'" (Psalm 2:1–6). He promises the Anointed One, "I will make the nations your inheritance, the ends of the earth your possession. You will rule them with an iron scepter. . . . Therefore, you kings, be wise; be warned, you rulers of the earth. Serve the LORD with fear and rejoice with trembling" (Psalm 2:11). Then He advises the whole earth, "Blessed are all who take refuge in him" (verse 12).

Yes, God has promised this planet to His Son, Jesus Christ, and someday it will be His. He will bring an end to all the injustice, the oppression, the wars, the crime, the terrorism that dominates our newspapers and television screens today. But before that time comes, the four horsemen are going to vent their storm of fury across the pages of history.

For the Christian believer, the return of Christ is comforting, for at last men and women of faith will be exonerated. They will be avenged. The nonbeliever will see and understand why true Christians marched to the sound of another drum. But for the sinful unbeliever, the triumphant return of Christ will prove disastrous, because Christ's return ensures final judgment.

21

SEVEN FINAL QUESTIONS

Seven Final Questions

Let's see if you can pass the examination God gives in First John.

The Gospel of John speaks of eternal life as manifested in the Son of God: "But these are written, that ye might believe that Jesus is the Christ, the Son of God; and that believing ye might have life through his name" (John 20:31).

The Gospel of John was written in order that we might believe that Jesus is the Christ. The First Epistle of John was written to people who believe that Jesus is the Christ but who have never come into full assurance of their present position or of the possession of eternal life. "These things have I written unto you that believe on the name of the Son of God; that ye may know that ye have eternal life, and that ye may believe on the name of the Son of God" (1 John 5:13). If you have any doubt concerning the atoning death of Christ or about His deity, read the Gospel of John, but if you have believed the message of the Gospel and you are still perplexed as to the question of assurance, read the Epistle of John.

So let us take the test. Let us examine ourselves. Let us check and see how we stand in the light of God's Word. Are you ready? Here goes!

Do You Believe on the Son?

"And this is his commandment, That we should believe on the name of his Son Jesus Christ, and love one another, as he gave us commandment," and His commandment is that we should believe on the name of His Son, Jesus Christ. "Whosoever believeth that Jesus is the Christ is born of God: and everyone that loveth him that begat loveth him also that is begotten of him" (1 John 5:1). Have you really, truly and definitely accepted Christ as your Savior? Has there come a period in your life when you were convicted of the Holy Spirit and you confessed Christ, not only as Savior, but as Lord? The word "believe" means to have trust in and to lean upon Christ, to confess Him as the Lord of your life and the Savior of your soul.

What Is Your Attitude Toward Sin?

"If we say that we have no sin, we deceive ourselves, and the truth is not in us. If we confess our sins, he is faithful and just to forgive us our sins, and to cleanse us from all unrighteousness. If we say that we have not sinned, we make him a liar, and his word is not in us" (1 John 1:8–10).

Do you hate sin as God hates it? Do you detest it? Is it loathsome, filthy, ugly to you? When you stumble and fall or yield to Satan's temptation in a moment of weakness, do you immediately confess?

Are You an Obedient Servant?

"And hereby we do know that we know him, if we keep his commandments" (1 John 2:3). The next verse says, "He that saith, I know him, and keepeth not his commandments, is a liar, and the truth is not in him." Do we say that we are Christians? Do we maintain that we are

God's children? Then we must prove it by our lives! The law had said concerning the man who keeps His commandments, "Which if a man do, he shall live in them." But under Christ the man who lives by faith will do His commandments. The person who is born of the Spirit will delight in obedience to the will of God. This doesn't mean that you are obedient in everything all the time! You should be, but in reality there is only one who can say, "I do always those things that please him." The one who knows Christ as Savior will find springing up within him a glorious love to do the will of God.

ARE YOU SEPARATED FROM THE WORLD?

"Love not the world, neither the things that are in the world. If any man love the world, the love of the Father is not in him. For all that is in the world, the lust of the flesh, and the lust of the eyes, and the pride of life, is not of the Father, but is of the world. And the world passeth away, and the lust thereof: but he that doeth the will of God abideth forever" (1 John 2:15–17).

God calls us to be a separate people. "Come out from among them, and be ye separate." We are a peculiar people—not, however, in the sense that we dress strangely or are eccentric. We are a chosen group. The moment you came to Christ you were adopted into the family of God. The old things you used to love you now hate. Things you used to hate you now love.

ARE YOU ANTICIPATING THE COMING OF CHRIST?

"Behold, what manner of love the Father hath bestowed upon us, that we should be called the sons of God: therefore the world knoweth us not, because it knew him not. Beloved, now are we the sons of God, and it doth not yet appear what we shall be: but we know that, when he shall appear, we shall be like him; for we shall see him as he is.

And every man that hath this hope in him purifieth himself, even as he is pure" (1 John 3:1–3).

The first coming of Christ is the greatest event in world history. At once it becomes the center of the two eternities. The mainspring in the clock of prophecy, the pivot around which revolves all the purposes of God.

Today the world faces another crisis: Christ's second coming. This time He is coming not in humiliation but in glorification to receive from this scene His own blood-bought children. Evidences abound that the time is almost here. Since "Ascension Day" when the heavenly witnesses said "This same Jesus . . . shall so come in like manner as ye have seen him go," the eyes of Christians have been turning heavenward. They look for Him and perhaps as never before expect Him at any moment.

DO YOU LOVE THE BRETHREN?

"We know that we have passed from death unto life, because we love the brethren. He that loveth not his brother abideth in death" (1 John 3:14).

The greatest need among professing Christians today is love. The one great command that is laid upon us by Jesus Christ is that we love one another; not that we should love one another as a husband loves his wife or as a mother loves her child; oh, no, far deeper than that. Our love for each other should be comparable to God's love for us. Is your love like sounding brass and a tinkling cymbal? You may know Greek and Hebrew. You may know church history, physiology and philosophy, but if you have not love, it profiteth you nothing. The kind of love that suffers, that is kind, that never envies, that does not puff itself up, that never seeks its own, that is not easily provoked, that never does evil, that never takes joy in sin, that is always happy and thrilled when the truth is presented, that endures everything—is this the kind of love you have?

DO YOU PRACTICE SIN?

"We know that whosoever is born of God sinneth not; but he that is begotten of God keepeth himself, and that wicked one toucheth him not" (1 John 5:18).

Now don't get alarmed! This verse should never have been translated as it is in the King James Version. Look at the words "sinneth not." The verse should read: "Whosoever is born of God doth not practice sin." In other words, if I see a man going on in sin after he has professed conversion, I have a right to doubt that man's salvation. He may stumble and fall. He may even yield to Satan and commit a sin in a moment of weakness, but he will immediately right himself and ask God for strength to be an overcomer.

BIBLIOGRAPHY

1947 *Calling Youth to Christ.* Introduction by Torrey M. Johnson. Grand Rapids, MI: Zondervan Publishing House.

1950 *Revival in Our Time.* Wheaton, IL: Van Kampen Press. "The Story of the Billy Graham Evangelistic Campaigns, Including Six of His Sermons."

1952 *The Chance of a Lifetime: Helps for Servicemen.* Fourth edition. Grand Rapids, MI: Zondervan Publishing House.

1955 *The Seven Deadly Sins.* Grand Rapids, MI: Zondervan Publishing House.

1955 *Peace with God.* Garden City, NY: Doubleday & Company, Inc..

1955 *The Secret of Happiness: Jesus's Teaching on Happiness as Expressed in the Beatitudes.* Garden City, NY: Doubleday & Company, Inc.

1960 *My Answer.* Garden City, NY: Doubleday & Company, Inc.

1960 *Answers to Life's Problems.* Dallas: Word Publishing.

1965 *World Aflame.* Garden City, NY: Doubleday & Company, Inc.

1966 *The Quotable Billy Graham.* Compiled and edited by Cort R. Flint and the Staff of *Quote.* Anderson, NC: Droke House Publishers.

1967 *The Wit and Wisdom of Billy Graham.* Edited and compiled by Bill Adler. New York: Random House.

1969 *The Challenge: Sermons from Madison Square Garden.* Garden City, NY: Doubleday & Company, Inc.

1971 *The Jesus Generation.* Grand Rapids, MI: Zondervan Publishing House.

1975 *Angels: God's Secret Agents.* Garden City, NY: Doubleday & Company, Inc.

1976 *Day-by-Day with Billy Graham: A Devotional Book.* Compiled and edited by Joan Winmill Brown. Minneapolis: World Wide Publications.

1977 *How to Be Born Again.* Waco: Word Books.

1978 *The Holy Spirit: Activating God's Power in Your Life.* Waco: Word Books.

1981 *Till Armageddon: A Perspective on Suffering.* Waco: Word Books.

1983 *The Evangelist and a Torn World: Messages by Billy Graham.* Delivered at the International Congress for Itinerant Evangelists, July 12-21, 1983. Minneapolis: World Wide Publications.

1983 *Approaching Hoofbeats: The Four Horsemen of the Apocalypse.* Waco: Word, Inc.

1984 *A Biblical Standard for Evangelists.* Minneapolis: World Wide Publications.

1984 *Peace with God.* Revised and expanded edition. Dallas: Word Publishing.

1985 *The Secret of Happiness: Jesus's Teaching on Happiness as Expressed in the Beatitudes.* Revised and expanded edition. Dallas: Word Publishing.

1986 *Angels: God's Secret Agents.* Reissue. Dallas: Word Inc.

1986   *Unto the Hills.* Waco: Word Books.

1986   *Angels.* Dallas: Word Publishing.

1987   *Facing Death—and the Life After.* Waco: Word Books.

1988   *The Holy Spirit: Activating God's Power in Your Life.* Dallas: Word Publishing.

1988   *Answers to Life's Problems.* Dallas: Word Publishing.

1989   *How to Be Born Again.* Waco: Word Publishing.

1991   *Hope for the Troubled Heart.* Dallas: Word, Inc.

1992   *Storm Warning.* Dallas: Word Publishing.

SOURCES

Scripture quotations in the following readings are taken from the Bibles listed in brackets, unless cited otherwise in the text:

Angels [KJV]
Approaching Hoofbeats [NIV]
Biblical Standard [KJV]
Calling Youth to Christ [KJV]
Challenge [KJV]
Chance of a Lifetime [KJV]
Facing Death [NIV]
Holy Spirit [NASB]
Hope [NIV]
Peace with God [KJV]
Revival in Our Time [KJV]
Secret of Happiness [KJV]
7 Deadly Sins [KJV]
Storm Warning [NIV]
Till Armageddon [NIV]
World Aflame [KJV]

The page numbers cited below refer to the first editions of the works, whether hardcover or paperback, unless otherwise indicated.

Actual Death of Jesus: *World Aflame,* 128-129
Adopted: *World Aflame,* 163
All of These Kids: *Facing Death,* 22-23
Angelic War: *Angels,* 60-62
Angels: *Angels,* 13-15
Angels as Executors: *Angels,* 99-100
Angels as Messengers: *Angels,* 111-13
Angels at the Cross: *Angels,* 128-129

New Man, Not Perfect: *World Aflame*, 167-168

Outward Journey: *Approaching Hoofbeats*, 100-101

Paid Ticket to Heaven: *Facing Death*, 215-216
Pale Horseman: *Approaching Hoofbeats*, 179-180
Paradise Lost: *Facing Death*, 219-220
Patience: *Holy Spirit*, re 195-196
Pattern for Prayer: *Hope*, 151-153
Peace: *Holy Spirit*, re, 193
Physical Burial of Jesus: *World Aflame*, 129
Power of Prayer: *Till Armageddon*, 153-155
Practice the Presence of Christ: *Till Armageddon*, 177
Practice with Prayer: *Till Armageddon*, 175
Praying through the Pain: *Hope*, 148-149
Preparation for the Journey: *Facing Death*, 194-201
Price We Must Pay: *Storm Warning*, 74-75
Pride: *Seven Deadly Sins*, 15-17
Promise of the Future: *Storm Warning*, 275-277
Promise of Peace: *Storm Warning*, 289-290

Rationalizing God: *World Aflame*, 90-91
Reality of Hell: *Facing Death*, 217-218
Red Horseman: *Approaching Hoofbeats*, 121-123
Results of the Atonement: *Calling Youth*, 112
Resurrection as History: *World Aflame*, 128
Revelation: *World Aflame*, 95-96
Revelation in Conscience: *World Aflame*, 98-99
Revelation in Jesus Christ: *World Aflame*, 101-102
Revelation in Nature: *World Aflame*, 96-97
Revelation in Scripture: *World Aflame*, 99-100
Rich Man and Lazarus: *Facing Death*, 218
Rich Young Man: *Storm Warning*, 260

Scarlet Thread: *Calling Youth*, 100-104
Science Doesn't Satisfy: *World Aflame*, 45-46
Searching in the Wrong Places: *Secret of Happiness*, 15-16
Secret of Joy: *Till Armageddon*, 141-142
Seer of the Unseen World: *Storm Warning*, 91-93

WILLIAM GRIFFIN has had long editorial associations with Harcourt Brace and Macmillan in both text books and trade books. He has reviewed books for the *Los Angeles Times, San Francisco Chronicle,* and *Christianity Today.* For a dozen years he covered religious publishing in the United States for *Publishers Weekly.* His previous anthologies include *The Joyful Christian: C. S. Lewis* and *The Newborn Christian: J. B. Phillips.* And he is the author of *C. S. Lewis: A Dramatic Life.*

RUTH GRAHAM DIENERT is the youngest daughter of Ruth and Billy Graham, and a single mother of three children. She has published *First Steps in The Bible* (Word, 1980), a children's Bible storybook, and articles in the *Saturday Evening Post, Moody Monthly* and *Decision* magazine. For nine years she was acquisitions editor for Harper Collins, San Francisco.

She lives near her parents in the mountains of North Carolina.